WIT AND THE WRITING OF HISTORY

Wisconsin Studies In Classics

General Editors
Barbara Hughes Fowler and Warren G. Moon

E. A. Thompson
Romans and Barbarians: The Decline of the Western Empire

Jennifer Tolbert Roberts
Accountability in Athenian Government

H. I. Marrou
A History of Education in Antiquity

Erika Simon
Festivals of Attica: An Archaeological Commentary

G. Michael Woloch
Roman Cities: Les villes romaines by Pierre Grimal,
translated and edited by G. Michael Woloch,
together with A Descriptive Catalogue of Roman Cities
by G. Michael Woloch

Warren G. Moon, *editor*
Ancient Greek Art and Iconography

Katherine Dohan Morrow
Greek Footwear and the Dating of Sculpture

Jeanny Vorys Canby, Edith Porada, Brunilde Sismondo Ridgway, and
Tamara Stech, *editors*
Ancient Anatolia: Aspects of Change and Cultural Development

Wendy J. Raschke, *editor*
*The Archaeology of the Olympics: The Olympics and
Other Festivals in Antiquity*

Paul Plass
*Wit and the Writing of History: The Rhetoric of
Historiography in Imperial Rome*

WIT AND THE WRITING OF HISTORY

THE RHETORIC OF HISTORIOGRAPHY IN IMPERIAL ROME

PAUL PLASS

THE UNIVERSITY OF WISCONSIN PRESS

The University of Wisconsin Press
114 North Murray Street
Madison, Wisconsin 53715

The University of Wisconsin Press, Ltd.
1 Gower Street
London WC1E 6HA, England

Printed in the United States of America

Library of Congress Cataloging-in-Publication Data

Plass, Paul, 1933–
    Wit and the writing of history.
    (Wisconsin studies in classics)
    Bibliography: pp. 167–170.
    Includes index.
    1. Rome—Historiography. 2. Historiography—Rome.
3. Latin wit and humor. I. Title. II. Series.
DG205.P53   1988   937'.0072   88-40193
ISBN 0-299-11800-2
ISBN 0-299-11804-5 (pbk.)

What an *elogium* is. An *elogium* is an inheritance in the bad sense, as Cornelius Tacitus says in his book of jokes: "When he died, the legacy of his character passed on to his sons." (Fulgentius *Explanation of Obsolete Words* 54).

There are no other traces of a joke book written by Tacitus, and the very idea may itself at first glance seem to be a rather good joke. But it is actually more than that, and this study in a sense is about what such a work might have been, had it existed. Fulgentius' report perhaps has Tacitus' epigrammatic style in view. In any case, the possibility of a *Liber facetiarum* put together out of material taken directly from him or other historians points to a phase of ancient history, rhetoric, and politics worth pursuing in its own right.

Contents

Acknowledgments

A Vilas Grant from the University of Wisconsin provided major support for my project. Thanks are due to members of the Vilas Committee and to then Chancellor Irving Shain. Professor Barry Baldwin of the University of Calgary not only generously took time amid his own busy schedule to offer criticism and encouragement but also passed along specific bibliographic items. Among other things I owe him Fulgentius' "quotation" from Tacitus' *Book of Jokes* which I have chosen as a motto. I found particularly helpful the remarks of one of my readers about larger perspectives on politics at Rome and on the more recent political thought which I have occasionally used as a point of reference for the Roman historians. Another reader had more substantial reservations about my emphases and organization. I have given them careful consideration, and though I at last decided that the present form best represents what I want—or perhaps am able—to say, I appreciate having been made to consider alternatives to my own approach.

My colleague Barbara Fowler has read the manuscript more than once. She, too, has given me specific suggestions along with encouragement as editor of the Wisconsin Studies in Classics. I thank her for that, as I do Warren Moon and Paul MacKendrick, Frank Clover, and Barry Powell for the help of various kinds which they gave. I am also grateful to Joy DeStefano and Tom Birch for encouragement and reactions from their own, different perspectives. Barbara Hanrahan, Ruth Melville, Carol Olsen, and Jack Kirshbaum have in every way been most helpful editors at the University of Wisconsin Press. I would also like to thank our department secretary, Norma Maynard, for her efficient work on the word processor. None of those whom I have mentioned is responsible for what has been done or not done with their advice and help.

I am very conscious that formal acknowledgments of this kind do not discharge but simply recognize debts. That is true above all of my wife, Lorry, to whom I dedicate this work: for her patience.

NOTE ON EDITIONS USED

References to Tacitus are from the Teubner editions of the *Annals, Histories,* and *Dialogue* (H. Heubner), *Germania* (A. Önnerfors), and *Agricola* (J. Delz). Citations of Dio Cassius follow E. Cary's Loeb edition. Those of Suetonius' *Lives* are by title of each biography and follow the numbering in Rolfe's Loeb edition. Translations are my own except for Suetonius' descriptions of the emperors, which are based on Rolfe's version. In most cases, abbreviations in the text and notes follow those in the *Oxford Classical Dictionary*.

WIT AND THE WRITING OF HISTORY

Introduction

I

Two faces which resemble each other, neither of which alone causes our laughter, make us laugh by their resemblance when they are together.

It is easy enough to think of an explanation for this interesting observation of Pascal's: we laugh because our expectations are violated. We instinctively see people as individuals, and since faces are a primary index of identity we are momentarily startled by abnormally close resemblance. There is another equally interesting aspect to Pascal's puzzle on which he does not comment: the effect of unexpected resemblance may not be outright laughter but something more elusive—amusement, bemusement, slight discomfort, or embarrassment (would open comment be tactless, as though the resemblance were a defect?). And beyond this, embarrassment may shade into a stronger feeling of absurdity or oddity, since even superficial loss of identity can be as disturbing as it is amusing. Twins, as Bergson remarks, look manufactured.

Incongruity, then, is so broad and elusive that it invites rapid shifts of response running from amusement to alarm. If twins are amusing, quintuplets seem bizarre, and a roomful of clones terrifying. Ancient rhetoric paid considerable attention to the "ridiculous" and to incongruity in the form of violated expectation. Ancient historians, in turn, were heavily influenced by rhetoric, and they too employ for their own purposes the full range of effects that can be produced by disrupted expectation.

Tacitus' *Annals* 2.51 is a particularly subtle case in point of norms played off against each other to subvert expectations and yield peculiarly witty political insight. Germanicus and Drusus support Haterius Agrippa (a relative of the former) for the praetorship, while a good many of the senators prefer someone with more children, as the law provides. If the next sentence is taken neutrally, "Tiberius was pleased that the senate was intervening between his sons and the law; the laws, to be sure, gave way, but not at once and by a small margin, just as they gave way also when they used to have force."

Laetabatur Tiberius, cum inter filios suos et leges senatus disceptaret. Victa est sine dubio lex, sed neque statim et paucis suffragiis, quo modo etiam cum valerent leges vincebantur.

3

In other words, Tiberius is pleased that, since the senate did not openly fawn on his sons, the law was compromised in a traditional, republican way. But this can also be read less charitably with respect to Tiberius: "he was enjoying the spectacle of the senate's futile gesture of independence; for the laws, of course, [as Tiberius wanted] were being overridden but with a show of free debate, as they used to be when they still had validity [and they have none now]."[1] Especially the slight oxymoron in *quo modo etiam cum valerent leges vincebantur* and its easy suggestion of "though they now have *no* validity" indicate a not completely straightforward point. One aim of irony is precisely to leave uncertain what is ironic,[2] and here the slight double take in thought is perhaps best left unresolved as a subtle jest about political duplicity and incongruity. The form of the wit is in that case displaced emphasis, as in Martial's epigram on Philo, the apparently popular parasite, "who [as Philo puts it] has never dined *at home,* because [in Martial's view] he never *dines* [at home, i.e., he goes hungry] if he has no invitation" (5.47). The point is his hypocrisy, not his poverty, and that depends on hearing what both Philo and Martial have to say. By the same token, Tiberius is both *"pleased* at the senate's *traditional* role in making *timely* exceptions to the *validity* of the law" and *"amused* at its *empty* role as it *abrogates* laws, which now have *no* validity." The effect is like people talking past each other, and that is a fair description of how Tacitus often assesses the politics of the time.

Annals 12.5–6 is a more elaborate case in point.

> The marriage of Claudius and Agrippina was being confirmed by rumor as well as by the illicit relationship itself. But they did not yet dare to take formal steps, since there was no precedent for an uncle marrying his niece. It was actually quite improper, and they were afraid that it might lead to political trouble, so no one acted until Vitellius used his special talents to handle the situation. When asked whether he would bow to popular demand and senatorial authority, Caesar replied that he was a citizen subject to public sentiment. Vitellius then ordered him to wait in the palace while he himself went to the senate [where, claiming national priority, he began by saying that] "the great burdens of the Princeps, who runs the whole world, require support so that he can devote attention to the public welfare without distraction from private worries. What better solace for our Censor's spirit than to take a wife—companion in good times and in bad—to whom he can entrust his most intimate thoughts and his little children? Claudius is not given to extravagance or self-indulgence, but is a man who has obeyed the laws from his youth." [After this opening was received with great favor by the senators, Vitellius went on to say that] "since there is unanimous agreement that the Princeps should marry, a woman notable for family connections, for promise of children, and for high chastity has to be chosen. It does not take much reflection to see that Agrippina is outstanding in status, that she has proved her fertility, and that her virtue is no less exemplary. Moreover, it is quite wonderful that by divine providence a widow [some thought that Agrippina had poisoned her previous husband] be joined to a Prin-

ceps who has limited himself to his own wives [faint praise, since the measure is his insatiable predecessor]. Everyone has heard of or has seen wives taken forcibly at Caesar's pleasure, but that is unacceptable to our current high moral standards. Instead, a precedent should be set for the ruler receiving a wife with the senate's blessing. It is true, to be sure, that marriage with a brother's daughter is new to us. But elsewhere it is lawful, and marriage of first cousins, though long unknown, has in time become common. Custom changes—as occasion demands—and this too will soon be ordinary enough."

Historiographically, the passage has the formal authority of a document (perhaps echoing some of Vitellius' words) which puts official policy on record and shows its dishonesty. The chief point, though, lies beyond immediate facts in the exquisite unction of Tacitus' version, which turns what Vitellius says into the special self-parody of people who in a way do believe what they know to be false. This is a moral and political phenomenon noted elsewhere by Tacitus (e.g., "the more false what they were doing, the more they did it," *Historiae* 1.45.1). The possibility that political reality lies precisely in falsity is caught in the slippery tone of Vitellius' talk about propriety, combining as it does witty cynicism with serious proposal. The former comes chiefly from Tacitus, but here the ancient historian's traditional right to express his understanding of events through speeches delivered by principals and composed by himself comes into its own. For insofar as his understanding is correct, or at least reasonable, its immediate, organic connection with events makes it real in a way that detached editorial judgment cannot be. Thus in Vitellius' mouth joke fuses with serious proposal to become official and create amusing incongruity or (in Syme's phrase) morbid "gaiety"[3] that is revealing and true, even if in a sense unfair.

Exegetical details aside, the effect of such writing on a large scale is to create an atmosphere of dry wit and ruthless penetration into a political and moral reality that is often irrational if not idiotic. The tone is at once amusing and dismaying. Both those who make history and those who write it are caught up in pervasive cynicism, though one of quite different sorts—the former an alarming moral cynicism that suggests disorder in high places, the latter an intellectual cynicism gratifying because it exposes the former. In the hands of Tacitus the two coincide to produce a powerful wittiness that convicts by its very manner of describing. It is doubly appropriate that Tacitus, as both rhetorician and politician of the first rank, should have taken political rhetoric to extraordinary levels of sophistication. When Otho decides to commit suicide in order to bring civil bloodshed to an end, the senate "felt admiration, was ashamed to ask any more questions and everybody went over to Vitellius" (*Hist.* 2.53.2). The situation, in fact, was delicate, and accommodation with the victor under the circumstances was only reasonable. Yet the derision in the (anti)climax at the end of the sentence is unmistakable, the more so since Otho's suicide is treated by Tacitus as a heroic gesture, while Vitellius is a scoundrel. The collapse of a normal sense of rightness which this implies gradually becomes a major theme as we are conditioned by the absurdity of one anecdote after another: Nero admiring the charms of his mother's corpse (*Ann.* 14.9.1); Nero's freedman Polyclitus "absolutely terrifying to our own troops but funny to the enemy, who as free men had no idea of a freedman's power" (*Ann.* 14.39.2; cf. *Ann.* 12.49.1); the man (in Dio Cassius) executed for taking a coin with Tiberius' image on it into a latrine (58, frag. 2).

I want to examine this stylistic aspect of the historiography of the early empire particularly as it is used by Tacitus. Style is in the first instance something to be observed and intuitively appreciated, a performance that, if done well, need not be talked about. Nor is it often easy to say much, since the workings of style are elusive just because their effects are so evident on the surface. Yet it is possible to specify some of the techniques that arrest attention by interfering with normal patterns of expectation, and I have chosen "wit" as a useful category to do so for several reasons. Though it, too, is often something too obvious to need comment, still, what is obvious may be anything but trivial. In the first place, although historians had no interest in the current rhetorical theory of wit for its own sake, their style was itself self-consciously rhetorical, and epigrammatic expression in particular had points of contact with the various kinds of wit discussed in handbooks. Moreover, although ancient rhethorical theory of wit was for the most part restricted to practical matters and did not include the far-ranging speculation characteristic of modern theories, wit was put to serious uses. Rhetoricians were quite aware of its important ethical aspects, and for historians like Sallust or Tacitus the rhetorical techniques (like history itself) were ultimately a means to insight into the moral lesson of events. Hence their use of wit provides a special perspective from which to observe both stylistic strategies and the substantive conception of history those strategies serve.

"Aphorism," "joke," "humor," "epigram," the "comic," and "wit" are, of course, vague terms, and examples in the historians range from subtly nuanced sentences to preposterous anecdotes. We can perhaps help ourselves define "wit" by combining "quip" with "epigram," the former being live, spoken repartee that solidifies into something more weighty when it is fixed in writing or quotation and placed in an anecdotal setting. Epigrams are thus quips on permanent display, their weight embodying the calculated, intellectual facet that makes wit of special value to the historians. And since historical writing, like most literature, was performed and heard, when epigrams were passed on anonymously from one person to another (and that is another point of contact with jokes), the link to a live setting which is indispensable for quips was preserved. In fact many epigrams were originally live political jokes later drawn into the literary side of political life. So far as their rhetorical form is concerned, aphorisms are a kind of knowledge typical in oral societies, and rhetoric was still largely oral. This is the aspect of epigrammatic wit on which Tacitus comments in the *Dialogue* (20.4): "the young who follow orators not only want to hear but to carry home whatever is worth remembering, and then pass it on [in conversation] or use it in their correspondence, if an idea flashed out in a sharp and brief epigram." It is also what Quintilian has in mind when he mentions the rule that "the best *sententia* is improvised under pressure" (*petatur a periculo, Institutio oratoria* 2.11.3). Hence the natural coincidence of political joke and rhetorical epigram.

Settling on a precise, exclusive definition would help determine what in Tacitus, Suetonius, or Dio is pertinent for our purposes. But I prefer to allow an impressionistic, discursive, and inclusive collection of the historians' actual practice to define the role played by wit in the hope that collection simultaneously shapes and is shaped by an ostensive definition coherent enough to throw light on this aspect of ancient historiography. My aim is description rather than prescription. Though rhetorical theory had a good deal to say about wit, in the historians wit has nothing like the status of an independent, clearly defined category that can be isolated for consideration in its own right. Nor is it part of a theoretical notion of the comedy or absurdity of political life, though that was a philosophic commonplace, and the futility of political action under the Principate is a motif in Tacitus. Wit is accordingly for the most part accessible only through empirical inspection of examples. The recent work of R. Saller on the typology of anecdotes is a useful approach to identifying structures that underlie historical narrative; and typology, too, is typically concrete rather than abstract, since it aims to define general classes through specific instances.[4] In these terms I am more interested in a single genus than various species, or rather in the many examples of wit belonging to one genus insofar as they all exemplify the chief historiographic role of wit as such, that is, exposure of the moral and political absurdity to which the Principate could lead. A welcome side advantage of using wit as an organizing category is its constant reminder that the historians (and this is most true of Suetonius and Plutarch) were also interested in entertaining. If the number of examples I have included seems needlessly large, a generous reader will grant that in this case quantity itself is an index of how important wit really was to the historians.

II

Wit is not merely hard to define precisely; it is something notoriously difficult to evaluate even for those closest to it. An anecdote of Seneca the Elder's (*Controversiae* 2.2.12) is in the first instance about poetry, but the point it makes applies to wit more generally: the three lines of poetry chosen by Ovid's friends as his worst turned out to be the same lines chosen by him as his best, and all three apparently attracted attention because of ostentatiously witty wordplay. The hazards of assessing wit are greater in the case of a foreign culture, and still more so when wit is put to special uses as it is in the historians. It is often uncertain in what sense something was intended to be amusing—if it was at all. In a discussion of the social conventions conditioning the reception of jokes Victor Raskin remarks that he had "often been misunderstood and believed to be making a capital joke [when he made the following statement about Richard Nixon], simply because, according to the still prevailing stereotype, Mr. Nixon cannot be commended for anything seriously:

> Richard Nixon was the best American president in this century with regard to foreign policy.[5]

Tacitus himself may have been the victim or perhaps the author of a similar misunderstanding. He describes how Nero delivered the funeral oration for Claudius written by Seneca. Everything went smoothly until he came to a passage on his predecessor's "foresight and wisdom"; speaker and audience had so far been serious *(intentus)*, but then "no one could help grinning, though the speech was quite elegant" *(Ann.* 13.3.1). It is not clear whether the section was an ironic joke appreciated by everyone present, though perhaps missed by Tacitus who thought it was meant seriously, or whether it was serious flattery which immediately struck everyone except Seneca as a ridiculous lie.[6] In any case, the incident and Tacitus' account illustrate the curious elusiveness of such things as well as the way in which uncertainty between seriousness and wit can point to deeper uncertainty about political reality and pretense. Just possibly that is a point Tacitus wants to make. Suetonius remarks that Claudius' stupidity in the affair of Messalina and Silius "was beyond belief" *(Claudius* 29.3), yet since it was presumably also a fact, it again lies in an area in which what is absurd to the point of implausibility overlaps with what is true.

Misunderstanding arises from the differing expectations through which everything we hear is screened (and often screened out). As a rule we take statements at face value; when that is impossible, they are most naturally taken as jokes and will be dismissed as lies (or madness) only in special circumstances. In a climate of extreme political hostility, for example, this last might well have been the fate of Raskin's assessment of Nixon and in fact was the fate of much that was said and done by or about the emperors. Conflation of these two alternatives to normal truth telling—namely, joking or lying—occasionally comes up in the ancient historians. Thus Tiberius' talk of restoring republican procedures was received as both dishonest and funny *(vana, inrisa; Ann.* 4.9.1). Caligula would first pretend that senators he had secretly executed were still alive by sending them summonses and then claim that they had taken their own lives voluntarily (*Gaius Caligula* 26.2). The claim is labeled a lie by Suetonius, and official invitations to dead men are not only false but absurd as well, amounting to an odd inversion of the familiar tactic of nonpersonhood: instead of being alive though politically dead and gone, Caligula's victims are dead and gone though briefly still politically alive.

These fluid possibilities of intention reappear in political invective at Rome. Cicero remarks that when slander is done with a heavy hand, it is merely insulting, done "more wittily [*facetius*] it is urbane." He treats slander in either case as something recognized for what it is and distinct from accusation, which requires evidence (*Pro Caelio* 3). The distinction between accusation and slander—between truth and falsehood—was not as clear as Cicero wants it to be here, but what he says reckons with the same two kinds of falsehood: amusing or merely insulting.

> Frequently, when difference of opinion developed between advocates or statemen, there seems to have been not much real argument about the *matter* in controversy; instead, the opponents devoted themselves to *slander* and castigation of one another, which may have been *amusing* to the judicial or comitial gatherings.[7]

This is the range in which many reports move. "Caligula is said to have wanted to appoint his favorite horse consul" (*Calig.* 55.3). Suetonius reports this initially as a *fact,* but "it is said" suggests a floating story, either a *joke* against the emperor or one by him ("We've had some asses as consul, why not a good horse?").[8] And insofar as a joke is taken seriously it has the force of a *lie,* in this case pointing to imperial madness.

Tiberius' hints at republican restoration or Caligula's absentmindedness could, of course, be interpreted more charitably. The problem, as Cicero notes in his discussion of ambiguity and wordplay, is one of context and intention. When Scipio Africanus had difficulty fitting a wreath on his head at a banquet someone remarked, "It's no wonder that it doesn't fit, seeing how big our head [of state] is" (*De oratore* 2.250). Cicero cites this as something said "not in jest but seriously"; it is, of course, a joke—one of the most obvious kind—though with a serious point which might sound like a plain statement in some contexts. That would be the case at a gathering of uncritical admirers (this is probably what Cicero means when he says that the remark was not a jest), and the flattery to which it then comes close again illustrates the importance of context and intention. The choice between truth (or at least sincerity) on the one hand, laughable flattery or lie on the other, is largely in the eye of the beholder, and in their hostility to the emperors the ancient historians often accentuate what they regard as dishonesty by conflating it with absurdity. When Claudius celebrated the Secular Games—held about once every century—he was greeted by a "virtuoso of flattery" with the remark, "May you enjoy many more!" (Suet. *Vitellius* 2.5). This is a joke in the pejorative sense only in the context of conviction that such a wish about Claudius must be dishonest. In a different context it is precisely the sort of thing to say as a charming jest (like the remark about Scipio) representing the truth with good-natured exaggeration. Context and intention thus constitute a continuum on which the opposites "lie" or "truth" may be mediated by "wit," though not without some confusion. Suetonius reports Nero's "marriage" to Sporus as a plain case of sexual perversion (*Nero* 28.1). But it may have been no more than an exotic initiation ritual, reports of which were then taken by the emperor's enemies as a lie designed to conceal the ugly truth, the two in turn being mediated by a fine joke: "the course of history would have been better if Nero's father had had such a wife." Like Nixon's foreign policy talents, Nero's marriage is potentially at once lie, truth, and joke.

The historicity of much of this material is, of course, dubious to say the least, since joke and event are now difficult to keep apart, but that is irrelevant for my purpose. Though the accounts of Gaius' military expedition to the north are little short of hilarious, his order of the day to his troops to collect seashells in their helmets (for example) may in fact have simply been a disciplinary measure and not comic madness as the accounts suggest (Tacitus refers twice to the expedition as a farce, *ludibrium*: *Germania* 37.4; *Hist.* 4.15.2). When Caligula built a huge causeway over the bay at Baiae (*Calig.* 19), some thought that he was imitating Xerxes, others that he was trying to intimidate Germans and Britons with the size of his projects. Suetonius then mentions a third explanation: an astrologer had said that he could no more rule than ride across the bay on a horse. Suetonius himself favors this view and with his partiality to omens may not regard it as a wholly unreasonable *aversio ominis*. But there is still an impression of a lunatic last laugh: the huge scale, the quipping quality of the original omen, and the queer pointlessness of the effort since the event it is supposed to avert—Caligula's not becoming emperor—has already not happened.

The emperors' frequently recherché legal procedures are another rich source of funny situations. And they, too, are often difficult to credit at face value, though legal systems naturally generate genuine oddities at some point, all the more so in times of stress when they are used as political tools. An observer of contemporary American society might well wonder about a recent petition to the Food and Drug Administration for a ban on use of lethal drugs in capital punishment until their safety has been established. Is this a serious issue of regulatory law, good material for satirizing activist abuse of the legal system, or itself a gesture of satire designed to bring out incoherence in policy? It is all of these, and we might question its authenticity if we found it in an anecdotal history because it has the sound of a "just so" story that would readily be invented if it were not true.

It often seems natural to think of the Roman historians as writing political theater. Since public entertainment or displays by the emperor could in fact be an extension of politics by other means, there was at Rome an element of real make-believe that could lend events a fictional quality.[9] The account of Nero's murder of his mother has been read both as sheer fiction patterned on Clytemnestra/Orestes and partly as real-life fiction staged by Nero in the role of Agave with Pentheus.[10] In the first case, the story is false and material for malicious wit about Nero the actor; in the second, it is true and a mad gesture by Nero the actor. Particular interpretations are at best speculative. What is certain is that fact on the one side, fiction on the other are frequently mediated by a miragelike, witty intermediate region that offers multiple, unresolved perception of political reality, much as the passages quoted above (p. 3f.) invite a stereoscopic view of senatorial debate.

The complicated question of sources can also for the most part be set aside.[11] My interest is in wit as it functions in the historians, whatever its original position on the chain running back to events and whatever the relation of different versions among themselves. The old question of who makes jokes up naturally has special interest in politics, involving as it does the social level from which discontent comes and what its target is. Reworking of sources, especially by Tacitus, must have led to changes in this respect as in others, though the need to save the point works as a natural preservative of much original political wit.

III

The plan of my study is this. The epigrammatic prose of the historians (especially Tacitus) employs specific logical structures to achieve its effect. "Logical" here is another word for "rhetorical" in accordance with Aristotle's understanding of rhetoric as often a form of syllogistic thought. The logic of epigrams, in turn, is close to that of familiar kinds of jokes. What they have in common is incongruity, and ancient rhetoric was quite aware of this connection. Both epigrams and jokes violate ordinary, expected patterns of thought in ways designed to catch attention by demanding momentary rethinking of what has been said. The early Principate is, of course, in the first instance singularly unamusing in the ordinary sense of the term, and Tacitus is an equally unamused historian. But Suetonius' or Plutarch's *Lives* are in a somewhat more obvious sense amusing, and the pertinence of joking becomes even clearer if we reflect that jokes are not simply amusing but may also be grim, bitter, black, sick, sharp, and cruel—all words often apt for the period and its historiography. Like the *philosophes,* Tacitus in particular is "both witty and humorless—the wit demanded by [his] profession, the humorlessness imposed on [him] by [his] belligerent status."[12] It is this serious aspect that makes wit something far more than a rhetorical device and turns it into an effective instrument specifically for dealing with the phenomenon of political and moral pathology. There is little that is very novel in this, but I will employ some models for analysis which highlight facets of epigrammatic wit in the historians from new points of view. And I intend to follow in detail the ways in which wit was used both rhetorically and historiographically. The former is interesting as a prime example of classical writers' extraordinary virtuosity in exploiting the properties of language. The latter touches on some broader features of wit implicit especially in Tacitus' conception of political reality and how that affects the way he writes about it. Taken together, these aspects of language constitute a major part of the linguistic dimension of politics, and so a study of wit is at the same time a study of what J. Pocock has called the "politics of language":

> . . . a series of devices for envisaging the varieties of the political functions which language can perform and of the types of political utterance that can be made, and the ways in which these utterances may transform one another as they interact under the stress of political conversation and dialectic.[13]

The first chapter takes up a special sort of incongruity, but one that is of considerable importance both for the historians and for the political life of the time. Outrage (in an active as well as passive sense), absurdity, and incongruity combine in the notion of political *ludibrium,* which, along with related terms like *contumelia,* marks out a political reality that helps set the tone for the historians' own rhetorical strategy of echoing an absurd state of affairs in barbed epigrams and incongruous anecdotes—that is to say, in a witty style. Against this background Tacitus' claim to be writing *sine ira et studio* can be assessed as an effort to keep the reciprocal relationship between history and historiography in proper balance, the latter legitimately reflecting the truly absurd, "abusive" nature of the former without itself becoming mere rhetorical *ludibrium.*

The second chapter deals with one facet of Tacitus' pointed style in particular: antithetic epigrammatic prose. I am interested in how its witty form makes epigrams "work" (much as jokes are said to do) to create a peculiarly Tacitean atmosphere of conflict between norms and how that, in turn, contributes to his broader purposes.

> When Otho was afraid, he was feared. (*Hist.* 1.81.1)

> What should we envy about informers: that they fear or that they are feared? (*Dial.* 13.4)

Epigrams of this sort go a long way toward creating the distinctive texture of language used by Tacitus to talk about events. Their effect depends on a surface grammar and logic which, in turn, point to the deeper political logic that is his real concern. For epigrams do more than talk about events; they also suggest a certain understanding of them. Tacitus' language is not a neutral tool but itself reflects and in a sense reproduces *in nuce* the substance of Roman politics, in this case, a peculiarly self-defeating dialectic of terror. Antithetic structure can be looked at from several perspectives: as conflict of codes; as parody of one code by another; as manipulation of the logic governing all language, not least political language.

The next chapter examines in more detail the technique of violated expectation *(para prosdokian),* especially in Tacitus and specifically as a form of political wit, that is, witty protest against improbable political reality. We expect "Otho did not yet have authority to prevent crime: he was already trying to do so," but we are first given "Otho did not yet have authority to prevent crime: he was already able to—order it" *(Hist.* 1.45.2: *Othoni nondum auctoritas inerat ad prohibendum scelus: iubere iam poterat).* To mark this effect I often insert a dash at the point where the thought sequence suddenly changes direction, the pause representing the moment of incongruity. The result is a cynical quip whose broader significance is that, if absurdity is a specific property of political events, the historian will naturally speak of them in a witty way.

Wit is typically verbal, but it can extend to behavior as well, much as "style" is a quality of both language and behavior. Physical action is also a species of expression, and chapter four traces violation of expectation in forms that extend beyond words to such things as the emperor's grotesque physical appearance or to bizarre events: portents, omens, or enacted jokes (absurd happenings in the reigns of "funny" emperors, e.g., Gaius' contest of cripples or strange legal procedures). Witty, anecdotal history is authentic even if not factually true, because in its incongruity it is history written at one of its most common denominators. To paraphrase Marx, for the ancient historians in its very first occurrence history may be farce in a strong sense of the word as well as tragedy. Quintilian's three sources of laughter thus correspond roughly to the first four chapters: (1) mental states revealed by deeds or words, (2) physical appearance, (3) external things *(Inst.* 6.3.37).

Ethical, social, and political expectations are embodied in norms that take a wide variety of forms at all levels of society. Violations are "funny" in the dual sense of "odd" and "amusing" in proportion to the sensitivity of the area covered by the code, and in the fifth chapter I deal with the declamatory and the pointed (Senecan) literary styles much in vogue during the first century for their amusing oddness of expression. The dependence of both on often bizarre cleverness is symptomatic of a grimly witty attitude toward contemporary political and social reality. The diffuse satirical atmosphere epitomized in Seneca's quip about a man "who can't be blamed even for being born in our times" *(De tranquillitate animi* 14.4) was at work also in historiography and served as its larger cultural context.

The world described by Seneca and the declaimers often seems quite mad, and the last chapter examines irrationality in the more formal guise of paranoid political logic.[14] That is a natural target of political criticism and a natural medium for political wit, modern as well as ancient. Modern political satire is pertinent to the ancient historians insofar as its medium is often a peculiar historical fiction or what has been called "faction" dealing with "factoids." George Orwell or Alexander Zinoviev incorporates highly specific details of irrational policy taken over directly from contemporary history and meant to be factual in important ways. (The procedure can be used effectively on any political system, the stripe of the system determining the nature of the irrationality, though it is natural to look for formal parallels between avowedly authoritarian societies.) In this respect satire comes very close to the rhetorical history written by Tacitus or Suetonius and as a technique is useful for highlighting some of its features. The ultimate nature of irrationality, though, may be understood differently in ancient and modern political thought. It can be seen either as a product of special, abnormal circumstances or as an objective ingredient of political order as such. In recent centuries, especially since Hobbes, the second paradigm in one form or another has come into favor. As moral norms have tended to lose their privileged position, the logic and contradictions of political systems have become largely matters of neutral, autonomous fact, for example, that public interest may be best served by free competition in private greed. Tacitus and Dio, too, realized that freedom at Rome was in point of fact best served by "slavery" to the Principate. But for the most part they take the normative view. Politics is applied morality, and so political contradiction is the consequence of moral failure in leadership—servility on the one side, brutality on the other—and therefore an occasion for witty indignation as well as theoretical insight.

I

Ludibrium and Political Wit

I

A natural starting point for examination of wit in the historians is the complex of political ideas centering on *ludibrium* and related terms like *contumelia, illudere,* or *inridere* (i.e., "nasty joking," "absurd playing," "insult," "abuse"). With slightly different emphases all of these words mark out a side of political life prominent enough to have a vocabulary of its own and covering a wide area well beyond wit in the ordinary sense. What is typical of wit is an intellectual element of deliberate cleverness. It is that, as Plutarch observes (*Quaestiones convivales* 631c), which can make wit actually seem more offensive than simple insult. "I remember when you wiped your nose with your arm" is rougher than "You're a fishmonger" because it wittily requires an inference from an omitted thought about fishmongers if it is not to be merely pointless. By the same token when Caesar spoke of his obligations to Nicomedes, Cicero's jibe, "Enough! We know what you two gave each other!" (Suet. *Julius* 49.3) is more effective than plain talk about rumors of a homosexual relation. The same point is implicit in an anecdote in Dio (59.26.8). As Gaius, dressed like Jupiter, was issuing oracles, a Gaul burst into laughter, and when asked by the emperor, "What do I look like?" he replied, "A big humbug!" Dio adds that "nothing was done because he was a shoemaker," for though this is formally a joke (by *para prosdokian*), what he ways is not really clever, has no political bearing, and is therefore not offensive. It would be all of these if he were a senator, and its merely amusing candor does become political wit when it is cited as an anecdote.

Since political wit is typically hostile, it is a species of *ludibrium,* the latter being aggressive though not necessarily clever, while political wit is both. The two are easily confused, and that leads Tacitus to dissociate the wit of his own rhetoric from mere *ira et studium,* that is, from the overt *ludibrium* to which it is both opposed and akin. He is aiming at something at once more and less, with more bite and less bark.

The word *ludibrium* has decidedly negative overtones, since the peculiarly derisive dimension to political events which it represents is tied to a breakdown in normal restraint and seriousness. As a result, its element of jest is often a vicious sport or ugly theater of the absurd (cf. *ut si in circo aut theatro ludicrum, Hist.* 1.32.1; 3.83). It displays the familiar ambivalence of the English "funny"—both disturbingly or shockingly "strange" and "amusing."[1] It ranges accordingly from direct acts of violence to witty and amusing political incongruity. And in one moment of discouragement it becomes for Tacitus a general quality of history itself (*Ann.* 3.18.4).

Latin usage marks out a spectrum of meaning for such words running from physical "outrage" to verbal "joke." *Ludibrium* and *contumelia,* often in tandem, cover both. Thus Thrasea was faced by outright physical *ludibria* and *contumeliae* (*Ann.* 16.26.1); on the other hand, though Claudius' intelligence was weak (*imminuta mens*), choice of a successor outside the family "might be the occasion for *ludibria* and *contumeliae*" (*Ann.* 6.46.2). This is clearly unwelcome political wit, and the dilemma was that Claudius' *imminuta mens,* too, was the subject of a great deal of such wit. The stages of violence in mutiny escalating from word to deed are carefully laid out along the same lines: first ridicule (*inrisus*), then insult (*contumeliae*), finally blows (*verbera, Ann.* 1.20.1). The notion of malicious wit even in the grossest abuse is inherent in *inridere* or *inludere;* and political slanging, though not on a high level of sophistication, would often involve more than mere name-calling. When Nero had aroused Tiberius' hostility, everyone abandoned him, while Sejanus' supporters "stayed around laughing at him" (*Ann.* 4.60.2; cf. *Hist.* 2.30.3); the naturally insolent urban plebs "had fun with the soldiers by taunting them," (*Hist.* 3.32.2); Nero "had fun with Sulla's detached head because of its premature grey" (*Ann.* 14.57.4); Galba's advanced years "were a subject of merriment and scorn for those who were used to Nero" (*Hist.* 1.7.3; cf. *Hist.* 2.74.1). This becomes vicious practical joking when it involves physically abusive "sport." Thus Galba's corpse as well as his age was subjected to *ludibria* (*Hist.* 1.49.1; cf. 2.49.3).

When *inludere* and *ludibrium* mean "deceive," "trick" (e.g., *Hist.* 3.10.3), the semantic field is extended more clearly in the direction of cleverness, and Seneca's mocking of Nero's singing voice (*Ann.* 14.52.3) or the *contumelia* in poems of Bibaculus and Catullus against the Caesars (*Ann.* 4.34.5) is political wit in a more normal sense. The power of wit to offend because of cleverness comes up again here. The "witty" (*dicax*) consul Fufius won Tiberius' enmity "because he had been accustomed to ridicule him with sharp jests, which are long remembered by those in power" (*Ann.* 5.2.2; Nero similarly felt the witty *ferocia* of Vestinus, *Ann.* 15.68.3).

Bitter amusement and jest, then, are a recurrent part of political reality. "Urbanity is a quality of language concentrated in a short statement and suitable for pleasing and moving men to any emotion, but especially suitable for defense or attack as situation or person might demand" (Domitius Marsus, quoted in Quint. *Inst.* 6.3.104). Many of the cases of laughter at political developments mentioned by the historians would have been urbane wit in this sense—clever in expression rather then merely abusive and as such capable of opening up insight into political absurdity at deeper levels. The heavy military guard at Augustus' funeral "excited much laughter" from those who recalled earlier stages of Roman servitude at Rome (*Ann.* 1.8.6). When Claudius performed ancient rites of purification on the very day on which one of his victims died, "everyone was amused" (*Ann.* 12.81). When he had a statue of Augustus removed from a place set aside for executions, he "was laughed at for watching what he forbade a statue to see" (Dio. 60.13.3). A senator who flattered his way into a one-day consulship "was the object of much laughter" (*Hist.* 3.37.2). When Vitellius cited his own disagreements with Thrasea as evidence for senatorial free speech, "some laughed at the impudence of the comparison with Thrasea" (*Hist.* 2.91.3).

This passive, defensive sense of amusement about politics on the part of those who are powerless is one side of the coin. The other is the emperor's aggressive exercise of political power in *ludibrium* and *contumelia* that often take the form of absurd abuse of supreme power. Augustus' consultation of priests on the legality of marrying a woman pregnant by her previous husband (*Ann.* 1.10.5) is *"per ludibrium"* because it trifles hypocritically with public decencies. This is not too serious, and Tiberius' "customary mixture of *ludibria* with *seria"* could be on occasion nothing more than amusingly ironic rejection of a proposal that would have compromised his security (*Ann.* 6.2.4). But Caligula's preposterous behavior on an expedition to the north is more disturbing *ludibrium* (*Germ.* 37.4; *Hist.* 4.15.2), and boundless senatorial obsequiousness in the face of Nero's crimes is farce *(ludibria)* "harder to bear now than the crimes themselves" (*Ann.* 14.59.4), that is to say, well on the way to becoming an overriding political reality. That is the case again when Messalina "ridicules [*inludere*] Roman politics" in her affair with Silius, which is in fact treated by Tacitus as farce with serious implications (*Ann.* 12.7.3). The savagery inflicted on Christians is *ludibrium* that was part of a maniac "circus game" (*Ann.* 15.44.4), and when Nero permits victims who are already dead to choose the manner of their death, he "is adding *ludibria* to murder" (*Ann.* 16.11.3). The dual sense borne by *ludibrium* is particularly effective in cases like this last. Legal action after execution is both a rational gesture of triumphant "mockery" and as such at a deeper level of insight also a symptom of true "absurdity." On another occasion, after a consul is taken summarily from a dinner he is hosting and executed by Nero, the terrified guests are held under arrest for a time fully expecting the same fate, only to be released to Nero's "laughing remark that they had suffered enough for their consular banquet" (*Ann.* 15.69.3).

The atmosphere of "playful," absurd violence in Roman political life is epitomized in the career of Vatinius, "among the foulest portents [*ostenta*] of Nero's court, deformed in body, skilled in vulgar wit" (*Ann.* 15.34.2). He was first taken on by the imperial entourage as a butt of ridicule, then proved to be expert at abusing others. The word *ostenta*—itself a touch of *contumelia* on Tacitus' part—in addition to the gross incongruity which it suggests, points to something that destroys the seriousness of Roman political life on a deeper, more ominously "funny" level. That is also true in a more specific way of the peculiar absurdity implicit in political censorship, whose futile efforts to control literature "should be laughed at for thinking that present power can blot out future memory" (*Ann.* 4.35.5). And Claudius' rise to power leads Tacitus to reflect on the effects of absurdity in human affairs on the very largest scale (*Ann.* 3.18.4; cf. *Ann.* 6.48.1):

> The wider my reflection on recent and ancient history, the more I am struck by the general absurdity of human experience [*ludibria rerum mortalium*].

This is then followed by a remark in which he sees the emergence of the comic Claudius much as Aristophanes sees the success of the Sausage Seller, though in this case the huge joke (by *para prosdokian*) is a matter of fate itself.

> In reputation, expectation, and esteem almost everyone else seemed a more likely candidate for power than the future emperor whom fate was keeping hidden.

In some of these passages, of course, the motif of political amusement may be an editorial addition of Tacitus' own, though the demonstrative nature of Roman politics and the limited means for expression under the emperors make it plausible enough. At any event, beyond particular cases political *ludibrium* is the general premise for historiographic wit insofar as a major aim of the pointed, epigrammatic style is to replicate the sense of derision that often attached to events. Tacitus' unusual language gradually builds up a distinct world of its own like a prism made of many faces set at different angles to the external world and reflecting it with varying degrees of distortion or precision. This counterworld has a surface hue or—to use ancient rhetorical terminology—a "color" determined by the texture of his language, and the images appearing in it are designed to distort only as they highlight what is actually in the original. Incongruity and absurdity should be reflected back from actual political life in such a way that reflection occurs at a higher level of insight,[2] and that is crucial for Tacitus' understanding of the legitimacy of his work.

II

The historians generally drew on a pool of often sensational material for their picture of what we now might call the "ludibristic" or derisive side of history. Anecdotes are of special value for political wit that is startling, but the perspectives and the effects achieved by Suetonius and Tacitus are quite different on that score. Tacitus' wit is the more penetrating because his aim is to unmask the political implications of moral irrationality. Suetonius is less ambitious. He is concerned chiefly with the personal evil of individual emperors, and he sees it for the most part in its own terms as personal scandal. "Suetonius too thinks that Tiberius' behavior was, in general terms, hypocritical (42.1), and states that Claudius' civility was a show (35.1). But his method (unlike Tacitus') does not allow him to expose the element of sham."[3] In Suetonius absurdity is episodic and often close to a dubious kind of disjointed psychohistory made up of anecdotal insights into character. We are not conscious of a witty rhetorical presence permeating everything—even the narrative—and unmasking everything as we are in Tacitus, who uses wit organically and at a much higher level. Suetonius is chiefly a collector of biographical facts, not a writer of historical narrative,[4] and the absurdity on which political wit depends tends to come in blocks of its own in the *Lives,* where it remains as the stuff of *ludibrium* with its potential as a genuine category of historical understanding largely unrealized.

Yet it seems too much to say that there is no exposure of sham in Suetonius. For one thing, though his style is far blander than Tacitus', Suetonius was not simply a collector of data. He took his facts from a variety of sources, including earlier historians, but he selected and arranged what he took, drastically reducing narrative and chronology to make both secondary to certain categories or rubrics (e.g., *Augustus* 9.1) designed to bring out the ethical reality of history. Though Suetonius does not work with a conflict between the political codes of empire and republic, his categories do create contrast between moral codes of virtue and vice. What is more, the gross moral incongruity that marks the lives of some emperors on a large scale is brought to light through a pattern of disappointed expectation: promising beginnings subsequently unmasked as illusion.[5] Suetonius' many sensational anecdotes initially are simply part of his sources and reflect interest in the drama of power (now centered in the emperor). Though they stand out in the biographies as raw data, from one point of view that isolation allows us to see all the more clearly the elements from which the witty and satirical dimension of history comes: violation of ordinary expectation in startling remarks, bizarre events, and absurd behavior. Seen in the perspective of each *Life* as a whole and of all the *Lives* together, "funniness" exposes, in a way that is bound to go some way beyond entertainment or information, the dissonance between ordinary norms and those that often come to dominate the political life of the Principate. To this extent the portrait of the earlier emperors is a statement of Suetonius' own about Roman politics in general and perhaps about the politics of his day, though without the large-scale engagement or focus of Tacitus and his extraordinarily thoughtful wittiness.[6]

III

Tacitus' conviction that a major part of the historian's task is to expose sham or something worse is what makes his claim to be writing *sine ira et studio* hard to assess (*Ann.* 1.1.3). The claim by itself is a commonplace and has to be seen against the larger tradition of political protest and political wit in ancient society.[7] For the most part such protest did not rise above the level of ordinary *ludibrium*. Tacitus defines his own position by insisting that his account will not replicate the absurdity of events in rhetorical excess of its own making. It is an essential task of the historian to portray the absurdity and abusiveness that are plain facts of history, but only as the property of history and not of historiography itself.

Direct physical violence is commonly restrained in society by rituals of one sort or another. In Rome rough-and-ready popular justice at one time took the form of verbal protest designed to bring infamy on the guilty party.[8] The insulting chants still being used later as a political tactic were an extension of this tradition of political abuse, which then reappears in still more refined form both in oratory and ultimately in epigrammatic wit as a means of political criticism in historiography. Ancient writers traced a similar line of development in the history of comedy. Farmers who felt wronged came to their village to denounce the guilty party. When this proved to be an effective check on injustice, the practice was formalized by being transferred to the theater. Comic poets subsequently took over the work of social criticism, and when their gross abusiveness was gradually restricted by law, it became indirect— that is, witty rather than merely abusive—until finally even that was halted.[9] Something like the latter stages was still important in its own way in politics and historiography at Rome.

The scheme is a product of Peripatetic and Hellenistic literary theory incorporating appreciation for the political dimension of wit. Integrating abusive joking as an acceptable social form of protest is followed by emergence of refined, indirect wit, especially in response to pressure from "the rich and powerful who want to do wrong with impunity."[10] Thus in comedy as a literary genre, increasing sophistication goes with decreasing political power of wit. The possibility that in accommodating itself to political restraints wit could actually become a more, rather than less, powerful tool of criticism and understanding was naturally something that concerned rhetoric and historiography in particular because of their direct connection with politics. Freedom of criticism was a live issue during the Principate. Stoics and Cynics were prepared to use gross violation of ordinary social norms as a method of criticism and reform. Their subversion of conventional decencies was embodied especially in the *spoudaiogeloios*—the "earnest buffoon"—and though the disdain felt by the wise man was usually far too overt for wit in the proper sense, Cynic/Stoic rhetoric may well have influenced the development of the more refined wit of the literary epigram. "It is hardily fantastic to see in the Stoic paradox the origin of the epigrammatic *mot* that distinguished Sallust from Cicero."[11] Whatever the exact truth of this suggestion may be, it is fair to say that the jarring effect and serious moral intention of Stoic paradox do reappear in Sallust, and what is true of him on this score is even truer of Tacitus.

Too direct violation of convention (as is often the case in satire) creates offense.

> There are in general two types of jokes—one illiberal, petulant, scandalous, obscene; the other elegant, urbane, natural, witty. (Cic. *De officiis* 1.103)

> Comedy [*kōmōdia*] differs from abuse [*loidoria*]; the latter openly brings out evils that are present, the former requires what is called "innuendo." (*Tractatus Coislinianus* VII)[12]

Wit arises from judicious probing of limits, from momentary breaches that create surprise or ambivalence rather than mere anger or incomprehension. Since the Stoic philosopher rejects any external restrictions on his freedom, he speaks his mind directly ("the wise man will speak right out," Cic. *Epistulae ad familiares* 9.22). He does so because he rejects all conventional codes, and to the extent that his outrageously frank language excludes urbane indirection it destroys the possibility of wit.

The need for sensitive balance between sharp wit and mere abuse is the background against which Tacitus' claim to write *sine ira et studio* must be set. The problem of abusive political wit is repeatedly mentioned by the historians of rhetoric, Cassius Severus, for example, being faulted by Tacitus and others for his harshness.[13]

> [Augustus was incensed by the] pleasure [*libidine*] which he took in insulting prominent figures through insolent writings. (*Ann.* 1.72.3; cf. Suet. *Aug.* 56.1 for *ioci invidiosi et petulantes* as a general political hazard)

> . . . more bile than blood . . . confused in his use of weapons, carried away by eagerness to hit, he did not so much fight as brawl . . . though compared to his successors he was superior in cleverness of wit. (*Dial.* 26.4)

> I [Cassius himself] remember that I entered his [Cestius'] lecture room just as he was about to speak against Milo; with his usual vanity he was saying, "If I were a gladiator, I would be [the great] Fusius; if I were a pantomime, I would be [the great] Bathyllus, if I were a horse, I would be [the great] Melissio." I couldn't restrain my anger and shouted, "if you were a sewer [*cloaca*], you would be the greatest [Cloaca Maxima]!" The students looked at me and wondered who the boor was. Cestius, who had intended to answer Cicero, could not think of an answer to me and refused to go on unless I left. I wouldn't go from the public

bath before I had washed. Then I decided to avenge Cicero on Cestius in the forum. I summoned him to court before the praetor, and when I had satisfied myself with jokes and insults, I demanded that he be indicted. (Sen. *Controv.* 3, pref. 16–17)

Labienus' abusiveness itself became the subject of a joke in the nickname "Rabienus" (Mad Dog),[14] and uncomplimentary references to both his and Cassius' social background can perhaps be taken as indications that the politics of resentment was suspected of playing a role in their methods ("he was of low origin and vicious life," *Ann.* 4.21.3; a man of "great poverty, great notoriety, and great hatred," Sen. *Controv.* 10, pref. 4). Seneca remarks that Labienus became a shadow cast by his enemies, fully as repressive in his way as they were ("such was his 'freedom' that he went beyond what can be taken as freedom," *Controv.* 10, pref. 5). This sounds like a description of Cynic extremism, and the joke about "Rabienus" may have been suggested by the well-worn pun on Cynic "dogs." Tacitus, too, had reservations about some of the symbolic resistance to the government in philosophic circles,[15] since he saw it as a misguided style of opposition bound often to duplicate the arrogance and absurdity it despised (*contumacia; inanis iactatio libertatis, Agricola* 42.3).

It is this excess, then, that he claims to avoid with his own refined wit, carefully poised between abusive hostility (*ira et studium* = *odium*) and compliancy (*metus, adulatio, Ann.* 1.1.2). That is the point again of the programmatic statement in *Histories* 1.1.2. Flattery and hatred are equally fatal to truth, but the latter is the greater danger given the human tendency to believe the worst: "of course, adulation suffers the ugly charge of slavishness, while there is a false appearance of freedom in malice." In the *Agricola* (1.4) he writes, "if I intended to denounce Agricola, I would not have to apologize for my biography of him." What lies between flattery and hatred is *ludibrium* transformed into tightly disciplined wit. For Tacitus the issue is not principally biased content; in his view the facts of official crime are plain enough. What matters is insight into the fundamental state of affairs beyond particular facts. In that light, tough-minded wittiness can be a category of serious historical thought if the historian repeats the active politician's task of finding a reasonable mean laid out with formal precision in *Annals* 4.20.3: "to walk a path free of ambition and danger between sheer insolence and ugly compliance" (cf. *Agr.* 8.3, 42.3).

At the beginning of the introduction we considered some cases (*Ann.* 2.51, 12.5–6) in which fixing a single meaning does not do justice to the force of Tacitus' language. Irony resists simple resolution, carrying part of the truth in its very equivocation between statement and jest. For that reason it is a fine way of being angry while avoiding *ira et studium. Annals* 6.50 is another example. The "report" that Tiberius regarded dissimulation as his finest *virtue* (*Ann.* 4.71.3) is a textbook case of sour wit, perhaps originally an actual jest making the rounds in Rome. Later, as death drew near, Tiberius' "body and strength were now giving out, but not yet his dissimulation" (*Iam Tiberium corpus, iam vires, nondum dissimulatio deserebat, Ann.* 6.50.1). Dissimulation in this case really is a virtue; Tiberius is showing good old-fashioned Roman toughness (*rigor animi*), and Tacitus has to admire it. At the same time, since it is still his *old* deviousness, which had "not yet" left him, it is a virtue oddly going under the name of a vice, and so we are vaguely conscious of the curious notion that Tiberius somehow did not even die candidly. Tacitus is interested not simply, or perhaps even principally, in getting the facts of Tiberius' last days straight but also in making a point about dissimulation. There is again no need to resolve the account into either malice or admiration.[16] The "tactless" choice of the word *dissimulatio* creates a stereoscopic perspective that fuses both angles into a deeper, witty antinomy that by itself makes a particular point about Roman politics.[17]

Tacitus' account of Curtius Rufus, the low-born overachiever who rose to proconsular rank (*Ann.* 11.21), is one last passage worth special attention for its coupling of sober historical judgment with derisory wit. After Rufus had begun to attract attention, Tiberius is said by Tacitus to have "veiled his scandalous origin by remarking, 'It seems to me that Rufus is his own ancestor'" (*videtur mihi ex se natus*). In a society as conscious of status as Rome even a euphemistic quip of this sort is bound also to be a witty put-down. It is, in fact, a fine example of the potentially insulting cleverness of wit. Tiberius himself was put down by an attempt of Augustus to defend him (*velut excusando exprobraret, Ann.* 1.10.7), and though Augustus apparently was sincere, the effect must have seemed amusing to many.

The point of Tiberius' whimsy is anticipated by a remark of Tacitus' own along the same line. "About the origin of Curtius Rufus, whose father is said by some to have been a gladiator, I would neither want to hand on lies, and I'm ashamed to pursue the truth" (*neque falsa prompserim et vera exsequi pudet*). This has a straightforward side: historians naturally want to avoid falsehood. But it is more than a neutral methodological statement; here judicious restraint is at the same time a dismissive, tendentious historian's jest to go along with Tiberius' politician's jest. And both hinge on incongruity: Rufus does not "belong";[18] he is a funny man whose incongruity naturally produces wit even as it is spoken about seriously. Despite accomplishments acknowledged by Tacitus, he finally exists in a political limbo drained of a good portion of any real worth. As a man without a past or a past best not spoken of, he is an emblem of larger political failure, of something absurdly *missing* at Rome. That is a note struck repeatedly by Tacitus, for example, in the epigram on the great future Galba had *behind* him and in a line on the false Agrippa, who in effect had future and past but no present (see below, pp. 62, 120). (To avoid arrest he has always just come or already left before word spreads that he really *is* anywhere; the tactic is reasonable enough for a man on the run, but Tacitus does not miss the larger suggestion of absurd unreality.) Tiberius' jest about Rufus is witty nonsense; Tacitus' own remark combines arch *praeteritio* (telling the truth by saying that he will not tell the truth) with *para prosdokian* (we do not really expect an historian worried about falsehood to avow that he is ashamed to tell the truth). The latter is further reinforced by the slight hitch between *neque* and *et,* with *neque* ("I would *neither* want to hand on lies") making us expect to hear something like "*nor* would I suppress the truth" along with "*and* [yet] I had better not tell the truth."

The epigrams on Galba, the false Agrippa, and the self-made Rufus thus all freeze and fix in our consciousness a peculiar pattern in Roman politics about which Tacitus is perfectly serious: less than meets the eye, empty, insubstantial, spurious. The point is driven home with another epigram about Rufus hinging on the notion of full and final reckoning. That is a topos commonly called up by inclusive formulas like "past, present, or future," "good, bad, or indifferent," "win, lose, or draw." In *Histories* 3.36.1, for example, Vitellius meets the threat to his imperial power by stuffing himself like an animal "forgetful of past, present, future." The fact that he dealt with the problems of power by heavy eating and drinking is worth knowing and perhaps rates ranking with other clinical cases of the era, but Tacitus' real point is carried in the inclusive, epigrammatic form of expression. For the suggestion of decisive, exhaustive, final assessment in "past, present, future" elevates Vitellius' behavior into the more general truth that contact with the real world may actually be wholly lost at the highest level of government. Not only is that true, but the idea of an emperor just *ignoring everything* makes a good joke, as does the later remark that he "would have forgotten that he had been emperor, if he had not been reminded" (*Hist.* 3.63.2). And taken together, truth and jest yield insight into political absurdity.[19] By the same token, derisory wit and historical judgment coincide in *Annals* 11.21 when Tacitus says that Rufus attained his improbable destiny only to "fawn grimly on superiors, bully inferiors, and be difficult with equals" (*adversus superiores tristi adulatione, adrogans minoribus, inter pares difficilis*). On a factual level we now know that he was an ungracious official. Beyond that, the fact is put in amusingly crisp language, whose precise, exemplary terms formalize the futility in Roman politics. It is easy to imagine a current joke about the "complete bureaucrat" behind the epigram, for what is amusing is the queer summing up of a successful career through an exemplary set of every possible professional *failing* (contrast *Agr.* 9). As witty expression cues insight into a deeper pattern, it screens out abusiveness while permitting the real *ludibrium* of events to come through in *contumelia* purged of mere *ira et studium* by rhetorical wit of a high order. The immediate background for Tacitus' claim to impartiality was the domination of historiography by writers hostile to the emperors. He was bound to use their material, yet could think that he was treating it in a fair way, not because he had eliminated the hostility but because he had nothing personal at stake prior to Flavian times.[20]

II

Antithetic Epigrams

I

Poetic epigrams may simply be versified jokes whose literary value is for the most part not of a high order. And since they usually have no specific context, their wit too is without significance beyond itself; like ordinary jokes they are no more than casual entertainment.

But wit becomes much more than mere diversion when it is no longer self-contained but deals with expectations seriously entertained in the real world. This dimension appears in prose and was the subject of considerable discussion in rhetorical theory. Rhetoric itself, of course, was often no more than witty diversion worked out on a larger scale than (say) Martial's epigrams but of no larger significance. Yet insofar as it dealt with actual legal and political issues and was "that quality in discourse by which the speaker or writer seeks to accomplish his purpose"[1] (and even so severe a critic as Plato conceded that), we should expect that epigrammatic wit might well be put to serious uses. The witty turn of phrase, the startling anecdote are, in fact, major features of historiography dealing with the early Principate, and they are important because in this setting incongruity helps shape our perception of historical reality itself.

Since we have defined wit particularly in formal terms—that is, as violation of expectation—it will be useful first to examine a more general aspect of Tacitus' rhetoric from a formal point of view.

II

One of the distinctive marks of classical historiography is the principle that history is a matter not simply of facts but of values. That is notably true for Tacitus, whose most memorable scenes are as much exemplary and dramatic as historical: the grotesque comedy of Nero's murder of his mother; the surreal battle in the moonlight near Cremona; Vitellius shortly before he is lynched wandering in bewilderment through the palace opening doors on silent and empty rooms; street fighting in Rome cheered on by the populace as taverns remain open and prostitutes move among piles of corpses. The peculiar power of such passages comes from Tacitus' awareness of the cruelty and irrationality just below the surface of political life. Vitellius' death is signaled by a kind of primitive shunning; street fighting in Rome exemplifies the degrading psychological link of normal pleasure with violence. A distinction between history and rhetoric (in the sense of "fiction") is, of course, observed by Tacitus, and however we may assess his success in maintaining the distinction, even the most dramatic scenes are always authentic history for him insofar as ethical truth is itself a plain fact among other facts and human beings are inescapably moral agents.

The rhetorician's primary tool is style, and the most important effect of Tacitus' style is creation of an epigrammatic atmosphere that has variously been described as "sinewy," "tense," "mordant," "angular."[2] Like highly dramatic scenes, style itself makes a substantive point in that its distinctive qualities embody the nature of historical reality and the ethical insight needed to understand it. Tacitus' compressed, elliptical syntax demands special effort for comprehension and thus draws his readers into the narrative. As they work to grasp the unusual form of expression they are subtly drawn to conspire with his view of events.[3]

> Appropriate style, too, makes what is said persuasive. For the mind is tricked [*paralogizetai*] into believing that what is said is the way things are, so that people think—even if it is not so—that things are as the speaker says. The hearer always is sympathetic with a dramatic speaker, even if he says nothing. (Aristotle *Rhetoric* 1408a19).

As is true for any good rhetoric, Tacitus' medium *is* in good measure his message; the very linguistic texture of his Latin suggests aggressive and ruthless intelligence exposing the hidden reality of events with tight-lipped indignation and distain. It is as though it were all so urgent that he has no time for observing ordinary grammatical courtesies. Demetrius' generalized description of brevity fits Tacitean Latin on this score exactly: "as wild beasts gather themselves before they leap, so words draw together and coil up to create force" (*On Style* 8; cf. Tacitus' own characterization of the compact explosive power of the pointed style whose "meaning blazes out in a bright and brief epigram," *Dial.* 20.4).

In the light of the status of rhetoric in ancient culture it is not surprising that form and style should have so important a role in relation to content, though in Tacitus they are bound together in an unusually fundamental way. In his case, content is political reality, and that depends on a code or set of rules which makes it possible for men to act intelligibly and for historians to evaluate their actions. Though he is no republican and concedes the necessity of the Principate, in his view the authentic code is in general that of republican values and its aristocratic *virtus:* above all, personal liberty, then discipline, concern for public welfare and public esteem.[4] The Principate accordingly is evil insofar as it violates that code ("hence when the system of government changed, all traditional and genuine values vanished," *Ann.* 1.4.1), and the importance of rhetoric for the historian derives from its ability, by structuring *language,* to help convey the *substantive* contrast between right and wrong. If political reality has in fact gotten out of joint, it must also be made to seem and sound so.

Some of Aristotle's views on the nature of rhetoric are instructive in this connection because they describe as a matter of theory what any rhetorician concerned about the dangers of *ira et studium* would be alert to in practice. At the very start of the *Rhetoric* (1354a16–55b7) he remarks that conventional rhetoric deals chiefly with "prejudice, pity, anger and other such emotions." For that reason rhetoric would be wholly useless if trials dealt strictly with objective evidence and left value judgment up to the jury. It would have to limit itself to facts, and under such ideal circumstances judgments, too, would be spelled out for the jury as much as possible by law to eliminate the influence of human passions. Passions, though, are in fact unavoidable. Politics entails emotional persuasion of some kind, and so political discourse is bound to reflect a society's ethos, for better or worse. In a corrupt society, then, a reasonable speaker takes his cue from the rhetoric currently setting terms for public discussion. And what he says will be responsible—even though it may be highly charged—if it is disciplined in the special logic of rhetoric, and fair-minded if it avoids excess.

The historian's rhetoric is thus bound to reflect the form and substance of current political reality even as it subverts them. In addition, as rhetoric it does more than express a moral code, since its own techniques themselves serve as another kind of code that shapes attitudes by generating and manipulating linguistic expectations.[5] As a result language and event (rhetoric and history) fit together in interlocking layers: (1) bare historical facts are (2) put into order in terms of a moral code that defines good and evil and expresses its values persuasively in (3) rhetorical structures embodying linguistic codes. Layers (1) and (2) are historical reality in its factual and ethical sides; (3) is the linguistic dimension of history, which Tacitus' rhetorical technique can deal with on any scale from phrases or sentences to entire scenes.

After first introducing Poppaea in an entirely factual manner (*Erat in civitate Sabina Poppaea . . .* , *Ann.* 13.45.1; this is level 1), Tacitus reveals the moral truth (level 2) about her in an epigram (level 3): "this woman had everything else except—character" *(huic mulieri cuncta alia fuere praeter honestum animum).*[6] Historical fact is divided into her external status at Rome (she had everything one might want) and her internal, moral character, and the latter is taken in hand by rhetoric. The familiar linguistic structure "everything . . . except" leads us to expect that the exception about to be mentioned is one among any number of things that Poppaea might or might not in point of fact have. But Tacitus has character in view, and by writing a sentence which sounds as though that were optional he reinforces his judgment that it is not. The epigram thus exposes and judges what the narrative states and describes. The arresting violation of expectation in "everything except—character" asserts the corruption of a society in which such a statement actually meets expectations because character is treated as optional. Between Tacitus and his reader the line is a bitter witticism. In the setting of public language though, it is a matter of ordinary fact, and Tacitus brings that out by embedding the epigram in the normal flow of the narrative so that we hear the words stereophonically as what he has to say and as a mocking quotation of how Poppaean Rome thinks. In this way epigrams achieve with supreme efficiency two chief aims of rhetoric: they make us *feel* gratified amusement at wit and make us *think* that the state of affairs targeted by the epigram is deplorable. They are both mirrors and windows, reflecting current reality in order to open up a view on alternatives. "The [political thinker] will be communicating with his fellow citizens . . . in terms of what he has done with their publicly approved paradigms of value and authority."[7]

The casual collocation of "virtue" and "dissimulation" in *Annals* 4.71.3 creates the same witty effect of dual focus: "of all his virtues Tiberius was believed to cherish dissimulation most highly" (cf. "vices which are his only source of—pride," *Hist.* 1.30.1). The tension between language and ethical codes that produces this startling statement has instructive parallels in Machiavelli. The confused political setting in which he worked had a similar blurring effect on language, as for example in a typically Machiavellian (and Tacitean) remark about Hannibal: "his inhuman cruelty . . . along with his infinite other virtue [*sua virtù*] made him always venerated and terrible in the sight of his soldiers, and without it his other virtue [*sua virtù*] would not have been enough to produce the effect."[8] If this is Machiavelli's own view, he seems to be playing cynically with the language of conventional norms by regarding inhuman cruelty as simply one among other virtues, much as dissimulation was viewed by Tiberius. On the other hand, if it is a judgment against Hannibal, the phrase is bitter wit unmasking the language of political ruthlessness. Machiavelli's *virtù* embodies an ambivalence in norms already present in the Latin *virtus,* which encompasses both "moral virtue" and "force" or "mastery." In the light of the latter, nonmoral sense of "virtue" the incongruity of a tribute to Hannibal would largely vanish, since forcefulness is consistent with other conventional virtues, notably with the courage and insistence on discipline which he displayed. But even with this proviso "inhuman cruelty" remains incongruous, and so the remark is more likely witty condemnation than witty recommendation. That is certainly the case with Tiberius' dissimulation, and the statement that he "was believed" to value it

highly suggests that Tacitus is reporting something commonly said about Tiberius. Perhaps he is quoting an actual joke about the emperor's favorite "virtue," but in any case, his own way of putting things is a genuinely witty case of
violated expectation: Tiberius counts dissimulation as his prime—virtue.

III

Like jokes, then, epigrams depend on rigorous economy of expression
to form thought patterns suitable for triggering wit. In the case of antithetic
epigrams oscillation is set up as two codes are pitted against each other, one
serving as a frame for the other. The resultant tension is what lends wit to the
epigrams on Poppaea and Tiberius and is also what makes epigrams formally
akin to parody. A parodied or "target" text establishes the context in which
expectations are created in order to be reshaped by the parodying text. Especially in political parody the shift in perception of the target text is intended to
reach subversively into the real world by affecting opinion. The parodist decodes the original text (understands it in its own terms), recodes it in new
form (creates parody) for his audience, which decodes it again (understands
the new form in its own terms) and is then in a position to appreciate the
parody by comparing the two (de)codings. The effect of this multiple framing
may be to define political identity.

> The use of slogans, clichés, and other words specific to . . . a group serve [sic] to
> give entrance to that group . . . [parody may also] critically analyse its own
> relationship to its model and the discourse represented by it, to distinguish itself
> from its model. . . . Here the subject's subsuming of his individual identity in
> that of another is reversed, and the identity of the target text critically laid bare
> before being made a part of the parody text. This analysis may also, as men-
> tioned earlier, serve a tendentious purpose in attributing a "false" identity to the
> target in order to caricature him, and can, in both cases, be subversive.[9]

It is in this sense that one set of values parodies or caricatures another in
epigrams like "Tiberius counted dissimulation as his prime virtue." They in-
corporate target texts into Tacitus' own text, they do so for a critical analysis
carried on largely through rhetorical forms, and they contribute to what is
undoubtedly in some measure a false, subversive identity created by Tacitus
for his targets. Tiberius is unlikely to have provided a target text himself by
saying, "My greatest virtue is dissimulation."

"Otho did not yet have authority to prevent crimes; he was already able to
order them" (*Hist.* 1.45.2). The second clause is the target "text" which speaks
for political reality debased by civil violence, and the familiarity of Tacitus'
audience with that reality permits him to make some assumptions about their

expectations in order to set the stage for parody. For as a plain statement becomes witty only when placed in a certain context (e.g., as response to a question that sets up the joke or in relation to an implicit premise), so the preformed original text is the indispensable premise for parody.[10] If we look at the epigram in this way, the parodied code or text is "[authority is] power to order what is politically desirable," the first clause is the parodying counter-code, and the epigram or parody itself springs from embedding the two to-gether to create a new, higher level of understanding from which one code (public crime) is made to seem incongruous as it stands next to the other.[11] The epigrammatic edge of the line comes from the move and countermove set up by tension between two norms, authority to prevent crime being as legiti-mate as "authority" to order it is "funny." This epigram on Otho is echoed in a parallel epigram (*Hist.* 3.25.3): "they call the deed crime and—do it." The parody of "authority" implicit in "Otho did not yet have authority to prevent crimes" is made fully explicit only in "he could already order them," since the sentence might (and should) have ended simply with "but he tried to do so." When it does not, we realize the criminal nature of authority at Rome, and in *Histories* 3.25.3 the parody works even more abruptly to turn realpolitik into overt criminality.[12]

Thucydides' Melian Dialogue works in much the same way on a larger scale: the complacently reasonable language of Athenian realpolitik is paro-died at a higher level of insight as it is set off first against the simple brutality that it unwittingly reveals itself to be, then against the equally brutal plague that unexpectedly mocks illusions of omnipotence. This extension of rhetori-cal structures to narrative was probably influenced by tragic drama and is exploited by Tacitus as well (e.g., the running ironic parody of rational state-craft in his highly impressionistic narrative of the nightmare battles at Bedriacum in the *Hist.*). The strongest form of parody is self-parody, for when no parodying text is explicitly provided, the target appears to be ren-dered absurd in the light of itself. "They call the deed a crime and do it" comes close to this in its extreme compression.

Tacitus perhaps employs the framing effect of irony and parody on a larger scale at the end of Maternus' remarks about the Principate (*Dial.* 40–41).[13] Under the Republic, rhetoric was usually abusive.

> That great and famous eloquence is the mother of license which fools call liberty . . . and which does not appear in well-run states . . . there was no peace in the forum, no concord in the senate, no restraint in the courts, no reverence for authority.

But Maternus' examples of good states include Macedonia and Persia, scarcely models of real liberty, and so far as the Principate is concerned, his praise of its political discipline is suspect.

> If a state were found in which no one does wrong, rhetoricians would be as useless there as doctors are among those who are healthy. . . . Rhetoric has little honor amid political discipline and willingness to obey the ruler. What is the need for long debates in the senate when the best men agree quickly? What need for public discussion when the one wisest man (and not many inexperienced people) deliberates about policy? What need for private accusations when crimes are so rare and minor? What need for contentious and lengthy defense when the judge's clemency is ready and waiting for those on trial?

If Tacitus is inviting a parodic reading of this declaration, it is a stellar example of the techniques of ironic wit we have been examining: political jargon quoted to be discredited by the veiled contrary intention that frames and thus transforms it into clever self-refutation. Maternus' language moves from a realistic, contrary to fact mood ("if a perfect state *were* found . . .") to a false indicative mood ("what *is* [now] the need for debate . . . ?") which unmasks the spuriousness of official ideals by simply stating them in their own terms. Long debates are indeed "unnecessary" when there is no real freedom, and the judge's clemency is naturally "ready" when it is wholly arbitrary. Both in logical structure and in the point it makes this comes close to the witty self-refutation of the formal epigram like the one in *Annals* 3.28.3: under Augustus "we had peace and—a master." "Master" works by *para prosdokian* to frame and parody "peace" and thus produce a sour joke given added edge by the derisive jingle in *pace et principe*.

IV

Some techniques of analysis worked out by linguistic philosophers help throw further light on the logical and conceptual substructure of Tacitus' rhetoric. Linguistic philosophy, of course, has its own agenda, yet it does touch on matters familiar from ancient rhetoric, and it has recently been applied with some success in political science and the philosophy of history.

We can begin with the distinction (originally drawn by J. L. Austin) between constative or locutionary language on the one hand and performative or illocutionary language on the other.[14] The locutionary phase of language is descriptive and factual and embodies literal meaning, that is, the immediate sense and reference of statements, whereas the illocutionary phase carries their larger force, point, or intention (this is roughly parallel to levels 1 and 2 discussed in sec. 2 above).

> With the constative utterance, we abstract from the illocutionary . . . aspects of the speech act, and we concentrate on the locutionary. . . . With the performa-

tive utterance, we attend as much as possible to the illocutionary force of the utterance, and abstract from the dimension of correspondence with facts.[15]

Communication is reliable because locution and illocution—meaning and intention—ordinarily coincide "felicitously" to produce "illocutionary uptake." When they do not, sense and intention fall apart "infelicitously." Thus the locution "I am going to do it" is misunderstood through ambiguity if it is assigned an incorrect intention from among the many possibilities (promise, prediction, threat, warning, intention).

An account of historical facts, then, is locutionary, whereas interpretation of the facts is illocutionary. What is of special use for our purposes is the connection between illocutionary force and, in the case of the ancient historians, the codes or norms in which their language was embedded and from which it took its "point." Norms are, in effect, the "social content" of statements extending beyond narrower "linguistic content," and social content—including the historian's bias—carries the illocutionary point.[16] In some cases that may depend directly on a very specific convention (e.g., "Strike three!" has point only in the context of the code of baseball). In other cases the larger setting of a statement's illocutionary force is created by vaguer conventions such as intonation, expression, or gesture. The problem of bias and rhetoric in ancient historiography arises, then, from the moral and political norms that determine the intention of what is said. Moreover, the traditional aim of rhetoric was persuasion, and speech acts can be not only commitments to an illocutionary intention on the speaker's part but also "perlocutionary" attempts to create commitment in others by convincing, persuading, or frightening.

Austin tentatively offers these illustrations of illocution and perlocution respectively:

> In saying I would shoot him I was threatening him.
> By saying that I would shoot him I alarmed him.[17]

We can accordingly say that part of a typical antithetic epigram is illocutionary. "They make desolation and call it peace" (*Agr.* 30):

> In saying that they bring peace the Romans intend to justify their power.
> In saying that they cause desolation Calgacus intends to repudiate the legitimacy of their power.

The epigram as a whole, on the other hand, is perlocutionary.

> By saying that the Romans make desolation and call it peace Calgacus is stripping the facade from Roman "peace" and persuading the Britons to resist oppression.

(This is, of course, ultimately a statement made by Tacitus, and its perlocutionary force in his own Roman setting is an interesting question. What
might have been his persuasive intention toward his Roman audience with so
powerful an anti-imperialistic epigram?) The illocutionary intention of "Poppaea has everything" is similarly undercut by Tacitus' "except character," and
the whole epigram is made to work as persuasive perlocutionary subversion
of official values.

The notion of performative language is especially useful in dealing with
the intrusive moral stance of the ancient historians. In performative language
a speaker not only says something but also does something in the very act of
speaking. That is why it could be dangerous to write history under the emperors. Verbs of promising or intending, for example, are at once descriptions of facts having to do with the circumstances of the promise and acts in
their own right. "I do" in the marriage ceremony is more a moral commitment
to the demands of marriage than a constative statement of facts about its
code. When a performative statement is not introduced by a performative
word, the norm it enacts remains implicit: "Strike three!" presupposes the
rules of baseball to make its point. "I declare that you are out!" on the other
hand, makes the illocutionary point explicitly and incorporates convention
directly in language. The commitment that makes performative language an
act comes out most clearly in the grammatical first person (as in "I do") and *as*
a commitment presupposes norms in the light of which description takes on
illocutionary force and becomes performative.

Linguistic philosophers see general analysis of language along these lines
as a tool valuable particularly for bringing to light what goes wrong with
philosophic discourse. As we have seen, that is a major aim also of Tacitus'
rhetoric in respect to political discourse, and what goes wrong is the fit between language and political or moral codes. "How do you do?" is by a convention built directly into language not a question but a greeting. Someone
who takes its illocutionary force to be "in what manner do you perform?" has
"taken up" an erroneous intention. Mistakes of this sort are often highly
amusing or highly embarrassing cases of the *para prosdokian* that plays so
important a role in the epigrammatic style and in wit generally. The foreigner
consulting his phrase book and selecting the wrong entry is a perennial source
of amusement, because language is one of the fundamental codes whose violation may immediately threaten rationality in astonishing ways. When a man
had been convicted of forgery in a court presided over by Claudius, someone
shouted, "His hands ought to be cut off!" and Claudius immediately called for
knife and block (*Claud.* 15.2). The upshot of the unhappy (in Austin's sense of
"infelicitous") foreigner's misadventures with language in a comic skit may
well be a visit to the local jail for public indecency. For there is, in fact, a
potentially serious side to these situations, and that is the deeper illocutionary
intention that Suetonius finds in the story about Claudius. It is a genuinely

witty case of conversation at cross-purpose in its own right, because Claudius fails to grasp the point of the remark not on an idiomatic level but on the level of his own abnormal intentions.

Hitches in thought sequence, then, due to failure of illocutionary uptake readily produce witticism, joke, or absurdity, and the breakdown is most often due to ambiguity among norms. "This contrast [between locutionary and illocutionary act] is most obvious in those cases in which the sentence uttered is ambiguous with respect to force."[18] In the context of football "Strike three!" is either absurd or a wittily odd way of describing something that can happen in the game. After a penalty one team may elect to give up three points earned for a field goal hoping for the six points of a touchdown, and an official might then waggishly instruct the scorekeeper to remove three points ("Strike three!"). This is trivial enough, but when conflict of intentions affects fundamental moral and political norms, the odd language that ensues is a serious matter. In the context of legal procedure it is absurd to think that what just anyone thinks "ought to be done" ought really to be *done,* as it is absurd to call something a crime and then just *do* it (*Hist.* 3.25.3) or for ordinary soldiers to undertake to transfer the imperium of the Roman people and just *do* it (*Hist.* 1.25.1).

Several of the examples used by Austin are peculiarly apt for our purposes.

> Again, suppose that, picking sides at a children's party, I say "I pick George." But George turns red in the face and says "Not playing." In that case I plainly, for some reason or another, have not picked George—whether because there is no convention that you can pick people who aren't playing, or because George in the circumstances is an inappropriate object for the procedure of picking. Or consider the case in which I say "I appoint you Consul," and it turns out that you have been appointed already—perhaps it may even transpire that you are a horse; here again we have the infelicity of inappropriate circumstances, inappropriate objects, or what not. Examples of flaws and hitches are perhaps scarcely necessary—one party in the marriage ceremony says "I will," the other says "I won't"; I say, "I bet sixpence," but nobody says "Done," nobody takes up the offer. In all these and other such cases, the act which we purport to perform, or set out to perform, is not achieved.[19]

All of this is again amusing or absurd to one degree or another. The instances of no response are good examples of deflationary *para prosdokian,* and "I will/I won't" could simply *be* a joke, either casual or, in the light of certain norms and intentions about marriage, a bitter witticism with serious point. Caligula's sudden use of a ceremonial mallet on one of the officiants instead of the animal during a sacrifice (*Calig.* 32.3) is an analogous and equally grotesque misfire of intention. A more interesting example is the witty turn of language by which Tacitus marks one instance of breakdown in political norms at Rome. Vitellius with some success had taken measures to arouse enthusiasm for his sinking regime, but when those who had offered support quickly began to desert, "in embarrassment at his futile efforts he turned down the offers of help that were not being made" (*Hist.* 3.58.4). Absence of one party to the normal dialogue between ruler and ruled results in illocutionary failure to grasp the correct point—as in the exchange "I will/I won't"—and the vacuum of intention is caught also at the linguistic level in the faintly absurd phrase about declining offers that are not being made (*quae non dabantur remisit*). If a challenge to a duel is merely shrugged off, "the whole code of procedure" is rejected.[20] That is what happens to Vitellius, and it happens again when Paetus refuses to speak in the senate and finally walks out, in effect voiding official political discourse as such (*Ann.* 14.12.1). The anecdote about Caligula's appointment of his horse alluded to by Austin takes all of this one step further to replace infelicitous or empty with truly mad intention.

Insincere statements are another form of language without true point. Someone may say, "I congratulate you" when he in fact denies credit, or he may make a promise or extend a welcome without genuine intention to do so. The direct tension between differing codes of honesty in these cases and the effect it has on language are again familiar from the numerous instances of political hypocrisy in Tacitus. Vitellius' support, as we have seen, was a matter of mere words, and so was Tiberius' false display of grief at the death of Germanicus (*Ann.* 3.2–6). In contrast, the people on that occasion "made no false display of grief, and *although* they did not avoid showing their grief openly, they felt it very deeply" (*Ann.* 2.82.3). Tacitus' language is again slightly odd in that it suggests some uncertainty about the correspondence between expression and intention in popular grief too. For under a habitually insincere regime any show of sorrow may be without genuine point, and that is what we are reminded of on the level of Tacitus' narrative by the subtle "although" implying surprise that in this case display *was* nevertheless genuine.[21] So far as false promises are concerned, Tacitus remarks that Tiberius' occasional talk of relinquishing power was taken as both lie and joke (*Ann.* 4.9.1). Tiberius, of course, did not say that he intended *not* to fulfill his intention, but everyone knew that that was (not) his intention, and so his statement seemed absurd. Since "I promise" or "I intend" is plainly a performative verb, it is very odd to say that one's promise has no point.

> "I promise that I shall be there, but I haven't the least intention of being there." Once again you can of course perfectly well promise to be there without having the least intention of being there, but there is something outrageous about saying it, about actually avowing the insincerity of the promise you give.[22]

Precisely because it outrageously violates expectation, language of this kind can be both witty and at a deeper level ethically disturbing—like epigrams that make political insincerity outrageously explicit and by doing so produce angry wit.

What Austin calls the "peculiar kind of nonsense" or "self-stultifying pro-cedure" in such language reappears in descriptions of imperial deviousness.[23]

> Gaius was the first to denounce and ridicule Tiberius, and so others did the same, thinking that it would please him. But later he also praised Tiberius and penalized some for their denunciation of him and hated both those who de-nounced Tiberius and those who praised him. (Dio 59.4.2)

Gaius' view of Tiberius evidently changed with time ("first . . . later"), and that hardly seems grounds for censure. And in fact this faintly amusing de-scription is not intended simply to be a factual account of Gaius' changing policies. Like similar passages in Dio (see below, p. 114), in its suggestion of something close to paranoia it points to moral and political absurdity. When Dio returns to the subject of Gaius' moods a few lines later, it is clear that this is the kind of juxtaposition he has in mind.

> He stopped charges of *maiestas* but put many to death for it . . . he burned incriminating letters but executed many on their evidence, since he had burned copies but not the originals. . . . He loved crowds and he loved solitude; he was angered both when requested and not requested to do something. . . . He both hated and liked both those who flattered him and those who were frank . . . so that no one knew what to say or how to act to him, and those who did so successfully were simply lucky. (59.3–6)

This may, of course, have been a deliberate political tactic, but for a hostile historical tradition intent on dramatizing political absurdity it is gross inco-herence (Gaius is "contrary", 59.4.1) leading to a preposterous state of affairs. Whatever the actual facts about the emperor's manner, the ultimate intention of Dio's description not only is to portray contrary character but to hint at a catch-22 logic of the kind that appears in political systems (see below, Chap. 6, beginning of Sec. 2) and is a natural target of political satire.

The issue of bias and impartiality in ancient historiography can now be restated by saying that even the most neutral locutionary language is shaped by the historians with a view toward their own illocutionary intentions and norms. As those norms are set into conflict with the corrupt norms of society or emperor, the facade of public meaning is unmasked and rendered absurd by its incongruity with the historian's rival intentions. As a matter of rhetori-cal form, sets of rival intentions are brought into play with most effect in epigrams. All of this naturally brings with it a considerable measure of judgmental bias, yet one that is not entirely the product of rhetorical tech-nique. Locutionary language is, of course, subject to the standard of ob-jective fact, and on this score the accounts in Tacitus, Dio, or Suetonius are often inadequate. Illocutionary language for its part is similarly subject to standards of fair and reasonable judgment, though in this case the standards can scarcely themselves avoid being intentions and judgments.

> But actually—though it would take too long to go on about this—the more you think about truth and falsity the more you find that very few statements that we ever utter are just true or just false. Usually there is the question are they fair or are they not fair, are they adequate or not adequate, are they exaggerated or not exaggerated? Are they too rough, or are they perfectly precise, accurate, and so on? "True" and "false" are just general labels for a whole dimension of different appraisals which have something or other to do with the relation between what we say and the facts. If, then, we loosen up our ideas of truth and falsity we shall see the statements, when assessed in relation to the facts, are not so very different after all from pieces of advice, warnings, verdicts, and so on.[24]

If John has no children, the assertion "All John's children are asleep" is infelicitous and *amusingly* irrelevant rather than simply false. This is another way in which statements can be rendered odd when placed into a larger and truer frame of reference that subverts their original intention. Something of the sort happens in the anecdotes about the absentminded Claudius making official appointments with people on the very day after he had condemned them to death and complaining at their tardiness (*Claud.* 39.1) or about Nero appealing to the judges for impartiality in a competition he had entered (*Ner.* 23.2f). "People say [of statements like that about John's children] 'the question does not arise.'"[25] Neither does tardiness due to late sleeping arise in the case of those condemned to death nor impartial judgment in the case of a competing emperor (or appointment to the consulship in the case of a horse). In each instance—whatever their original intentions—the remarks are made amusingly irrelevant rather than merely false by a larger truth. Of course, the emperors' intentions were in context perhaps quite reasonable. Nero may have been genuinely anxious about his chances, Claudius genuinely puzzled about absentees, Caligula simply jesting about his horse being consul (as he was obviously jesting when he wished that the Romans had one neck to cut, *Calig.* 30.2). In that case, it is the question of imperial hypocrisy or absurdity that does not really arise, and though they may actually have said such things, the reports are false but in an amusing way. All of this goes to show how its complex logic could cause language to take on a life of its own, all the more so in a rhetorically conditioned culture and in the hands of those with an ax to grind.

Inconsistency among criteria of meaning is brought into sharpest focus in epigrams because of the narrow restrictions imposed on their form, especially when they are antithetic. More discursively, Tacitean insinuation has the same effect of drawing attention to an alternative, true political "point." Although insinuation is not illocutionary in the proper sense because its intention is veiled, in the case of Tacitus it is perhaps overt and systematic enough to permit his bias to be defined as the illocutionary and perlocutionary intention running implicitly through his narrative on a large scale and occasionally surfacing in explicit performative avowals.

> It is my intention to treat only senatorial motions which are remarkable for shame or honor, since I think that the special duty of history is to assure that virtue be recorded and shameful acts or words be deterred by fear of evil reputation among posterity. (*Ann.* 3.65.1)

What precedes this is typical third-person narrative for the most part recounting facts but with occasional touches of judgment which are then made explicit in this first-person performative statement. As the English idiom "to make a statement" indicates, Tacitus is here not in the first instance passing on information; he is doing something as a historian by saying something. If he did not envisage concrete political consequences from his act of writing, he did see part of its ultimate point as an ethical act and would probably have regarded an impartial account as itself an expression of political absurdity, rather like Nero's cool assessment of the nose of one of his victims (*Ann.* 14.59.3).

> If an author was what we call "creative," "seminal" or "revolutionary," we can ascribe to him a definite effect (and perhaps intention also) of changing the paradigm structure by some force which his utterances exerted.[26]

Tacitus was scarcely revolutionary, but his rhetoric was creative as well as seminal, and his resourceful use of multiple frames of meaning and intention in language was in its own way aimed at changing the paradigm structure of his audience.

V

Each of the three models we have considered is a way of schematizing the epigrammatic style and throws light on a different aspect: codes on its use of moral and political norms; parody on its polemical function; linguistic philosophy on its logical and linguistic workings. Of course, "norms," or "illocution" is not the language of ancient rhetoric, which instead approached this aspect of epigrams in its own more familiar terms of contrast and antithesis.

Polarity of one sort or another was deeply embedded in Greek and Roman ways of thinking. When Aristotle recommends the periodic style for some relatively abstract reasons having to do with the structure of thought itself, he remarks specifically on the role played by antithesis. Periods break sentences into parts that are intelligible because they are limited and thus permit creation and satisfaction of expectation. "[The periodic style] is pleasant and easily understood because it is the opposite of unstructured. The hearer always thinks that he is grasping something and that he has reached an end. It is unpleasant not to anticipate [*pronoein*] and not to complete anything" (*Rh.* 1409b1). The effect is further enhanced when periodic units are antithetic: "Such a style is pleasant because opposites are most easily known by being placed side by side, and because it resembles a syllogism; for refutation is bringing opposites together" (1410a20). Aristotle's point is that the relation between opposites is transparent, and in this respect the effect of the periodic style, especially if it is also antithetic, is identical to that of the syllogism itself, which similarly "gets more applause and is most gratifying" when the hearer quickly sees the connection between the components and anticipates the conclusion (1400b29). Thus rhetoric and logic share with wit a special pleasure derived from "getting the point" in one way or another.

Apart from such highly specialized analysis along the lines of logic, antithesis was in any case a familiar pattern, ready-made for organizing historical data into Tacitus' own antithetic patterns: past/present, republic/empire, freedom/slavery, integrity/corruption, virtue/vice, good/evil.[27] To revert to the terminology of linguistic analysis, these antitheses are the multiple and potentially conflicting norms at work in the illocutionary intentions of political language. Since the historical material that Tacitus uses takes on meaning as it fits into patterns, style is itself historiographically essential insofar as it is designed to reflect and reinforce those patterns. To use a geological analogy, style is a surface feature shaped by deep formations. Tacitus' text is accordingly saturated with antithesis ranging from simple two-word contrasts to elaborate patterns whose effect is all the greater because of the mosaic patterns into which Latin tends to fall naturally.

> Galba's remark was good for the state but dangerous for himself: he said that soldiers were chosen by him and not bought. (*Hist.* 1.5.2)

> [Otho's freedmen and servants held up to him the vices of Nero] as his own if he was daring, as others' if he was not. (*Hist.* 1.22.1)

> [He was aware that] the greatest crimes are begun with peril, completed with profit. (*incipi cum periculo, peragi cum praemio, Ann.* 12.67.2)

> [In war] everyone claims victory for himself, only one is blamed for defeat. (*Agr.* 27.1)

> They should act carefully rather than quickly, because he wished to be at war rather than wage it. (*Ann.* 15.3.1)

> And so by virtue in obedience and modesty in speech he was free from envy but not from glory. (*Agr.* 8.3)

> The greater my hope of success if I were choosing to live, the more glorious my death when I die. (*Hist.* 2.47.1)

> Others may hold power longer, none will give it up more bravely. (*Hist.* 2.47.2)

> He should face life bravely and never forget or too much remember that Otho was his uncle. (*Hist.* 2.48.2)

> In terror whether it was a chance outburst of the soldiers or a trick of the emperor, whether it was more dangerous to stay and be caught or flee and scatter, at times they pretended coolness, at times they were revealed by their fear. They watched Otho's face, and as happens to suspicious minds, when Otho was afraid he was feared. (*Hist.* 1.81.1)

In the last example, which contains no fewer than eight explicit or implicit pairs, antithesis goes well beyond rhetorical effect and directly imitates the wild, pendulum-like swing of events. Moreover, most of these instances are *sententiae*—"the craze and curse of his [Tacitus'] generation as of several generations preceding."[28] Yet while it is fair to say that few people were so infatuated with words as were Greeks and Romans, it is also fair to say that few were so aware of their infatuation. In Tacitus *sententiae* become a calculated secondary syntax as essential as grammatical syntax (which he in fact also bends for rhetorical effect), because they are not a mannerism but answer to the nature of political reality, which is in good measure made up of what people say and how they say it. Words have consequences; "Augustus was sensible that mankind is governed by names."[29]

Since Tacitus both describes and judges, his antitheses span both true-and-false and right-and-wrong. As a rhetorician, he is especially aware of the important role played by language in shaping political reality and illusion.[30] Those who were critical called Vitellius "vulgar" *(humilis)*, his supporters spoke of his "affability and good nature." In reality, Tacitus says, he squandered both his own and others' property, but "his very faults were taken as virtues" (*Hist.* 1.52.2). By moving from Vitellius' apparent virtues existing merely on a verbal level to his actual faults, the analysis of language here dispels the former in order to expose the latter. The underlying pattern is thus very close to that of formal antithetic epigrams designed to uncover false political language. In discussing public opinion about the "old-fashioned" Piso, proposed as successor to Galba, Tacitus similarly remarks that by some he was fairly regarded as *severus,* less sympathetically by others as *tristior* (*Hist.* 1.14.2; cf. 1.38.1). *Severus* is the complimentary ("disciplinarian"), *tristior* the pejorative term ("repressive," "sour," "harsh"). A few pages later (*Hist.* 1.18.3), when he calls Galba himself a "stingy old man" who damaged his own cause by "old-fashioned rigor and excessive severity," *parcus* has a pejorative sense and severity is a fault. But Tacitus is speaking only of excessive severity; severity itself is a virtue, and the use of the adjective "old-fashioned" hints at some sympathy for Galba. A final, typically indirect clause further reinforces "old-fashioned" to move the balance in Galba's favor; Tacitus speaks of rigor and severity "to which we are no longer equal," and earlier (*Hist.* 1.5.2) he had mentioned the fame that Galba's severity had once enjoyed. The interplay between proper and improper severity is thus linked to a contrast between good past and evil present, and Rome's unhappy state is epitomized by Tacitus' resort to praise by faint damnation: Galba had serious faults, but he was not a wholly bad man, though in degenerate times it was easy to think and *speak* of him as though he were.[31] Tacitus finally resolves the issue with a curious turn of phrase of his own: Galba "did not so much possess virtues as lack vices" *(magis extra vitia quam cum virtutibus),* and he once more remarks on the linguistic aspect of the situation. His high birth and "the terror of the times served as a veil so that what was sluggishness was called wisdom" (*Hist.* 1.49.3; cf. 3.75.1 on Sabinus: "Some thought that he was sluggish, many that he was moderate"). The point of these discussions of political and moral vocabulary is not simply to clarify its use but to bring out its high semantic tension and potential for sustaining false political reality.

In the light of this, Tacitus' occasional allusions to political ghostwriters take on added significance (*Hist.* 1.90.2 [Otho]; *Ann.* 13.3.2 [Nero]).[32] Otho's speech is a masterpiece of euphemism designed to mask awkward facts. He speaks of the legions' "ignorance rather than rashness" and is careful to avoid abuse of Vitellius, evidently because his anonymous writer is hedging his own bets by creating multiple levels of intention in official language. Nero was the first to use prepared speeches, and though that naturally makes us suspect his official statements, it also prepares us for the insincerity of his private conversations. If language can create illusion it can in the hands of the historian also unmask it, and many of Tacitus' antithetic epigrams are accordingly formed along the axis of true and false language.[33] It was a trick of Tiberius' to cover "recent crimes with old words" (*Ann.* 4.19.2); young men pretend to "higher studies" in order to cover "idleness" with a magnificent word (*Hist.* 4.5.1); what others would call "crimes" Galba called "remedies"—"brutality" was "strictness," "avarice" was "frugality," "punishment" and "abuse" were "discipline" (*Hist.* 1.37.4); some men do not weigh good and evil in their own terms but on the basis of words, and no one ever sought power for himself and enslavement for others without invoking "liberty and other specious words" (*Hist.* 4.73.3).

As we have seen, the significance of such ambiguous language is that it arises from a false code of values existing side by side with a true code. What is more, ambiguity affects communication in the broad sense including nonverbal communication.[34] It thus poisons relationships on all levels and strikes at the foundation of civilized life. "Whatever mood of the day Tiberius had assumed, Caligula put on the same and spoke much the same language" (*Ann.* 6.20.1).

When Otho's position was being threatened by Vitellius and spies were suspected everywhere, men did not choose just their words carefully; they also
chose their facial expression *(vultus)* in public so as not to seem too joyful or
too sorrowful at news. Senators stepped gingerly between too much speech and
too much silence and carefully twisted their proposals to take account of any
eventuality in the struggle for power. Those who were most cautious used only
ordinary abuse against Vitellius, spoke only during an uproar, and "drowned
themselves out in a confusion of words" *(Hist.* 1.85.3). Their aim was noncom-
mittal neutrality that spoke without saying anything.[35]

Tacitus returns several times to the theme of empty political expression and
uses it with special effect in his portrayal of the reigns of Tiberius and Nero.
He observes that in his effort to undermine Galba Otho would drop ambiguous remarks *(Hist.* 1.23.1). Evasiveness in this case was merely a tactic;
Tiberius' language, on the other hand, was much more deeply ambiguous and
led senators (never certain what he meant) to be terrified of *understanding*
him *(Ann.* 1.11.2)[36]—an exact corollary to the technique of remaining silent
or speaking so as *not* to be heard described in *Histories* 1.85.3.[37] They had
good reason to do so, because Tiberius misconstrued statements and expressions *(verba, vultus)* as crimes *(Ann.* 1.7.7; cf. *Hist.* 2.52.1). Later, Nero's
mother had learned the same lesson and knew that the one defense against
treachery is to pretend not to notice *(Ann.* 14.6.1). Tiberius further reinforced
ambiguity by keeping his own expression unchanged *(Ann.* 3.44.4; cf. *Hist.*
1.81.1) so that worried senators could read his face no better than his words.

The most sinister instance of false expression occurs during Nero's murder
of Britannicus. The young man was given poison, and as he began to die in
agony those at the table "knew what was happening [but] sat motionless,
Agrippina trying to control her features as all eyes were focused on Nero,"
who casually remarked that it was simply "an epileptic fit" *(Ann.* 13.16.3).
The same motif occurs in connection with Domitian. Tacitus first signals the
conflict between true and false expression in an antithetic epigram that unmasks the truth (he was "affable in face, anxious in mind": *fronte laetus,
pectore anxius, Agr.* 39.1), then goes on to remark on other facets of the conflict between expression and reality. Domitian feared that the silence imposed
on public speaking could be circumvented by military accomplishment (39.2),
the honors he granted to Agricola were decked out with (mere) laudatory
words (40.1), and Agricola himself was ordered to come to the palace at night
to be dismissed with a brief kiss and no conversation (40.3). Finally the pallor
of his victims is set against the perpetual ruddiness of his own face which
(Tacitus suggests) prevented him from blushing for shame (45.2).

All of this is highly rhetorical and raises problems of historical accuracy;
the remark about Domitian's complexion sounds very much like a mere malicious joke. But for Tacitus it is precisely in the rhetorically dramatic contrast
between expression and reality that the truth about political falsity comes to

light. The false expression imposed by bad emperors must be systematically
set against true expression. The false Stoic who "assumed a [false] expression
[*imago*] of integrity" (*Ann.* 16.32.3) contrasts thematically with the followers
of Thrasea Paetus, whose very expression *(vultus)* and manner could be construed as a justified reproach to Nero (*Ann.* 16.22.2; cf. 1.7.1) The absence of
protest against Nero's crimes by most senators contasts with the denunciation
by a solider caught in conspiracy. Nothing about the affair offended Nero's
ears more than his free speech ("the glory of confession"), since the emperor
was "as free to commit crimes as he was unaccustomed to hear about them"
(*Ann.* 15.67.3). Plain talk is a special virtue always celebrated by Tacitus because of its rarity; the candid speech of a senator, he says, was the "beginning
of his great glory" (*Hist.* 4.4.3). Candor is glorious because it unmasks false
silence or false language, and that brings us back to the antithetic and epigrammatic style. Because antitheses run in two directions, they formally embody the historian's task of unmasking officially masked falsehood.

The technique of unmasking hypocrisy through antithesis is mentioned as
a polemical rhetorical technique by Aristotle in *Rhetoric* 1399a30 ("the most
effective of the topical paradoxes"):

> Men do not praise the same things in public and in private; in public they praise
> what is just and noble, in private what is expedient, and so one should try to
> infer the opposite from each.

Thus a man may say that honorable poverty is preferable to dishonest gain
but really want the opposite.

> If his words agree with his wishes, their contradiction with public norms must
> be brought out; if he agrees with public norms, his words must be made to
> contradict his wishes. (Arist. *Sophistic Refutations* 12)

Contradiction is readily exposed in the form of antithesis, and some examples
given by Aristotle illustrate how a euphemistic facade concealing political
reality can be torn down by reading in the reverse direction (*Rh.* 1405a25).
"Pirates" calling themselves "purveyors" are in fact purveyors who are mere
pirates. Insofar as such dishonest language is in a way metaphorical, metaphor is a useful tool for political euphemism.

> It is possible to say that the man who has "committed a crime" has "made a mis-
> take" or vice versa, and that a thief has "taken" or that he has "stolen" something.

This again is the reciprocal movement of antithetic epigrams. One of the
directions, along which the language of false political reality moves in order to
mask the truth, is epitomized by Orwell's "war is peace; freedom is slavery":

True/Real		*False/Illusory*
actual evil (war)	is masked as	apparent good (peace)
actual good (freedom)		apparent evil (slavery)

The other direction uncovers falsehood:

False/Illusory		*True/Real*
apparent good (peace)	is unmasked as	actual evil (war)
apparent evil (slavery)		actual good (freedom)

In Tacitus' own terms (*Agr.* 30.4):

actual desolation	is masked as	apparent peace
apparent peace	is unmasked as	actual desolation

Such language is, of course, metaphorical only in a restricted sense of the term, corresponding to the understanding of metaphor as simple substitution of one notion for another, that is, an unexpected transfer of something to a new category (Arist. *Poetics* 1457b5; for "metaphor" applied to dislocation in the logic of jokes, see *Rh.* 1412a19). The revelatory effect of metaphor entails a great deal more than mere substitution, though the larger political context in which substitution occurs does lend even simple interchange of euphemistic and candid language the power to open up new understanding, even if it is not metaphorical in the full sense.[38]

VI

Phrases like "pirates are purveyors," or "thieves don't steal, they take," or "desolation is peace" have several interesting properties. They are not only crude metaphors, but also tendentious ones carrying a hidden agenda. By the same token they are genuine jokes of a kind especially useful in political wit (cf. "private property is theft").[39] Moreover, in its most compact form the reciprocal pattern produces the powerful rhetorical device of oxymoron, which as the sharpest possible antithesis serves as a species of abbreviated epigram confronting one norm directly with another: "savage peace" (*Hist.* 1.50.2; cf. 1.2.1), "wretched peace" (*Ann.* 3.44.3; cf. 1.10.4), "wretched happiness" (*Hist.* 2.45.3). In "arrogant modesty" (*Ann.* 1.8.5) imperial power veiled by Tiberius as republican restraint is instantly unveiled and called by Tacitus the imperial arrogance it is. "Those who think of revolt, have revolted" (*qui deliberant desciverunt, Hist.* 2.77.3) is a masterpiece of compression and epigrammatic logic. The idea itself is a commonplace (Plut. *Gal-*

ba 4.4; Sen. *De Beneficiis* 5.14.2; *De constantia sapientis* 7.4; *De ira* 1.3.1);
what is striking here is its witty form. On the one hand, deliberation and
decision are antithetic notions: to do one is precisely not to do the other. And
so the faintly paradoxical sound of saying that they are the same is what forces
unmasking of another, higher norm (that of absolute loyalty) under which
they *are* the same, and the verbal jingle neatly reinforces the point.

More commonly the dual movement of masking/unmasking is somewhat
less abrupt and is signaled in Tacitus by explicit remarks about mistaken
language. Britons began to wear Roman dress, then "gradually took up
pleasant vices—porches, baths, rich dinners—and so what naive people
called 'culture' was really part of their slavery" (*Agr.* 21.2). "No one [in
Germany] laughs at vice, nor is seducing and being seduced called 'modish'"
(*Germ.* 19.1). That is to say, adultery is veiled as "fashionable," unveiled as
"adultery." In its very form the epigram functions as a correction of false
language and a revelation of truth.[40] Tacitus does not so much "avoid
ordinary public language . . . [because of] pathological aversion from the
half-truths of his society,"[41] as he quotes public language to bare its illusion.
When Otho, for example, appeals to his unruly soldiers to check their
"bravery" and "virtue," both words are transparent and probably current
euphemisms for "mutinous violence" (*Hist.* 1.83.2).

Tacitus, in fact, provides what amounts to a small glossary of false
language and values, defined with epigrammatic point on the pattern of antithesis. Freedom: in civil war victors have the "freedom" *(licentiam)* only of
killing (*Hist.* 3.66.3; this is like Otho's "authority" to order crimes, (*Hist.*
1.45.2); friendship: if one did not have an enemy he would be destroyed by a
"friend" (*Hist.* 1.2.3); courage: victorious troops publicly demanded to be led
on to take Cremona at night—"pretty words, but what each said to himself
was that a city on a plain is stormed easily, no more courage is needed to break
in at dark and there is greater freedom to loot" (*Hist.* 3.19.1).[42] The "courage"
unmasked here as greed made the Flavian generals afraid of rather than confident in their troops—so much for "leadership" in civil war—since "any
slaughter, wounds or blood was outweighed by greed for booty" (*Hist.*
3.26.3). When things reach such a pass that Nero's crimes are celebrated with
offerings, Tacitus stops to address his reader directly: "Anyone who learns
about the events of that time from me or other historians should be sure of this
. . . what once were signs of prosperity then were signs of public disaster"
(*Ann.* 14.64.3). Religious ritual is, of course, still another form of communication, and it too must be read in reverse order in a false society.

The corollary of evil masquerading as good is good treated as evil. Soldiers
come to hate industry and honesty as though they were vices (*Hist.* 1.45.2);
Galba's severity was resented by troops who loved the vices of emperors no
less than they had once revered their virtues (*Hist.* 1.5.2); authority, vigor, and
experience were all grounds for—accusation (*Hist.* 1.87.2); "the certain fate of

virtue was—death" (*Hist.* 1.2.3; cf. *Ann.* 3.55.3). Strange things happen to language itself under these circumstances, and the double take forced on the ear by such sentences unmasks what is wrong. "They were *convicted of loyalty* as the worst of crimes by the rebels" (*Hist.* 1.59.1); "Celsus confessed to the crime of firm *loyalty* to Galba" (*Hist.* 1.71.2); "Vitellius believed in their treachery to Otho and therefore *acquitted them of loyalty* to him" (*Hist.* 2.60.1; cf. Lucan 2.519–21: the worst punishment is that a citizen be *pardoned* for defending his country; 4.230: an honorable cause allows one to hope for— *pardon*). Unmasking false virtue is more common than uncovering an apparent fault for the virtue it really is, perhaps because the ethical effect seems greater. As Tacitus remarks, the historian who flatters is suspected of servility, but one who slanders is admired for free spirit (*Hist.* 1.1.2). Slander or flattery aside, human nature is pleased to think evil of others and therefore is more gratified when spurious virtue is exposed as a fault than when a supposed fault is seen to be a virtue (e.g., patriotism or loyalty). The former is outrageous; virtue stigmatized as vice is pathetic, and even soldiers who were angered when they thought of Celsus' loyalty to Galba as a crime could admire it too (*Hist.* 1.71.2).[43]

VII

Perversion of the legal process under the emperors is another rich source of material for the technique of exposing official language through antithetic inversion of intentions. In this case revelation of falsehood usually does not take place in epigrams but in incidents narrated in a way designed to bring out contradiction or incongruity. In this sense, the incidents are themselves "epigrammatic" in their effect, exposing the truth through official actions or words made to work unwittingly against themselves. The complexity of such situations suggests that Tacitus relished the ironic wit they dramatize.

When a praetor is accused of spreading ugly stories about Tiberius, the informer makes his charge "inescapable" by detailing the nastiest aspects of Tiberius' character, "aspects that were believed to have been talked about because they were true" (*Ann.* 1.74.3). That is to say, so far as official political reality is concerned the accusation is unanswerable because the rumors are mere slander. But if in fact the charge of treason against the praetor is itself slander, it is the legal proceeding that is false. And if things never said about the emperor are effective because they are true, the official legal evidence of the praetor's guilt actually depends for its plausibility on the emperor's guilt.

Here it is a complex inversion of falsity and truth in an entire absurd situation that does the work of unmasking otherwise done more directly by epigrams. In fact, a line in *Histories* 1.45.1 comes close to reducing the peculiar logic of this situation to an epigram: so hypocritical were senate and people

alike that "the more false what they did was, the more they did it." The values
that political hypocrisy reverses can safely be read backward: official zeal is a
sign of dishonesty, official complaint about slander a sign of the truth. What
matters is not so much particular facts as the state of affairs in the grip of
reverse logic. The same point is made against Domitian in an epigram in
Agricola 43.4. His "blind and corrupt" mind was delighted when he was
named in Agricola's will, ignorant that "only a bad princeps is named heir by a
good father." When extortion by corrupt rulers is veiled as "inheritance"
freely given by good men, things are inverted and good donor becomes an
index of bad donee, as false evidence is of innocence.

In another case, during the trial of a "noted wit," a witness repeats ugly
stories about Tiberius so frankly before the senate that the emperor considers
abandoning attendance at meetings where he must hear "things that were true
and serious" (*verae et graves, Ann.* 4.42.1). Against the background of official
hypocrisy *verae* again has an amusing suggestion of self-incrimination, since
if the charges are true Tiberius knows that they are true and is made to admit
as much on the level of Tacitus' narrative by his reluctance to hear what is
being said about him. To demonstrate his tolerance of free speech for others
Tiberius himself once ordered public reading of a will that denounced him
bitterly (e.g., as a "senile imbecile"), and Tacitus is led to conjecture that he
may also have done so "through indifference to his reputation" (*patientiam
libertatis alienae ostentans et contemptor suae infamiae, Ann.* 6.38.3). The
startling chiastic phrase ("toleration of freedom for others and for himself
indifference to a bad name") is a combination of contrast and coordination
that puts everything at sixes and sevens through multiple insinuation. "Toleration of freedom" is a good thing and could go with admirable acceptance of
the consequences of free speech on Tiberius' part. But the word *contemptor*
does not suggest admiration; "contempt of reputation means contempt of
virtue" (*Ann.* 4.38.5), and so virtuous "toleration of freedom" is oddly tied to
"bad name." And, in fact, something has gone awry here: in an effort to display a virtue he does not have Tiberius exposes faults he does. In his apology
for benign despotism in Dio, Maecenas warns Augustus not to respond at all
to some charges, true or false, since anything he says will either make them
seem true or prove that they are (52.31.7). The emperors were admittedly in a
difficult position, and Tacitus also wonders whether Tiberius was perhaps
trying to discover "through [courting] insults" the truth of what was being
said about him. This is a reasonable tactic, but one that also makes things
worse by publicizing charges.

At other times Tiberius followed a contrary, more obvious policy of self-
defense, and Dio draws attention specifically to the absurdity of the situation
which this created (as Maecenas had warned). He was led either into "re-
peating insults as though they were eulogies" (58.25.3) or into complaining
about charges that had never actually been made (so the emperor is

slandering *himself*) but were in fact true (so he is not *slandering* himself) and now revealed for the first time.

> When Tiberius would investigate in detail rumors spread about him, he would call himself all the ugly names which others used of him. Everything was put on the public record, and he often added true details about himself even though no one had brought them up, in order to justify his anger. He charged himself with things he punished others for saying and seemed ridiculous for doing so. When people denied that they had said certain things, he would swear that they had and in this way more truly slandered himself. (Dio 57.23.3)

Dio adds that some thought him mad (though not really) for in effect being guilty of *lèse-majesté* against himself.[44]

On another occasion, when Labeo committed suicide, Tiberius complained that his death was a reproach to the emperor to cover Labeo's own crimes (*Ann.* 6.29.2, *culpam invidia velavisse*). The crimes apparently were real, but when Tacitus introduces the paragraph with a remark on "continuing slaughter at Rome," a reader is bound to reflect that suicide was indeed often a reproach to the emperor, and so even in this case Tiberius' righteous indignation implicitly draws attention to his own guilt. Shortly before this (*Ann.* 6.26.1) one of Tiberius' intimate friends decides to commit suicide, though he is in excellent health. The emperor pays him a visit and after attempting dissuasion finally reminds him that the suicide of a close friend without reason will be a serious matter for "my conscience and my reputation." On the level of events the motive remains implicit because the friend refuses to discuss the matter. On the level of Tacitus' narrative it is revealed as his "fear and anger" at the course of public life; and so though the situation is unclear insofar as the motive is concealed from Tiberius, it is after all revealed by Tacitus and again by Tiberius himself in the remark about damage to his reputation, which in its unwitting truth makes the incident into another witty anecdote about imperial self-exposure.

Nero's complaint about the ugly things people will say of him if Seneca retires (*Ann.* 14.56.2) is yet another variant, as is *Annals* 3.16.2, though the text there is uncertain. In the former Seneca appeals for permission to transfer his wealth to the emperor and retire but quickly gets into deep waters. When he suggests that his wish to retire will be to the emperor's credit, since it will show that "you raised to the highest power men who could also bear lack of power" (54.3), Nero counters by saying that self-denial in this case would be self-service and an insult to himself, since any virtue that gains glory for Seneca is bound to be a reproach to Nero. "All men will talk not about your moderation if you return your wealth, not about your retirement if you leave the emperor, but about my avarice and fear of my cruelty." Nero's fear of *infamia* is in one way unexceptionable and in accord with a sober precept like that in *De clementia* 1.15.5 ("rulers must give much consideration to their reputation, too"). But in context it clearly works as self-indictment. For Nero is unwittingly stating the plain truth about himself: men will indeed speak about his avarice and cruelty. The conversation thus has the effect of an unmasking epigram, in this instance again put into the mouth of its target,[45] and Tacitus underscores the point by adding that Nero followed the exchange "with an embrace and kisses, since he was by nature and habit accustomed to veil his hatred with false kindness." If we know this, we know what the kiss means; if we know what that means, we know that his *infamia* is deserved. The account of Germanicus' death is Tacitus' masterpiece of insinuation. Throughout Piso is cast as Tiberius' pawn, though Tacitus remains vague about the evidence. After Piso commits suicide (or is executed) under pressure of Tiberius' withdrawal of support, the emperor "assuming an expression of grief complained about the reproach caused him by such a death" (*Ann.* 3.16.2). What Tiberius protests is presumably talk about his own responsibility in the affair, but "feigned grief" once again unmasks self-defense against reproach itself as unintentional self-reproach.

VIII

Correlative phrases (not so much . . . as, no (more) . . . than, rather . . . than) are inherently antithetic and for that reason naturally suited to epigrammatic expression. The first member marks out a field (e.g., Lepidus' supporters claimed that he was "gentle," *Ann.* 3.32.2) which is then momentarily held in suspension as the comparison begins ("gentle rather than . . .") until it is completed as the second member drops into place (". . . rather than cowardly": *mitem magis quam ignavum*). What is more, contrast is combined with comparison, and the latter often carries with it an implicit value judgment that is especially useful in dealing with the nuances of political language.[46] Thus the claim that Lepidus was "gentle rather than cowardly" has a slightly defensive accent and as a political epigram about him is witty dismissal. Gentleness is a good thing and cowardice a bad thing, but by taking the edge off the antithesis the remark insinuates that "gentle" may after all also in a way be "cowardly." *Magis quam* is "more X than Y but still Y" as well as "X rather than Y." The abrupt antithesis in *Histories* 1.3.3, "our preservation is not a concern of the gods, our punishment is" (*non esse curae deis securitatem nostram, esse ultionem*), would be softened and rendered ironic in the correlative form, "the gods care no more for our preservation [as they do and as we should expect] than for our punishment." This says wryly that confidence in divine care may well be misplaced, the former simply that it is illusory.

The various possibilities in such constructions are exploited to the full by

Tacitus.[47] At times he uses *magis* or *potius quam* to mark more or less straightforward alternatives:

> [Tiberius praised Germanicus] *more* with specious words *than* in convincing expression of his deeper attitude. (*Ann.* 1.52.2).

> [Plancina paid an] overdue *rather than* undeserved penalty. (*Ann.* 6.26.3)

> [War was waged against the Germans] *more* to recover the reputation lost with Varus' army *than* to extend the empire. (*Ann.* 1.3.6)

The first is a clear-cut contrast between what Tiberius said and what he thought. The second is a clear-cut choice between possible assessments of Plancina. The third is a subtler hint that recovery of reputation was a more real and also in comparison a less impressive motive than was extension of power. *Magis quam* can accordingly be used to draw attention to the camouflaging of political reality through language which so interested Tacitus:

> Nights were given to celebration [*laetitia*] *rather than* to license [*lascivia*]. (*Ann.* 14.21.3)

> [Tiberius knew] how things were *rather than* how they were being talked about. (*Ann.* 3.70.3)

Insofar as it is antithetic, *magis quam* sets right against wrong, true against false ("celebration" against "license"). And because it is at the same time corrective ("celebration" is a dishonest substitute for "license"), it also has an unmasking effect that touches on the conflict between norms that underlies the corruption of political language. Occasionally the unmasking is made explicit. Thus the corruption of language in "nights given over to celebration *rather than* to license in *Annals* 14.21.3 has already been marked a few lines earlier in 14.21.1: "most people enjoyed the license of the celebration and nevertheless covered it with decent words." *Annals* 13.31.3 uses the same method: "subjects were hurt *no less* by such gifts *than* by the extortion of officials who cover [*propugnant*] with political favors [public shows] the crimes they committed from greed." The incongruity (i.e., that gifts could be harmful) in the first clause is resolved by the straightforward statement in the second that the "gifts" were mere "bribes."

As we have seen, unprincipled shifts in political morality during the scramble for survival put language under stresses that could lead to strange dislocations:

> When Vitellius was satisfied that they had been treacherous [to Otho], he acquitted them of loyalty. (*Hist.* 2.60.1)

The *magis quam* formula is brought in with great effect when Tacitus says in this connection that the defendants "used a defense *more* necessary *than* honorable." That is a witty way of talking about necessity, coolly conceding the imperatives of politics, then undercutting them with the greater imperatives of integrity. What is more, since the claim of the Othonians to have been traitors to Otho was probably false as well as "necessary," the situation has a double twist: not only in treason that earns acquittal but in the false claim to treason (cf. the double reverse in Petronius' "vices or imitations of them" *Ann.* 16.18.2, which might well have been "*more* imitations of vice *than* real ones").

Comparison of this sort, then, typically blurs or softens the antithetic contrast between norms to produce a pleasing effect of witty, oblique rather than head-on conflict. One member of the correlation is not only antithetic to the other (e.g., necessity to honor) but also incongruous in the light of ordinary norms (necessity in comparison with honor). It is only to be expected that Agrippina would attempt to influence the emperor through persuasion, and so the phrase about the influence she actually exercised "*more* by threats *than* by pleading" (*Ann.* 12.42.3) is unexpected. But since what is normal (i.e., "pleading") is kept in view, the language avoids simply saying that "she used threats," and it is this ironic tact about her unprecedented power at Rome that turns the words into a cynical quip. The tone of understatement verges on that of Sallust's sly "she danced and sang *better than* was necessary for a decent woman" (*Catiline* 25.2), though without the added touch of Sallust's "necessary" replacing "proper" in a witty mock politeness that avoids the blunt "than any decent woman would . . ." We naturally expect that anyone would want to rule, but Piso's modesty suggested that he was "*more* able *than* willing to hold power" (*Hist.* 1.17.1). His detachment is perhaps admirable, but in the case of Vitellius comparison is clearly invidious. We again expect that he would want power, but when he was urged to seize it, "his sluggish nature was moved to desire *more than* to hope" (*Hist.* 1.52.4). Piso's reluctance disappointingly overrides his real ability. Vitellius' desire is a ludicrous substitute for the real self-confidence called for. The scandal of civil war is similarly exposed in the very language of the Flavian leaders to their troops: they should "wish not to capture *rather than* save" Rome (*Hist.* 3.60.3). We expect *servare; capere* should not even be mentioned, and its use lends a touch of bitter wit (cf. *Ann.* 1.41.1 for talk of "capturing" one's own cities in civil war).

Inversion of the legal process is yet another motif that fits in easily with the formula. Men were deprived of rank "not because they hated the emperor but because they were thought to do so" and therefore were exiled "*more* because they were discredited *than* because they were convicted" (*Ann.* 15.71.2). When we read that as soon as charges were entered the accused "were regarded *more* as condemned *than* as defendants" (*Ann.* 16.14.3), the false inference that those charged are guilty is again exposed by the formula itself inasmuch as it reverses terms by implying that what is "more" the case is what we should have expected to be "less" (cf. *Ann.* 15.71.5 for the absurdity of guilt before conviction). *Magis quam* in this respect is a particularly concentrated form of the indirection that often goes with epigrammatic brevity and makes it witty.

> . . . abrupt and allusive [*suspiciosae*] *sententiae* in which more is to be understood than is heard. (Sen. *Epistulae* 114.1)

> . . . you say as much as you want and you mean more than you say. (*Ep.* 59.5)

> . . . we think it better to mean more than we say. (Quint. *Inst.* 8, pref. 24)[48]

Magis quam can also muffle a potential compliment through invidious comparison.

> [Valens acted in mimes] with *more* style *than decency* (*scite magis quam probe, Hist.* 3.62.2).

> In money, status and talent Vibius Crispus ranked *more* among the notable (*claros*) *than* among the noble (*bonos, Hist.* 2.10.1).

The style and the celebrity were real enough, but neither really amounted to much. That is what is said, and what the corrective comparison ultimately means is that at Rome style was often mistaken for genuine taste, while people could be (in the contemporary phrase) famous for being famous rather than for worth.

By the same token, *magis quam* is a good way of conveying the air of vague futility or indecision to which Tacitus often draws attention (see below, chap. 6, sec. 4). The same Valens

> was *more* sure of what to avoid *than* of what to trust. (*Hist.* 3.43.2).

This is as much cynical wit about, as it is description of general political fecklessness, and that is true of numerous other instances of the formula.

> [Mutineers were] *more* cowed *than* pacified. (*Ann.* 1.39.6)

> [Because Vitellius thought that friendship could be bought] he was *more* owned it *than* actually had it. (*Hist.* 3.86.2)

> [At Vitellius' death] war stopped *more than* peace began. (*Hist.* 4.1.1)

> [Galba was] *more* a man without vice *than* one of virtue. (*Hist.* 1.49.2)

> [Armenians were] *more* leaderless *than* free (*Ann.* 2.4.2)

Some of these epigrams come close in their effect to amusing (if sour) jokes. There is, at any rate, something genuinely amusing about a political system in which a procurator ("sluggish in spirit, absurd in body") "plundered Rome's allies *rather than* her enemies" (*Ann.* 12.49.1) or in which a man could survive "*more* from the emperor's forgetfulness *than* from his clemency" (*Ann.* 6.14.2). The idea that power is arbitrary is a commonplace; here the way it is expressed is witty because *magis quam* syntactically sets up expectation dashed when the appropriate member of the comparison suddenly comes in the wrong place. We expect to hear that people survive because of imperial clemency rather than (or at least more than) administrative inefficiency. In *Germania* 37.5 the formula again conveys cynically amused disapproval: "in recent times the Germans have provided occasions *more* of triumph *than* of victory." We are perhaps intended to hear official euphemism in "triumph." At any rate, official pretense or just this score was evidently a familiar occasion for political joking: "Domitian was aware that his recent false triumph in Germany was laughed at" (*Agr.* 39.10), and other passages ridicule sham prisoners from sham wars (Dio 67.7.4; Pliny *Panegyricus* 16.3; cf. Suet. *Calig.* 47).

After providing some typical ethnographic information about the inferior quality of pearls in Britain perhaps due to lack of skill on the part of those who gather them, Tacitus adds, "I could *more* easily believe that what is lacking is quality in the pearls *than* greed in us" (*ego facilius crediderim naturam margaritis deesse quam nobis avaritiam, Agr.* 12.6). Chiasmus, antithesis, and a variant of the *magis quam* formula all work to underscore the sour judgment on Roman greed. And with its sly comparison of probabilities the epigram is a genuinely witty warning that Roman greed precludes making a *virtue* of necessity. The very number of examples of the formula and its variants makes another important point: the confusion in standards it marks seemed so pervasive to Tacitus that it was more a natural way of speaking and thinking than a stylistic mannerism.

IX

These various methods for setting up interplay between virtue and vice, truth and falsehood through antithetic epigrams are interesting in their own right as rhetorical techniques. But the pattern they embody on a verbal level reflects something that lies also at a deeper, conceptual level.[49] In one passage Tacitus touches on the common idea that events move in cycles: "Perhaps there is a certain cycle in all things so that as the seasons change, so do moral standards" (*Ann.* 3.55.5).[50] But he is not at all doctrinaire and never develops the notion of historical recurrence with any precision. His own view seems close to that of Thucydides: human nature remains at bottom the same, hence any cyclic movement is transformed into a pattern of waves with periods of advance succeeding periods of decline, and so on. The result is endless but similar variations that in the long run tend to level out events without resolution in either direction. The general pattern of epigrammatic masking and unmasking fits into this scheme and is to some extent a function of it.

In periods of good government language, institutions, and values are authentic; in periods of corrupt government they become debased. In dealing with the latter the historian's task is not simply to describe but to expose, and he can do so by inverting what is politically and morally false. The long-term historical sequence that Tacitus has in view is republican government succeeded by repressive Principate, interrupted, in turn, by occasional good emperors. Since the course of history *is* this ongoing conflict between values on a large scale, an antithetic pattern of thought and language is itself an indispensable tool for historical insight because it answers to the texture of history itself. "Jews regard as *profane* all that we hold *sacred,* and conversely *permit* all that we *abhor";* their *clannishness* is the obverse of their *hatred for others,* and so "though they are given to *lust,* Jewish men *abstain* from non-Jewish women" (*Hist.* 5.4 and 5). This is not merely jaundiced rhetorical abuse (though it is that, too); it is understanding of another culture in terms of a structuralism that in its own way genuinely attempts to do what recent forms of structuralism try to do, employing as its key category not simply neutral binary opposition but binary incongruity in the pattern of events.

History on a large scale, then, is a condition with chronic recoveries and lapses: we should be grateful for the former; we can live with the latter but cannot hope for a true cure (*Hist.* 4.8.2, 4.74.2). History's opposing rhythms are a function of the human nature which creates history, and human language itself naturally plays an important part in the process. In *Histories* 2.38 Tacitus introduces a broad outline of the course of Roman history with the comment that the "old desire for power long ingrained in humans broke out as the empire grew" (*Hist.* 2.38.1). Ambition has not always been so ruthless but varies from era to era and was exacerbated in Rome by loss of foreign enemies. This leaves open the possibility of improvement through return to an earlier standard of political life, though changes are only a matter of degree since the evil tendency is ingrained in human nature.[51] Periodic inversion of authentic values and of the language through which they are expressed follows from this as a natural by-product of history as well as of human nature, and Tacitus is quite conscious of the shifts in political and moral language that occur.[52] By the same token, a major task of historiography is counterinversion or unmasking to reestablish during periods of bad government the authentic language and norms that go with good government. To this extent Tacitus' view of history on a large scale can fairly be seen as a background consciousness reflected directly in his rhetoric and helping shape the ways in which it is appropriate to speak about particular things, that is to say, in terms of parody, epigram, and antithesis, which bring conflicting codes and intentions to light.

III

Techniques of Wit

I

With these rhetorical techniques of the epigrammatic style as a general background, we can now turn to the more specifically witty facets of the historiography of the early empire as a whole. Witty, that is to say, in the sense of "amusing," though not always pleasantly so, since the wit we are concerned with lies at a level deep and broad enough to touch on serious issues. One notable feature of Tacitus' and Suetonius' history is its pervasive cleverness: the principals seem never at a loss for striking things to say or do, someone is present to remember, and (in the case of Tacitus) the historian's own epigrammatic style lends a final witty bite. It is precisely this quality, of course, that often creates problems of historical credibility, but whatever the historians' own attitude on that score may have been, their intention in the first instance was to uncover the deeper, exemplary meaning of events—what has been called the moral "inscape" of character rather than the external "landscape" of fact.[1]

> It is my intention to treat only senatorial motions which are remarkable for honor or shame, since I think that the special duty of history is to assure that virtue be recorded and shameful acts or words be deterred by fear of evil reputation among posterity. (*Ann.* 3.65.1)

In another passage Tacitus connects his own work specifically with catastrophic collapse of ordinary norms of behavior and then remarks that history which honestly takes account of this quickly becomes offensive to many because it often strikes close to home.

> Few can distinguish what is honorable and what is dishonorable, useful and harmful . . . my subject will be useful but not pleasant. Accounts of countries, various battles, dying commanders hold the interest of readers; what I offer is savage orders, endless accusations, false friendships, destruction of the innocent. . . . Some people think that reports of others' evil deeds are a criticism of

themselves. Even fame and virtue have enemies since they prove the opposite [i.e., reveal disgrace and vice] by coming too close to home. (*Ann.* 4.33.2)

An incident recounted by Tacitus illustrates in a simple way the link between historical insight and perception of ethical incongruity. So contemptuous of the difference between right and wrong were victors during the civil war that a soldier killed his brother and then demanded a reward for doing so. His superiors found themselves in a double bind, being "prevented either from rewarding him [on grounds of common decency] or punishing him [on grounds of military policy]." So they put him off with the excuse that his merit was beyond their ability to repay on the spot, and Tacitus says that he does not know what finally happened (*Hist.* 3.51.1). The story is queer in a dual sense; it shocks ordinary ethical feeling and at the same time there is also something grimly amusing about the way in which those in power are quite unable to deal with the consequences of a situation they have created, and nothing is in fact done. Tacitus' account appropriately fades away into silence because finally the truth is that under such circumstances there can be nothing more to do or say. His own moral agenda comes out openly in a final remark about the value of "solace against evil and examples of good" in the light of such incidents.

We do not expect anyone to value a reward higher than the life of his brother. The political truth of the story (as distinct from its historical authenticity) lies in the profound dissonance of norms, and when that is put in precise linguistic form the tension between language and reason produces a formal joke or epigram.

Antony's reply to the Megarians who had proudly pressed upon him the attractions of their senate house was, "It's small but—shabby" (*mikron men, sapron de, Antony* 23.3). Plutarch introduces the story with the remark that at first Antony was not improper (*atopos*) in his behavior toward the Greeks, but then rebuffed the Megarians. The anecdote evidently is an instance of impropriety; *atopia* is a word that in its literal sense of "out of place" precisely catches the notion of breach of norms, and the joke is in fact a neat put-down sprung by violating the expected negative/positive antithesis set up by *men/de*. When Alexander played the lyre at a party, Philip asked him "whether he was not ashamed of playing so—well" (*Pericles* 1.5). The (apparent) incoherence arises from witty tension between ordinary language in which shame goes with playing badly and the aristocratic code against manual skills. Plutarch's own remarks in *Alexander* 1.1 recognize not only that historical insight may be triggered specifically by incongruity between norms, but also that the occasion for such insight is often jesting relaxation of the restrictions that define public norms. Then "men can discard the official uniform and show the human being."[2] That is evidently what Antony does, and the wit of Philip's bon mot, too, lies in startling dissonance caused by subversion of one code by another.

II

The general principle of violated expectation *(para prosdokian)* that underlies these anecdotes and many other forms of wit attracted a great deal of attention in ancient rhetorical theory.[3] Though violation of expectation is only a species of wit, in ancient theory it tends to stand for the entire genus.

> Most jokes [*asteia*] come from dislocation [*metaphoras*] and deception . . . [wit] occurs whenever something is unexpected [*paradoxon*] and in violation of our previous assumption . . . as is the case with wordplays, since they too deceive. . . . "He trudged onward, and under his feet he had—chilblains": the hearer assumed that what would be said would be "sandals." (Arist. *Rh.* 1412a19).

We expect that others will behave and speak in accordance with the objective world—in fact, we define normalcy in those terms. Wit occurs when we are startled by deliberate or casual illogic, and so long as illogic remains at that intentional, socially acceptable level it is amusing, that is to say, is what Aristotle in defining facetiousness *(eutrapeleia)* neatly calls "cultured insolence" *(hybris pepaideumenē, Rh.* 1389b11). As the balance shifts from "culture" to "insolence" (as it notably does in the ferocious wit of the Roman historians) wit takes on a serious or ominous dimension: it becomes offensive, threatening, and ultimately insane.

Public rules of one sort or another are always a factor in wit, and wit is notoriously risky because in some forms (sexual, ethnic, political) normally restrained factors may reach an offensively overt level. Social life in general depends on a variety of codes that establish expectations and thus permit us to relax our guard against surprise.

> One will readily see that the great part, if not all, of everyday conversation maintains subjective reality. Indeed, its massivity is achieved by the accumulation and consistency of casual conversation—conversation that can *afford to be* casual precisely because it refers to the routine of a taken-for-granted world. The loss of casualness signals a break in the routines and, at least potentially, a threat to the taken-for-granted reality. Thus one may imagine the effect of casualness on an exchange like this: "Well, it's time for me to get to the station." "Fine, darling, don't forget to take along your gun."[4]

This account of the assumptions about meaning that underlie ordinary language is doubly to the point in that the typically conversational form of jokes aims precisely at creating a routine situation in order to set up violation of expectation. At the same time, this particular exchange between husband and wife could well be a serious political statement about law and order as well as a joke. Routines or codes of behavior are what Plutarch, too, has in mind when he says that wit mixed with wine relaxes inhibition to destroy "form and pattern" (*to plasma kai ton schēmatismon, Quaest. conv.* 645b; cf. 621e).

Para prosdokian accordingly is the natural pattern for what Tacitus wants to say about civil war and the collapse of military discipline that goes with it. Both violate the code of political rationality in which the difference between order and disorder, friend and foe is clearly defined.

> Those who could not be controlled could be—punished. (*ut contineri non possent qui puniri poterant, Hist.* 4.27.3; cf. the military epigram on discipline, "we can't make you do it, but we can make you wish you had")

> The remedy of one disturbance was—another one. (*Hist.* 2.68.2; perhaps "remedy" was a familiar euphemism like the current "liberation")[5]

> [As Valens' army passed through Gaul the inhabitants placated its irrational violence] and though they were not at war, they tried everything to attain—peace. (*Hist.* 1.63.2; cf. 2.12.2)

The formula reappears wherever political irrationality is to be found.

> [Several Romans who had won political credit in unsuccessful campaigns against the African leader Tacfarinas were honored] with three crowned statues in the city and he was—still sacking Africa. (*Ann.* 4.23.1)

> [Tiberius was jealous of Germanicus and so] since Germanicus was forbidden from completing the war, it was taken as—completed. (*Ann.* 2.41.2; cf. the curiously similar mixture of sham, realism, and jest in the proposal that the war in Vietnam be declared won and the United States withdraw)

> Astrologers are a race of men, untrustworthy to those who have power and deceitful to those who want it, which in our city will always be both banned and—consulted. (*Hist.* 1.22.1)

> The same people love idleness and hate—quiet. (*Germ.* 15.1)

> The legions from Moesia recalled that they had helped those from Pannonia to take vengeance, and the Pannonians, as though excused by the mutiny of others, were delighted to—repeat their crime. (*Hist.* 3.11.2)

> Because that way was faster, Tigellinus won the rewards of virtue through—vice. (*Hist.* 1.72.1)

> Otho acted like a slave in order to be—master. (*Hist.* 1.36.3; *omnia serviliter pro dominatione:* "everything slavish for—masterhood")

> In his sixth consulate Augustus was secure enough to cancel the powers of his

triumvirate and pass laws under which we could have peace and a—prince. (*Ann.* 3.28.2; *pace et principe* = "master").[6]

[Two ordinary soldiers] undertook to transfer the imperium of the Roman people and they—did it. (*Hist.* 1.25.1)

The effect depends on a shock, usually at the end, which would be further enhanced in actual delivery. Any punch line is better in the telling, and Tacitus was a practicing orator of the first rank. The structure is that of jokes set up by a perfectly normal grammatical form then completed with content that cancels what went before and turns the statement into nonsense. Thought sequence is broken abruptly, and in the case of ordinary joking the dislocation typically gives what is said an amusingly incoherent sound.

Paula wants to marry me, but I won't have her because she's too old. I would, if she were—older. (Martial 10.8)

I can resist everything but—temptation.

Quintilian (*Inst.* 6.3.84) cites several examples from Cicero:

What did he lack except wealth and virtue?

Cicero meeting the freedman of an enemy whose death has been falsely reported:
    How are things?
    Fine.
    Oh, he *is* dead then?

In *De oratore* 2.281 Cicero himself describes the first of these witticisms as an example of "incongruity." The members are *discrepantia* and make an epigram much like Tacitus' "Poppaea had everything else except—character." Such jokes or epigrams admirably illustrate the two features of *para prosdokian* mentioned by Demetrius (*On Style* 153): they are amusing because they end in an unexpected way and because they display logical incoherence (*anakolouthia* is the equivalent of Cicero's *discrepantia*). His word for the type is *griphos,* literally a creel of intricate construction, an image that brings to mind the absurd involutions in legal logic dealt with in declamatory rhetoric and the similar portrayal of political irrationality in the historians.

The technique works through what Freud calls "unification": joining of incompatible members.[7] In the first two examples from Tacitus quoted above a "disturbance" may be a "remedy" of sorts but a startling one to say the least, and "punishment" is a sorry partner of "control." Vitellius' enemies "had no freedom [*licentia*] other than to—kill him" (*Hist.* 3.66.3): the absurdity of "freedom" in realpolitik is again brought out by the startling synonym. A joke circulating about Caligula quoted by Suetonius is another case in point (*Calig.* 10.2). His pretense of indifference to the oppression he suffered at the hands of Tiberius was so great that it was said that there "never had been a better slave or a worse—master" (*servum meliorem . . . deteriorem dominum*). On the initial verbal level this is a clever antithetic (and chiastic) epigram perfectly ordinary in meaning if Caligula is slave and master at different times. But it has a faintly nonsensical sound if "master" and "slave" are taken together. Then it is an oxymoron whose parts provoke reciprocal unmasking: slave is in fact master, and master, slave. With that comes realization that the supreme absurdity of the Principate is its combining the worst of both worlds, and Suetonius goes on immediately to portray Caligula's "savage and vicious nature."

Tacitus' remark about German and Roman morality is another typical instance of unmasked language: "No one in Germany laughs at vice, nor is seducing and being seduced called 'modish'" (*Germ.* 19.1). Though not exactly a formal epigram, the point of this is a common subject of wit by *para prosdokian,* and Tacitus may have been borrowing from a wide range of current jokes, quips, and epigrams on the new morality and its language, some perhaps originally self-indulgent and euphemistic rather than satirical (as "they make desolation and call it peace" turns "peace" against its original use). Seneca has several epigrams on this theme. "Does any woman blush at divorce when celebrities count years not by consuls but by husbands and leave home to marry, and marry—to divorce . . . no woman has a husband except to irritate her—lover. Chastity is proof of ugliness . . . she is a simple, old-fashioned woman who doesn't know that having only one lover is called being—'married'" (*Ben.* 3.16.2). "[Decency] is in bad taste, insensitive and boorish . . . the most respectable form of marriage is—adultery, and . . . a man takes a wife [*duxit*] only when he takes her—[*abduxit*] from another man" (*Ben.* 1.9.3). All of this sounds like a canvass of current bons mots. That the situations might in fact be in accordance with Roman law is for Tacitus or Seneca part of the joke. Dio (60.31.1) mentions Messalina's plan to have all her lovers legally made—"husbands" (cf. *Annals* 11.26; Juvenal 6.141: "a rich woman is a widow if she marries a greedy man" [i.e., he will grant her sexual freedom]; and Martial 6.90: "Gellia has only one lover, and what is really disgraceful is that she is the wife of two men [husbands]" [cf. 6.7]). Caligula had the bride brought from a wedding to his own house, then "divorced" her a few days later and subsequently banished her on suspicion that she had been seeing her first husband. In another version of the incident he is said to have warned the groom sitting opposite him at the celebration, "Hands off my wife!" and then promptly made off with her (*Calig.* 25.1; cf. Sen. *Constant.* 18.2). Various versions of the Otho/Nero/Poppaea triangle were current material for amusing stories. Poppaea lived with or was married to Otho before marrying Nero, whom the two fended off for a time. When he finally broke up their relationship and assigned Otho to a distant post, a couplet circulated about "Otho exiled in phony honor because he began to have an affair with his—own wife."

III

Other techniques permit political anomaly to appear more subtly in nothing more than a slight wrinkle in logic or syntax. Orwell's famous "all animals are equal, but some animals are more equal than others" is the paradigm case. In *De tranquillitate* 11.12 Seneca's theme is the unpredictable changes of fortune, and he wittily marks the improbability of Croesus' escape from the pyre by speaking of it as an impossibility: he found himself "a survivor of his own death." In *Agricola* 3.2 Tacitus turns the same idea into a tribute to the survivors of Domitian's terror, when he says that the few who remained alive "not only outlived others but—if I may say so—themselves." One cannot properly speak of surviving oneself, and so the phrase "if I may say so" apologizes for the offense to common sense which makes the remark amusing and at the same time suggests that political oppression renders the very language that must be used to speak about it absurd. In *Annals* 3.66.4 the paradox has its full force: Bruttedius' impatience led him to "outdo his equals, his superiors, finally—*his own* ambition." In addition to pitting Bruttedius against himself this epigram is a simple instance of the locked sequence forcing a train of thought in a set direction only to lead it to an odd last member. The Latin is written to reinforce that effect: *dum aequales, dein superiores, postremo suasmet ipse spes antire parat.* It is also an ingenious variation on such tripartite inclusive formulas as "past, present, or future" discussed above (see end of Chap. 1), with Bruttedius himself replacing the expected "inferiors" whom his ambition has left behind. Memmius Regulus was a man of such unquestioned probity that Nero once identified him as a worthy successor—"and he *nevertheless* lived on after the remark" (*Ann.* 14.47.1).

Tacitus puts unreal subjunctive conditions to equally suggestive uses, for example, in one of his finest epigrams: [*Galba*] *omnium consensu capax imperii, nisi imperasset* (*Hist.* 1.49.4). This is not exactly—or not only—contrary to fact ("he would in everyone's view have been capable, if he had not ruled") but works as a deflationary combination of fact and hypothesis held together by an omitted clause: "he was in everyone's view capable of ruling [and would have kept that reputation]—if only he had not ruled." His reputation, of course, would have been false if he had not ruled, and the effect of the omission here is as elegant as the quip cited by Freud: "he has a great future behind him."[8]

The most familiar form of wittily dislocated language is double entendre. That is especially effective in sexual or political humor because it plays two meanings or codes off against each other, one veiling the other for appearance's sake. Double entendre figures for the most part in Suetonius simply as a form of wit (usually invective) that was part of actual political life and occasionally worth remembering.[9] Tacitus uses it sparingly. He allows himself a pun on Domitian (*Domitiani indomitae libidines, Hist.* 4.68.1) and another on Mucianus (*famosus* = famous/notorious, *Hist.* 1.10.1). When monuments were built in Rome for expected victory, then left standing when defeat ensued, "appearance was considered, knowledge [*conscientia*] ignored" (*Ann.* 15.18.1), and *conscientia* is "guilty conscience" as well as "knowledge." He also quotes a witty double entendre that admirably catches the hypocrisy of autocracy: "the condition of imperial power is that account be rendered only to one auditor" (*Ann.* 1.6.3). This is not only epigram but pun (political/financial "account") and bitter joke insofar as there is in a sense no accountability if one person ultimately holds power (cf. "the best committee is a committee of one").

Equivocation is especially useful in official language, but as we have seen, it is also vulnerable to unmasking when recast in antithetic form and read epigrammatically in the opposite direction. That is what Tacitus does when he calls the only "remedy" Galba could think of for his constitutional crisis an "imperial election" or "congress" (*comitia imperii, Hist.* 1.14.1). Conflation of republican and autocratic categories produces amusing and revealing double-talk, which in form is identical to self-refuting epigrams like "savage peace" (*Hist.* 1.50.2) or "arrogant modesty" (*Ann.* 1.8.5). A remark about Nero's literary activity (*adfectavit studium carminum, Ann.* 14.16.1) probably again plays on both senses of the verb *adfectare* (take up, work on/affect, pretend to), while *annum sibi ultimum, rei publicae prope supremum* (*Hist.* 1.11.3) comes very close to wordplay and makes a fine joke: "Galba's and Vinius' final year was nearly the end of Rome" or "their last year was just about terminal for Rome." When Nero eulogizes Poppaea's "other gifts of fortune *pro virtutibus*," the preposition *pro* is a simple wordplay: for Nero it means "as," for Tacitus it means "in place of" (*Ann.* 16.6.2).

When ordinary ways of thinking are no longer adequate to political reality, language itself comes under tension. Orwell's "All animals are equal, but some are more equal than others" is an epigram because of the oddity in grammar, and it is odd because it tries to make ordinary language adequate to the public reality of a society falsely parading equality. By the same token, Tacitus' epigrammatic style helps make the point that ordinary language is inadequate to the queer reality of Roman politics. There it is possible to "outlive oneself," or it may be that "the worst enemies are those who—praise you" (*Agr.* 41.1). *Pessimum inimicorum genus, laudantes* is an odd as well as clever thing to say, because it is trying to speak to a situation in which normally antithetic terms (friend/enemy) are in apposition to each other. At the immediate linguistic level Tacitus seeks to create a slightly out-of-focus image that deliberately distorts reality in order to bring it back into focus at a deeper level. The incongruity forces us to resolve the dissonance, and as we do, an alternative code comes into play to rectify language and unmask political falsehood.[10]

Epigrams employing simple violation of expectation produce wit that is direct and immediate, and are the more effective for it. There are a few cases worth mentioning of a somewhat more indirect wit that comes from language whose normal, casual sound disguises nonsense. The effect arises from delayed action: we initially accept what is said only to realize the nonsense pointing, in turn, to a larger sense. The joke on capitalism and communism is a well-known example in epigram form: "In capitalism one man exploits another, in communism it's the other way around."[11] Cicero has a joke of the same kind on a woman claiming to be only thirty: "That's true; I have heard her say it for twenty years." Quintilian mentions the sly irrelevance of the remark by a Knight criticized by Augustus for wasting his inheritance: "But I thought it was *mine*!" (*Inst.* 6.3.74). Perfectly normal language about rights is impertinent in both senses of the term under autocracy, as Augustus is bound to admit in any response he might make. We might compare with this anecdote Nero's complaint to Seneca in *Annals* 14.56.2 ("If you give me your wealth, everyone will talk of my greed") recast as repartee: "It's unjust that you people should criticize the gifts I receive / But we thought that you were being *greedy*!" Suetonius has a similar indirect protest by a man thanking Claudius for permission to defend a client: "After all, it *is* usual" (*Claud.* 15.3).

The wit of such language comes from a framing effect in statements subverted by larger, momentarily concealed contexts. In the epigram on capitalism and communism the true equivalence of the systems is initially hidden by an apparent contrast between the two in "the other way around." A potentially serious political point is then made when the actual force of the phrase is felt. For its effect is to bring out *two* facts: not simply exploitation in both cases but, beyond that, disguised falsity in the system specifically disclaiming "exploitation." And this added fact is the larger context at once concealed and disclosed precisely by the witty form. Implicit mathematical reckoning is the subversive frame for Cicero's quip, as it is again for the flattering remark addressed to Claudius as he was celebrating the Secular Games (held every hundred years or so), "May you have many more!" (*Vit.* 2.5). The picture of freedom in the Knight's language ("But I thought . . .") is similarly framed by the implicit repression, Nero's picture of innocence ("But then people will say . . .") by his implicit guilty greed. The idea that the pleasure of wit comes from grasping hidden connections could be especially fruitful for historians to whom history was largely about dishonesty and self-deception.

IV

It is natural that many anecdotes would deal with perversion of the legal process in particular since that, as the primary code embodying expectation of public rationality, is a rich source of wit.[12] Claudius' "funny" practice of on occasion hearing only one side of a dispute is a paradigm case (*Claud.* 15.2; the chapter is largely devoted to his "frivolous and deranged" legal ideas; cf. Seneca *Apocolocyntosis* 12.3, 10.4).

In *Annals* 3.25-28 Tacitus gives special attention to breakdown of the legality in which Roman society took pride. He remarks on the failure of one major law to achieve its aim, though informers were thriving to such a degree that "as previously Rome suffered from crimes, now it suffered from laws." This strange state of affairs leads him to a deeper examination of the origins of law and of its immense growth at Rome. An earlier stage of simple life was followed by violence and ambition manageable only through legal systems. But during the Republic the system at Rome proliferated into a vast body of inconsistent *(multa et diversa)* laws so that at last "the most corrupt state has the most laws" (27.3). This absurdity continued even during Pompey's efforts at reform, when "remedies were worse than abuses" (28.1), and during the civil wars, "when the worst deeds went unpunished, while honesty was a death warrant." He then ends his sketch studded with sharp epigrams about the law's ineffectiveness with an ironic quip on a more recent stage of Roman legal history. Finally under Augustus "we had peace and a—master" (*pace et principe*, 28.2; the effect in context is something like "order and—no law").

The peculiar legal irrationality that he has traced through the Republic is then a recurrent theme in Tacitus' picture of the Principate. It is specifically the point of many of the best anecdotes and a key ingredient in their amusing effect. *Annals* 15.71 is a collection of stories on the theme of Nero's legal lunacy, ending with a fine specimen of witty omission. His victims "first learned that they had been defendants when they learned of their penalty" (*Ann.* 15.71.5). If accusation and defense drop out between crime and penalty, penalty becomes (legalized) crime (cf. Messalina's conviction before her defense, *Ann.* 11.28.2), and Tacitus is clearly trying to make the same joking suggestion of insanity as the Red Queen's "sentence first, verdict afterwards." In fact a related, though less drastic proposal had been made earlier that Tiberius evaluate each candidate's character before appointment. "Crimes are punished by laws; how much better to see that there is no crime!" (*Ann.* 3.69.1). This is not at all unreasonable and is, in fact, the sober policy of Agricola (*Agr.* 19.3). But since it was introduced by way of flattery, the powers it hints at are quite unreasonable, and the emperor in this case refuses in the name of realism. Since he cannot see fully into another's character, "punishment must follow crime."[13] The remark that someone had to be "appointed [*designatur*] as defendant" in a trumped-up indictment (*Ann.* 14.60.2) has the same suggestion of absurd reversal, the more so in view of the legal overtones of *designatur.*

Wit along this line becomes more elaborate and grim (Tacitus calls the incident "brutal farce [*ludibria*] added to murder") in *Annals* 16.11. Three victims of judicial suicide under Nero—grandmother, father, and daughter—pray to die first "to leave their loved ones still living and about to die" *(suos superstites et morituros).* The anomaly of Neronian jurisprudence is marked here by the simultaneous death of three generations, while the futility to which it reduces its victims is marked by the delicate oxymoron "still living and [but] about to die."[14] The peculiar quality of "declamatory" absurdity (see discussion in chap. 5, sec. 3) is then taken a step further and the account becomes scarcely intelligible when the victims are indicted after death, though Nero graciously intervenes to permit them free choice of the manner of death. The possibility of trial in the case of treason even for those who had committed suicide does not lessen the absurdity that Tacitus' account suggests (cf. expulsion of senators who are already dead, *Ann.* 14.59.4). On other occasions Nero would send doctors to "take care of" those who had been condemned, "for that is what he called [*vocabatur*, with *iocabatur* as an apt variant] opening veins" (*Ner.* 37.2).

Caligula, too, has in Suetonius a section devoted exclusively to unusual legal methods. Having "expedited" justice by condemning under one sentence forty defendants charged with different crimes, he went home and told his wife Caesonia that while she had been taking a nap he had gotten a great deal of work done (38.3). In Seneca (*Ep.* 77.18) his response to a wretched prisoner's appeal for death is a genuinely witty put-down: "What makes you think you're alive?" He might execute the fathers of his victims to "spare them grief" (Sen. *De ira* 3.19.5), then again he might have them executed if they tried to close their eyes when forced to witness the death of a son (Dio 59.25.6). He spoke tactfully of signing warrants for execution as a matter of "clearing his books" (*Calig.* 29.2); and when it became too costly to feed cattle to the beasts used in spectacles, he decided to substitute criminals, whom he reviewed in a long line, and then without examining any of the charges against them selected all of those standing between two bald men (27.1).

The legal procedures of Tiberius ("clever inventor of new laws," *Ann.* 2.30.3) were equally bizarre. An imprisoned man who requested death was refused because "we haven't become friends yet" (Suet. *Tiberius* 61.5; Dio generalizes this incident into the joking dictum that under Tiberius life could be punishment, death a favor, 58.23.6, and Seneca uses the idea in *Agamemnon* 994–96). Elsewhere Dio tells of a man executed for taking a coin with Tiberius' image on it into a latrine (58, frag. 2; cf. Sen. *Ben.* 3.26.2). In another case Tiberius had had a man severely tortured, and when he learned that his victim had been falsely suspected, had him speedily executed on the ground that he was too dishonored to live any longer (Dio 58.3.7). This is peculiarly striking because Tiberius' attitude does make a certain sense under the Roman code of honor and thus gives a doubly startling facade of reason to unreason. At any rate, Suetonius reports that one of the conspirators against Nero justified the attempt as a *favor* to him, since only by death could a man so disgraced by vice be helped (*Ner.* 36.2). Sejanus' daughter posed a finer point of law and had to be duly raped before execution, because it was illegal for a virgin to be executed (*Ann.* 5.9).

The grotesquerie of all of this again comes from a large-scale shaping of events in accordance with the structure of wit to dramatize sudden moments of unreason. The case of self-incrimination during sleep mentioned by Tacitus is a particularly interesting instance of truncated political logic that is bound to seem absurd in a normal world.

> Suillius added two well-known Roman Knights to those accused . . . the reason for their death was that they had made their house available for meetings of Mnester and Poppaea. But what they were charged with was a dream which occurred in the dead of night [and which was taken to portend trouble or death for Claudius]. . . . What is not in doubt is that a dream of some sort was fatal to both. (*Ann.* 11.4.1)

It is most improbable that anyone was executed at Rome simply for having a dream, and Tacitus admits as much when he says that the cause of death was Poppaea's use of the brothers' home. But public interpretation of dreams would have been another matter. That might well have political motives, and it is likely that something of the sort happened in this case. Though Tacitus notes that the dream was connected with Claudius' death, by omitting any mention of subversive use of dream interpretation he juxtaposes "dream" as closely as possible with "execution," short-circuits ordinary reasoning, and turns the incident into a bizarre non sequitur of despotism. One can actually dream oneself into the hands of the executioner, and the assurance "there is no doubt that some sort of dream . . ." does not so much reiterate the facts as make a witty point about the larger, absurd reality of repression, whatever the exact facts may have been.

The formal technique here is omission, which as applied to history means telescoping events to make queer connections.[15]

> An advocate at whom Claudius had become angry was thrown into the Tiber on his order. When one of his clients later consulted another advocate, the latter asked, "Who told you that I swim better than he does?" (Dio 60.33.8)

That is to say, who told you that (since practicing law at Rome is hazardous, I have a better chance of surviving because) I swim better? By the same token, a dream about Claudius (had unfavorable political implications, which when discussed openly) meant death for two Knights.

This telescoping effect becomes more extreme in one of Suetonius' stories about Caligula's gambling. While strolling in the atrium during a brief absence from the game he spots two wealthy Knights, instantly has them arrested, confiscates their money, and returns to the game boasting that his luck has never been better (*Calig.* 41.2). It may still be possible to make sense of this astonishing sequence of events (cf. Dio 59.22.4), but it seems hopeless to do so with the story that goes from Caligula routinely officiating at a sacrifice directly to Caligula for no reason sacrificing his fellow officiant instead of the animal (*Calig.* 32.3). Political jokes based on this technique were evidently common and in some cases are perhaps directly retold in the historians. The young poet Montanus was exiled "because he showed talent" (*Ann.* 16.29.2), and nothing is said about Nero's envy; Paetus Thrasea was executed for a "grumpy pedagogue's expression" (*Ner.* 37.1), and nothing is said about what his demeanor meant; Seneca was nearly executed "for pleading a case well" in Gaius' presence (Dio 59.19.7); Julius Graecinus was executed "simply because he was a better man than was convenient for a tyrant" (Sen. *Ben.* 2.21.5); and a family of three was doomed because "simply in virtue of being alive they were hateful to the emperor" as a reproach for one of his other murders (*Ann.* 16.10.1).

The entertainment value of all of these preposterous stories is plain enough. Aside from that, though, and aside from their plausibility even at the time, they are rooted in the actual logic of Roman political life, and that is what gives them historiographic value. The Principate, in fact, was not a pure autocracy; it governed in accordance with a wide range of legal restrictions, and such power as the senate had lay largely in its legislative activity. For that reason legal procedure assumed great importance as a symbol of legitimacy. But power was often symbolic also in the sense of being merely nominal, and that made legal procedure itself into an oddly natural medium for pretense and parody. Hence the point of many of the stories comes from disparity between form and content. For insofar as law was an authentic symbol of political rationality, it was especially vulnerable to imperial caprice, in the same way as Cynic subversion of norms through random gestures of absurd behavior was most effective and most amusing when aimed specifically at prime embodiments of conventional values.

IV

Enacted Wit

I

The menacing fact behind the vast collection of bizarre anecdotes in the ancient historians was the emperors' power to transform witty *ludibrium* into reality. "Remember, I can do anything and to anybody" (*omnia mihi et in omnes licere, Calig.* 29.1); "no emperor has yet realized what he could do" (*Ner.* 37.3). When Claudius, a favorite subject for stories about legal eccentricity, heard someone in court shout that a convicted forger "should have his hands cut off" (*Claud.* 15.2), he instantly called for an executioner with knife and block. His call for immediate performance of a figure of speech is a good instance of metaphor taken literally, and the story goes to show how readily eccentricity could turn into terror or absurdity under the Principate. The 120-foot statue and other oversized features of Nero's Golden House are similarly, for Suetonius, madly literal metaphors of grandeur (*Ner.* 31.1). Tiberius, too, has his little joke by actually sending someone with a message to the dead. After he had neglected to pay largess promised by Augustus, someone whispered something into the ear of a corpse being taken out to burial. When asked what he had said, the man replied that he was sending a reminder to Augustus, and Tiberius had him executed so that he could deliver the message in person (Dio 57.14.1).

In the atmosphere of undefined terror during Tiberius' reign no one could be trusted, "and even voiceless things—roof, walls—were viewed with suspicion" (*Ann.* 4.69.3). This makes a powerful metaphor, and one with a certain "cartoon" quality to it. Taken literally, it becomes a poster of walls growing hostile mouths and ears, a surreal picture driving its lesson home with absurdity. But in Rome that picture becomes plain fact when informers actually do hide in the space between ceiling and roof to eavesdrop (4.69.1). Cartooning of this a sort is often implicit in jokes with a strong visual element, for example, the story of Caligula's wish that the Roman people had a collective neck for easier cutting (*Calig.* 30.2). Visualized literally, this again becomes a political cartoon of Emperor slaughtering the People; taken seriously, it becomes evidence for his madness. Suetonius uses it as both, though it may

69

originally have been no more than a disgusted jest. Caligula's sacrifice of a fellow officiant (32.2) makes another fine cartoon (of Lunatic Imperial Violence), in this case, one that is supposed to have actually happened, a surreal photograph rather than a cartoon.

A symbolic, cartoonlike quality similar to that in Caligula's wish for a Roman Neck appears in an incident under Commodus which Dio claims to have witnessed himself (73.21). During one of his public performances as a gladiator—itself a living caricature of sorts—Commodus cut off the head of an ostrich. Then brandishing it in one hand and wielding the bloody sword in the other, he approached the senators' section with a nasty grin on his face. Dio says that many senators "would have died by the sword on the spot, since it was amusement and not distress that we felt," if they had not on his suggestion taken laurel leaves from the crowns they wore and chewed them vigorously to conceal their laughter. In the first instance this astonishing account presents itself as a literal fact: the emperor threatened senators with death; they thought that he was funny and only by suppressing their amusement did they escape. Since Dio claims to have been present at this and other incidents (73.18.3), it is hard to question the facts. But even when it is taken literally, Commodus' gesture is by itself also symbolic, though a symbol verging in his view on the real world (hence the senators' genuine danger) and in their view also on mere absurdity (hence the laughter). The latter is happily foremost in Dio's account; Commodus was presently assassinated, and so the whole affair in a sense after all comes to no more than a striking political picture (again of Lunatic Imperial Violence).

Insofar as anecdotes, then, typically deal with what happens they are enacted jokes. Commodus is symbolically *doing* what Gaius is *saying* in his quip about a single Roman neck, and the gesture is accompanied by signs of ludibristic amusement on both sides. This connection between word and deed helps throw light on another peculiar, much more important feature of ancient historiography: the prominent role played by oracles and omens. Both have a prima facie similarity to enacted wit on several counts: they are typically incongruous because they violate ordinary expectations; they are signs of deeper political disorder; and as actual happenings omens are, in effect, practical jokes of a sort.

It is difficult for us to appreciate political interpretation of omens in a society which took them seriously. Even when they were rationalized or simply recorded by skeptical historians, that had to be done consciously and was another way of interpretation rather than outright elimination. As the denial of rhetoric may be a form of rhetoric, so mention of omens may be a *praeteritio* by which they are preserved as a factor in political understanding. And the factor they tend in one way or another to embody is anomaly.

Dio mentions the case of an oracular response pictured by a sketch of a boy strangling two serpents (73.7.1–2). When he later came to see that the boy was

Commodus, who had two brothers executed (as Heracles strangled two serpents), religious omen in effect assumes the form of political cartoon. What permits this to happen is the pervasive fusion of religion and politics through which emperors become vaguely divine figures. Several other instances of "ominous" political riddling come up in connection with Commodus. Dio says that his appearance as Mercury, golden wand and all, "was taken as an omen" (73.19.4). Presumably someone saw a grim joke about Mercury Psychopomp (cf. 73.19.5: "what came next [in Commodus' show] was no longer a game but entailed the death of many"). Again, when Commodus' helmet was taken out of the arena by the same door through which corpses went (73.21.3), "it was generally believed that he would shortly die." There is nothing amusing about this, but even here political omens are still caught up in a political theater alive to the riddling side of events. And the point they conceal is in fact often amusing. For it was easy to jest with omens, and in fusing religion with politics the emperor as a living representative of divinity was always perilously close to caricaturing and parodying himself. Public amusement at absurdity on that score was a familiar feature of Roman political life. Commodus was aping Heracles when he struck the senators as irresistibly funny, and the story is introduced by a typical set of anecdotes that sound like malicious jokes or exaggeration treated as fact. The general populace was afraid to attend Commodus' games because of a rumor that he would pick off a few spectators in his role as Heracles shooting the Stymphalian birds. And that rumor was believed because he had in fact earlier gathered everyone who had feet missing, equipped them all with serpent tails and with sponges to throw as rocks, and then arming himself with a very real club beat them to death, this time as Heracles fighting the Giants (73.20.2–3). The logic and language of omens thus fit in with a larger political idiom of *ludibrium* in which reality and metaphor, mad anomaly and ordinary fact, verbal and visual funniness all run into and out of one another.

II

It is common enough for omens to seem witty or amusing because they play out the implications of language. When the first letter of "Caesar" in an inscription was melted by a stroke of lightning, the omen was taken to mean that Augustus would live 100 days (roman numeral C) and then become a god (*aesar* means "god" in Etruscan, *Aug.* 97.2). The event thus in a very exact sense enacts a witty statement: "take 100 days from Caesar and you have a god."

Transition of this kind between word and event is implicit in Aristotle's analysis of the logic of metaphor in the *Rhetoric*. His example of an effective metaphor is Pericles' description of the loss of young men in war as "a year without a spring" (1411a1). As an actual event rather than a rhetorical meta-phor the loss of spring would be an omen, and one naturally taken as a sign (say) of the imminent death of young men in war. Aristotle is not actually concerned here with the link of metaphor to reality, but it is elsewhere illus-trated in the story of Periander's advice for preserving power: he walked in silence through a field of grain lopping off stalks that stood higher than the rest (*Politics* 1284a26).

When an event takes its meaning from unexpressed language (in this case the implicit statement, "Cut down your rivals"), it is in effect, a wordless oracle, that is, an omen or portent. On the other hand, when language is explicit but the referent obscure, it becomes a verbal omen or oracle, and in either case the result is a living pun of the kind most familiar in the oracles from Delphi. The complex mechanisms of meaning in all of this make it natural enough to look for truth as something to be detected behind and through things by reversing and decoding them. The Athenians were advised that "Zeus grants Athens a wooden wall which will not be taken by the Per-sians": "wooden wall" also means "fleet," because a fleet can act as a wall. Cyrus is the "mule" (half-Mede, half-Persian) that actually does become king of the Medes; Apollo speaks of "white ravens," which do appear after some drunken men cover ravens with white paint. When Croesus destroys "a great kingdom" or when Oedipus destroys his "parents" each is a victim of implicit or omitted premises that turn ordinary language into grimly witty metaphor. When Crassus set off from Brundisium, he failed to construe the true syntax of a man hawking Caunian figs (*Cauneas = cave ne eas*, Cic. *De divinatione* 2.84). Augustus, on the other hand, carefully avoided starting anything im-portant on the Nones (*Nonis = non is =* "[you] don't go." *Aug.* 92.2).

The importance of oracular responses for the historian was enhanced by their ability to embody the uncertainty in human expectations about events themselves. The old consciousness of a deep gulf between gods and men ex-presses itself here as doubt whether humans ever do receive a clear answer about the future. The enigmatic quality of oracles suggests that we do not, that destiny at the very moment of revelation remains after all unrevealed; and so the self-canceling, punning ("funny") syntax of oracles dramatizes the car-dinal fact that our norms of historical truth may be overriden by a higher norm that generates a curious kind of joke as it does so. One response quoted by Tacitus (*Ann.* 12.63.1) sounds very much like a local joke raised to oracular dignity. The Greeks were told to found Byzantium "opposite the city of the blind," that is, the inferior site chosen earlier by the Chalcedonians, and Herodotus does in fact attribute the remark to a Persian (4.144). From this point of view oracles and omens are divine wit dislocating the ordinary hu-man syntax of both language and event. And it is the witty dislocation, quite apart from questions of a divine source, that made omens serious historical material for Tacitus.

Many of the oracles and ominous events mentioned by ancient historians accordingly have a peculiarly surreal quality, and it is worth considering the specific sense in which surrealism can help define the extraordinary effects that omens create. Though surrealism as a metaphysical theory is foreign to the ancient thought-world, the ethical and political criticism it mounted is another matter. On that score there is a very real point of contact with a taste for the grotesque in imperial Rome, and the saturation of the historical records with astonishing incidents placed on the same level as ordinary events is so thorough that it is easy to forget how remarkable the events really are. To take an example at random: Dio says that when thunderstorms came along, Caligula worked a machine that replied to what Jupiter was saying (59.28.6). If this is made of whole cloth, it is an extravagant joke about Caligula, surreal in the full sense of the term. If it is not, it describes something that is equally surreal, and anything in between these two possibilities is no less puzzling. Was there evidence of an actual device? How would it have been worked? What could its true purpose have been? Almost any concrete scenario to account for what Dio says seems unreal, and that is in fact the one historiographic certainty underlying such incidents, namely, that under the Principate it was hard to tell the difference between real and unreal, between policy and insanity.

Surrealism aimed at assaulting false reality, and to do so it used a method formally much like the technique of creating incongruity between frame and content (see above, p. 64). Some of Magritte's paintings—for example, a bright, blue, sunlit sky over the dark trees and lighted lamps of an evening street scene—are good cases in point. In other paintings reality itself (e.g., a scene visible through an apparently real open window) may be framed by an easel and thereby transformed into a mere imitation of reality. The result is confusion through multiple levels of reference, or in terms of linguistic analysis, invitation to "infelicitous illocutionary uptake." What is pertinent for our purposes is the technique of creating a sense of ordinary reality as a frame of reference in order simultaneously to subvert that reality through gross incongruity. When verbal as well as visual elements work together, incongruity takes the form of seen wordplay, for example, Magritte's meticulous picture of a pipe with the inscription, "This is not a pipe" (because it is a painting). This is in principle much like the technique of epigrams in which one moral or political norm ("Poppaea had everything else") is subverted when it is framed by another ("except character," i.e., "everything else" is in reality not much). It is also akin to the technique of riddling oracles and omens: Apollo's "white raven," it turns out, has the sur-reality of a *painted* raven.[1]

The aim is to display something from an angle that renders it, or our normal view of it, strange. The implausibility that justifies dismissing many omens as religious illusion is what at the same time guarantees them a place in hard fact as emblems of the deeper absurd texture of events.[2]

Tacitus speaks of Claudius' rise to power as a joke (*ludibria, Ann.* 3.18.4) and reports that at his funeral no one could suppress a smile when his intelligence was praised (*Ann.* 13.3.1). In Suetonius Claudius is portrayed as a genuinely ludicrous figure. Augustus fears that he will be ridiculed by the public and that he will make a fool of himself because of his odd behavior (*Claud.* 4). He was spared by Caligula only for ridicule (*in ludibrium, Calig.* 23.3) and after he became emperor was a favorite victim of practical jokes *(contumeliae)*. When he fell asleep at dinners (a sign of his dullness), people would throw olive or date stones at him or put slippers on his hands, then wake him to watch as he rubbed his face (*Claud.* 8). *Para prosdokian* of a grossly comic sort marks his elevation to power, too. In terror at Caligula's assassination, he hid in the drapes; a common soldier saw his feet, pulled him out, and recognizing him—hailed him emperor as Claudius fell to *his* knees in fear. We are clearly intended to see in this an enactment of the absurd relationship between power and slavishness which runs deep in the imperial system. Suetonius treats the incident as amusing in a stronger sense by remarking that Claudius became emperor "by a marvelous event" (*mirabili casu, Claud.* 10.1), and he thinks it worthwhile to include so vulgarly comic an aspect of Claudius' life as a fat-man joke. As a young man he was encouraged by Livy to write history. When he gave his first public reading, several benches broke under the weight of a portly member of the audience. Claudius spoiled his own debut because he could not help thinking of what had happened and breaking down in laughter (*Claud.* 41.1).

The affinity of all of this to the category of what is funny in a deeper, "ominous" sense is marked by Claudius' mother's use of the term *portentum* (sign/strange event) in speaking of him (*Claud.* 3.2), and it appears elsewhere as well. When Suetonius introduces the subject of Caligula's often unaccountable behavior with the remark "so much for Gaius as emperor; the rest is about Gaius the *monstrum*" (*Calig.* 22.1), *monstrum* is again at once "inhuman," "absurd," and "ominous." The word bears the last meaning in particular in Suet. *Galba* 18.1: "great and frequent omens [*monstra*] from the start of his reign foretold the end he in fact met." So too Vatinius is "among the foulest portents [*ostenta*] of Nero's court" (*Ann.* 15.34.2), and even as a great, ominous *(prodigiosum)* flock of black birds flew over Vitellius to blot out the sun he was, in his incompetence, himself "the chief portent" (*ostentum, Hist.* 3.56.2; cf. *monstrum* of a blind flatterer in Juvenal 4.115, and *portentum* of a depraved person in Sen. *Quaestiones naturales* 1.16.3).[3]

Omens in the form of prodigies are inherently grotesque (cf. *Ner.* 46).[4] They lie at the outer edge of ordinary human experience and typically appear at moments of crisis—transitions of power, the birth and death of emperors. These are times of anxiety when expectations are most at risk, and from this point of view the strangeness of omens is a ready-made instance of the deeper strangeness in the syntax of events. In *Annals* 16.13 Tacitus remarks that in the year "foul for its crimes and marked even by the gods with storms and diseases" the epidemic of deaths among the upper classes seemed less lamentable, "inasmuch as the victims were forestalling the emperor's savagery by a normal death." *Annals* 15.47.1 is a companion piece: the close of another year saw many prodigies announcing disaster, including a comet "which Nero always expiated with noble blood." The force of each of these epigrams comes from a latent dialectic that is felt rather than spelled out in the compression of thought. In the first, ominous *abnormal* deaths by natural causes are so outbid by *normal* political brutality that they seem *normal* and natural in comparison with its true *abnormality*. In the second, *abnormal* murder becomes a *normal* means (i.e., ritual expiation) for restoring *normality* in face of *abnormal events (cf. Ann.* 4.70 for political repression as religious ceremony). In both cases portents define a category in which political and religious anomaly come together—or are brought together by Tacitus—to yield bitter political wit. Something of the sort happens when Nero vows that Vindex will "pay the price" for his rebellion and the audience roars back the ambiguous response, "You will do it, Augustus!" (*Ner.* 46.3), that is "you will make *him* pay the price" and "*you* will pay the price." But it is not clear whether this is supposed to be a deliberate or providential pun. Suetonius includes it among the portents of Nero's downfall, and it might well have seemed political support, witty protest, and omen all at once.

To this extent, then, the nature of political reality is mirrored also in portents and omens, whatever their authenticity. They serve as an appropriate backdrop for actors who may themselves be *ostenta* and, as signs of absurdity, constitute a special dimension of grotesque historical wit. Tacitus' frequent depreciatory remarks about their authenticity are a fair warning against overestimating their role. They are not prominent in all parts of the *Annals;* when they do occur, they may receive only brief, passing mention; he is aware of the temptation to interpret chance events falsely as omens and of the connection they have with ordinary political stress (e.g., war panic: *Hist.* 1.86.1).

> The secrets of fate and the fact that Vespasian and his sons were marked out for power by signs and oracles we believed—after his success. (*post fortunam credidimus, Hist.* 1.10.3)

Initially the point is simply that Vespasian showed no hostility to Galba, and so his future career could not be foreseen. But Tacitus also mentions "signs and oracles" and does so in two voices. One is that of traditional belief that men often lack foresight to grasp the significance of signs, the other that of skeptical jesting about twenty/twenty hindsight. Together these two voices form an interlocking pair, each serving as a premise for the other: seeing signs only after the event is failure of insight if they are real; but signs, of course, *are* credible only after the event if they are illusory to begin with. The latter seems closer to Tacitus' usual view.

In *Annals* 14.12.2 he introduces some spectacular prodigies by remarking that they were useless and obviously not of divine origin, inasmuch as Nero enjoyed many more years of crime. At the same time, he is prepared to integrate their oddness, if not their truth, into the fabric of events. That is why he reports them in the first place, and in this very section, after making the shrewd observation that the face of nature is not so easily changed as is human expression, he says that the sight of the landscape where Agrippina had been murdered was "troublesome" to Nero, and that "there were those who believed that sounds of trumpets in the high hills and groaning from his mother's grave were heard" (*Ann.* 14.10.3). Signs are largely demythologized in this psychological interpretation of the effect of guilt. Yet they are not dismissed out of hand, but precisely by being queer serve as an index of Nero's monstrosity (which also "was beyond everyone's protest," *Ann.* 14.11.3), much as political figures can themselves become incredible portents.

The impressive opening passage of the *Histories* again establishes a link between prodigies and political disorder (*Hist.* 1.3.2; cf. *Ann.* 12.43), and whatever theological meaning Tacitus may have attached to the phrase, he assigns omens a place of some importance in history when he speaks of them as "divine vengeance" (*Hist.* 1.3.2; cf. 2.50.2 for his reluctance to repudiate the widespread tradition supporting them). Perhaps he means little more than that political disaster is often richly deserved. In any event, as far as historiographic function is concerned, their empirical reality is largely subsumed in the rhetorical reality of history. On this level portents need only be reported in order to have the effect of conveying anomaly, and here the question of factual truth is simply not an issue. They can be taken seriously as a historiographic category without being taken literally as a religious or historical category.[5]

The sense in which portents are absurd is plain enough; it seems less natural to speak of them as witty or amusing and to connect them with epigrams. As we have seen, the most specific point of contact with verbal wit is their punning quality, and the importance of this for reinforcing incongruity as a general property of history is especially marked in Suetonius. The familiar pun on "mother-land" appears in Caesar's dream of raping his mother (*Iul.* 7.2)—i.e., "mastering" Rome. A stray dog drops a human hand under Vespasian's table (*Vespasian* 5.4) as a sign that he will be given "imperial power," that is, will be "given a hand" by destiny. Shortly before Caesar's assassination by senators in Pompey's Hall for regal ambition a small "king bird" flew into the hall pursued by other birds that tore it to pieces (*Iul.* 81.3). The old principle of *nomen/omen* lends itself to oracular double entendre of this kind. Alone in the temple of Serapis, Vespasian sees his freedman "Basilides" (*basileus* is "King" in Greek) offer him sacred objects, though Basilides at the time was far away (7.1). When Vitellius was killed by a man nicknamed Becco (rooster's beak), an earlier omen (a rooster had perched on him) came true. What is more, *gallus* also means "rooster," and Becco was Gallic (*Vit.* 18).

That these plays of meaning could be thought of as a type of wit is made clear in Suetonius' account of how Vespasian, even as death approached, treated omens as jokes. He turned the appearance of a comet and the mysterious opening of Augustus' Mausoleum into a multiple pun by applying the comet ("hairy") to the long-haired king of Parthia and the open tomb to a member of Augustus' family named Junia Calvina ("baldy," *Vesp.* 23.4; Dio 66.17). Tacitus says that Nero's dedication to Jupiter "Vindex" of a dagger that had figured in an unsuccessful plot against him was later taken to be an omen of "Vindex's" revolt against him (*Ann.* 15.74): as the god and the man become metaphors of each other their names form a wordplay, and that in turn is *enacted* in the dedication and in the revolt (for another pun on *Vindex* cf. *Ner.* 45.2).

In some cases the wit implicit in omens invites outright bantering with destiny in a game of "capping" one oracular wordplay with another. To cap a prophecy that he would no more become emperor than ride over the Bay of Baiae on a horse Caligula built a causeway several miles long (*Calig.* 19.3). Caesar is credited with neat repartee when he fell as he was disembarking but escaped being the butt of a joke of history by crying, "Africa, I embrace you!" (*Iul.* 59). Faced by the evil portent of a sacrificial victim lacking a *cor,* he again attempted to finesse the situation, this time with a double pun: "it is no portent [surprise] if an animal has no *cor*" (both "heart" and "mind," *Iul.* 77).

When Caligula ordered dirt dumped in Vespasian's lap for not keeping the streets of Rome clean, the insulting practical joke was taken by some to mean that his "country" (native soil) would some day "come into his protection" (*Vesp.* 5.3). And when Caligula was later warned to beware of "Cassius," he executed the proconsul of Asia, forgetting that the name of another man, who did in fact assassinate him, was also Cassius (*Calig.* 57.3). Failure to grasp potential double entendre in oracles is a classic case of witty displaced emphasis.[6] Nero similarly failed to get the point of a warning to "watch the seventy-third year," referring as it did not to his own age but to Galba's (*Ner.* 40.3).

As Tiberius marched an army through Philippi, altars set up by earlier victorious legions spontaneously flared ("brilliant prospects," *Tib.* 14.3), and when he threw golden dice into a fountain the highest ("winning") number came up (14.4). When his pet snake was eaten by ants, he took it as a warning against the "power of the multitude" ("teeming masses," 72.2; cf. Nero's dream of being covered with flying ants, *Ner.* 46.1). Vitellius' equestrian statues all collapsed with broken legs ("feet of clay," *Vit.* 9), and "fall" from power is a recurrent metaphor in omens. Thus an inscription on a triumphal statue of Domitian torn off in a storm fell on a nearby tomb (Suet. *Domitian* 15.2); as Nero, the last emperor connected by family to Augustus, was about to die, lightning hit the temple of the Caesars, heads fell from all the statues, and the scepter was dashed from Augustus' hand (Suet. *Galb.* 1).

Omens or oracles, then, involve factors that go beyond purely religious considerations. The equivocation on which they often hinge is rooted in language itself, and so "the ominous" can be a permanent element in human understanding. For in moments of crisis people have always been sensitive to impending ("superstitious") hidden meanings. Shortly before the Battle of Midway comment was occasioned aboard the Japanese flagship by a menu including a dish whose name meant both "served with miso" (bean paste) and "to make a mess of things." On the other side, American fondness for acronyms produced a flood of new terms including CINCUS (Commander in Chief United States Fleet). After Pearl Harbor, "sink us" proved to be notably inauspicious and was quickly dropped. An outright joke in circulation at the time about reviewing the Pacific Fleet from a glass-bottomed boat is no better a jest, but because it was deliberate it did not share the unwelcome accidental funniness of CINCUS. For even when omens no longer carry a weight of public religious meaning, such things, after all, are noticed and felt in some way to be a sign of events, especially of their painful incongruity. They are accordingly worth mentioning by the historian whatever his view of their authenticity may be. The story of the ill-omened Japanese dish in fact looks suspiciously like a typical retrospective prophecy; the CINCUS incident is a minor, faintly amusing problem of morale, but both are formally witty and just in that respect say something serious about the ironies of power, as such things did for the Roman historians.

III

We have up to this point examined several major techniques for triggering a sense of anomaly in order to disclose the nature of political reality.

1. Metaphor (e.g., imperial power "falls"). Metaphor is punning of sorts, but the extension of meaning from one level to another which it executes (from physical "fall" to "loss" of power) is part of ordinary language and a commonplace of style.
2. Wordplay (e.g., Nero dedicated a dagger to "Vindex"). "Vindex" again does double duty, and since one of its meanings is outside Nero's immediate intention, the ironic double entendre reveals the true state of affairs in the form of an unconscious jest.
3. Omens (e.g., imperial statues actually fall). As a literal event this lies outside ordinary laws and is an enacted pun that in its very oddness unmasks the true state of affairs, much as epigrams or puns do on the level of style by violating linguistic expectations.

At this point language shades into event—metaphor becomes fact—as is true in two other forms of subversion of norms in ancient historiography: caricature and political events of surpassing absurdity.[7] We are intended to read accounts of odd physical appearance as statements—in the case of vicious emperors, statements revealing true character and doing so by physical anomaly as striking as that of omens. The "incongruity" *(minime congruens)* between Otho's questionable life and admirable death was regarded as preternatural *(miraculo)*, and the evidence for Otho's life is Suetonius' description of his appearance (bad legs and feet; bewigged, hairless effeminacy, *Otho* 12). Physical defects can lend a specifically ominous dimension to political figures inasmuch as the potentially religious implications of odd appearance would naturally enrich political fear and loathing. Vatinius, an evil omen *(ostentum)* of Nero's court, has a "twisted body" *(Ann.* 15.34.2); Paelignus, though not called a "portent," is "contemptible for his absurd body" *(Ann.* 12.49.1); Juvenal's Crispinus is a "feeble" *monstrum* (4.2), his Catullus a "blind" *monstrum* (4.115). Domitian was accompanied during gladiatorial shows by a small boy "who had an abnormally small head [*parvo portentosoque capite*]" and with whom he occasionally discussed affairs of state *(Dom.* 4.2). A good part of the amusing portentousness of the story is that Suetonius offers no further explanation: such things are a matter of course at Rome.

Apart from occasional specific suggestions of monstrosity of this sort, descriptions often have the more general tone of case studies in abnormality.

> He possessed majesty and dignity of appearance, [but only] when he was standing still or sitting, and especially when he was lying down; for he was tall but not slight, with an attractive face, white hair, and a solid neck. But when he walked, his weak legs gave way under him and he had many disgusting traits both when he relaxed and when he was busy. His laughter was unseemly and his anger still more so, for he would foam at the mouth and trickle at the nose; he stammered besides, and his head, which was very shaky at all times, was especially so then at his every move. *(Claud.* 30)

Incongruity between attractive and ugly features points to incongruity of norms at a deeper level as well, and especially in the case of Claudius, caricature is a natural extension of Suetonius' preceding account of personal eccentricity.

Physiognomy had attracted a good deal of attention at the time and seemed to offer a method of solving the perennial difficulty of reading character from physical appearance. Taken in conjunction with the view that character does not change much but simply comes to light in time, physiognomy could provide yet another useful tool for unmasking the truth, in this case the truth behind personal appearance. It is not clear to what extent Suetonius' vignettes are actually influenced by physiognomic theory,[8] but they are in some cases designed to embody moral judgment with startling effect. There is no precise correspondence between ugly and evil or attractive and good. The physical vigor of the good Vespasian is offset by his expression of perpetual strain as though he were on a toilet (*Vesp.* 20). This is, to be sure, quoted as a noted wit's good-natured remark, but it is scarcely complimentary. Yet for the most part, good emperors are physically attractive, bad ones repellent. The latter become, so to say, living omens—at once grotesque prodigy and moral monster—subverting common norms.

> Caligula was very tall and pale, with a huge body, but very thin neck and legs. His eyes and temples were hollow, his forehead broad and grim, his hair thin and entirely gone on the top of his head, though elsewhere he was hairy. Because of this to look upon him from a higher place as he passed by, or for any reason whatever to mention a goat, was a capital offense. His face was naturally forbidding and savage, and he purposely made it savage by practicing all kinds of terrible and frightening faces before a mirror. (*Calig.* 50.1; cf. Sen. *Constant.* 18.1: "his appearance was a rich source of amusement").

The effect in this case is wholly negative, and the passage is followed by a discussion of the emperor's mental disease. A description of his style of dress (*Calig.* 52) is again cast in terms of violated expectation *(usus):* Caligula is *ludibrium* incarnate, a walking cartoon, beyond all norms—Roman, masculine, or even human.

Such descriptions constitute a form of political wit familiar to Romans as *contumelia,* personal abuse. In terms of physiognomic theory, Caligula's appearance might be linked to the goat's and panther's cunning lechery.[9] Suetonius mentions that he had a writer of Atellan farces burned "because of a line of ambiguous wit" (*Calig.* 27.4), and the stage may itself have also used physiognomic principles to satirize and unmask political targets.[10] Verbal and visual wit would have neatly reinforced each other in the theater, and for historians, too, a verbal portrait could serve much as costumes or masks did in comedy.

In the case of Nero (*Ner.* 51) the portrait again creates an impression of abnormality, whereas the description of the enigmatic Tiberius combines attractive with sinister elements. So far as the latter is concerned his arrogant physical mannerisms were so noticeable that Augustus would publicly excuse them as natural and not character weaknesses—a distinction that presupposes the general truth of physiognomic inference. Tiberius' reign began well; at first he expressed disgust at flattery while himself flattering the senate and permitting free speech (*Tib.* 29–32). But it was all sham (30, 33, 42, 57, 67): his true self emerged later (cf. *Ann.* 4.57.2).

He was large and strong and of a stature above average; broad in shoulders and chest; well proportioned and balanced from head to foot. His left hand was more nimble and stronger, and its joints were so powerful that he could bore through a fresh firm apple with his finger, and break the head of a boy, or even a young man, with a snap. He was of fair complexion and wore his hair long at the back to cover the nape of his neck. That seemed to be a family trait. His face was handsome but would break out on a sudden with many pimples. His eyes were very large and, strange to say, could see even at night and in the dark, but only for a short time when they first opened after sleep; then they grew dim again. He strode along with his neck stiff and bent forward, usually with a tense expression and for the most part in silence, never or rarely conversing with his companions, and then with great deliberation and a kind of gentle movement of his fingers. (Suet, *Tib.* 68)

Like Tacitus, Suetonius accepts the necessity of the Principate, but, more than that, takes it institutionally as a matter of course. He has, in fact, little interest in institutions. As is natural enough for a biographer, his sense of the absurd is moral rather than political, individual rather than official and does not contribute to any very large ideas about politics or history. His assessment of emperors is generally more balanced and realistic than Tacitus', and by the same token, also less focused, more neutral, and merely entertaining. In view of this, caricature is perhaps too strong a term for these portraits. They are more like cartoons or selected unflattering photographs. Many of the details are probably accurate, and there is no rhetorical reason why they should not be, since caricature comes from picking out and arranging actual features. The effect of the abnormalities selected would have been further strengthened by the Roman instinct for political abuse of defects (e.g., *Vit.* 17.2, where ridicule of the emperor's defects is followed by his brutal physical torture). Suetonius could thus depend on the descriptions to work like a Rorschach image, with the verbal picture of oddity drawn in the rest of the biography helping to shape what the hearer would see in these more literal pictures.[11]

Caricature in any form is a particularly clear case of the degrading function of wit. It is typically political, and the hostility it expresses symbolically takes the form of actual physical appearance made to reveal ugly truth. It serves as a substitute for actual physical degradation, and in this respect is like both wit *(le ridicule tue)* and the "ominous" accidents that befall emperors' statues or the deliberate violence they suffer.[12] As we have seen, from one point of view omens serve as divine wit or *ludibrium* directed against those in power. As violations of norms they are for the historians an index of absurdity in political life, and like wit they both make and have a sharp point. Insofar as this is true also of the portraits, they are yet another weapon of witty criticism.

IV

Grotesque emperors and bizarre omens embody political absurdity as physical reality and that brings us to the final form of wit: actual events or "happenings" (in the contemporary sense) of lunatic oddness. "They call the deed a crime and—do it" epitomizes the link between queer language and queer political behavior. When absurdity of this kind intrudes into history, events themselves degenerate into black comedy carrying with it an acute problem of credibility frequently posed by the historiography of the Principate. It has in fact been argued that Tacitus' account of Nero's comic opera plot against his mother is largely fiction patterned on the story of Clytemnestra and Orestes,[13] though it seems unlikely that wholesale fabrication would have become part of the historical tradition so quickly. Caligula issues invitations to dinner in the name of his horse and considers it for a consulship (*Calig.* 55.3); he imagines that he sleeps with the moon, not simply in her light (22.4); at a sacrifice he suddenly takes it into his head to dispatch one of the officiants instead of the animal (32.3); after marshaling an army along the seashore without giving the vaguest idea of what he wants to do, he orders the troops to collect seashells in their helmets (46).[14]

This is total subversion of all norms, sheer lunacy whose effect is like that of the offense to sane and sober reason in some of the best jokes.[15] And in some cases it is difficult not to suspect that what is described as an actual event *was* originally a very good joke.[16] A manner of speaking—especially a widely circulated witty remark—could easily at last be taken literally in circles inclined to be hostile to the emperors. At a lavish party given by Messalina someone who had climbed into a tree as a prank and was asked what he could see announced, "Storm clouds over Ostia!" (where Claudius was staying). Tacitus suggests that either a storm was visible or a "chance remark" turned out to be prophetic (*Ann.* 11.31.3). The latter could be an excellent example of the inherent double entendre (stormy weather = irate husband) which is a property of omens, but is seems more likely that the reply was meant to be a joke about the erratic Claudius ("as easy to fool as he is quick to be angry," *Ann.* 11.26). The ease with which witticism could exchange places with fact is perhaps marked here by Tacitus' surprising failure to consider the possibility that the remark was a joke (unless that is included in "chance remark").

Under the circumstances it is hard to say where wit stops and deliberate falsehood begins, for that, too, can be a weapon of political opposition, as the rhetoricians knew: "When will the orator speak falsely even though his audience knows that he is doing so? When it does them good to hear what he has to say."[17] When Hermogenes adds that "because of their own self-interest they do not refute the speaker," he recognizes a bond analogous to the conspiracy that binds the joke teller and his audience when he tells a joke at the expense of a third party (see above, chap. 2, n. 3). It is hostile intention that helps confuse the lines separating joke, exaggeration, falsehood, and lie.

Suetonius' remark that Claudius' stupidity in the affair of Messalina and Silius (*Claud.* 29.3) "exceeded all belief" is a figure of speech, but one that still points to something lying between plain fact and mere fabrication, since he presumably does believe it is true. (The marriage, though, was perhaps only part of a religious celebration.) Tacitus' version of the affair is a particularly vivid vignette, and he probably has its moments of genuine hilarity in mind when he speaks of a "fictional" *(fabulosum)* and "fantastic" *(miraculi causa)* quality to the account, though insisting that it rests on solid evidence (*Ann.* 11.27.1). The somewhat ambiguous status implied by such qualifications is perhaps also a factor in some of the "reports" cited by the historians. It was "reported" that Augustus had appointed Tiberius as successor so that he himself would be all the more missed (*Tib.* 21.2).[18] If the report was in fact a joke making the rounds, it is a fine case in point of Hermogenes' unbelievable but edifying "just so" story ("Tiberius is so bad that Augustus must have . . .") turned to good use by the historians. The idea does actually appear as a topos in Aristotle (*Rhe.* 1399b29): "It is said in Theodectes' *Ajax* that Diomedes chose Odysseus not because he held him in high regard but so that his companion would be inferior." Topoi of one sort or another may well lie behind other jokes and anecdotes.

The technique in this case is what Aristotle calls "giving as an actual reason a possible reason," and his subsequent remarks on the plausibility of anecdotes are directly pertinent to Suetonius' remark about Claudius' stupidity "exceeding all belief."

> Another topos is things that apparently happened, though they are unbelievable; they would not have been believed, if they were not true or close to it. In fact they are all the more believable since people believe what is either true or probable, and so if something is unbelievable and improbable, it is likely to be true, because it does not seem so in view of likelihood or probability. (*Rh.* 1400a5)

If the general improbability of a report makes it probably true in fact, the violation of expectation on which wit depends can be promoted into a principle of historical truth. For in terms of this rhetorical logic, the very improbability that makes many anecdotes amusing also could be a sign of their truth. Of course, historians did not appeal to ingenious reasoning of this sort to authenticate anecdotes. But they did work with a more general principle of the probability of improbability which turns political wit into material for serious historiography in another way. In its various forms ranging from anecdote to epigram wit *typifies* the absurdity and unreason that are literal

facts of political life, much as in Aristotle's view poetry may typify truths of
history at a higher level of generality even when it is not specifically true.[19]

It is one thing to suspect that political jokes lie behind some incidents reported as sober fact by the historians, another to identify them. Suetonius
himself expresses doubt whether stories about Galba's stinginess were true or
simply hostile jesting (*per ludibrium, Galb.* 12.3). A typological approach
seems of little use here.

> When Marcellus [a fussy grammarian] had criticized something in a speech of
> Tiberius, Asteius Capito insisted that it was good Latin, and if it wasn't, it *would*
> be from then on. Marcellus replied, "Capito lies; Caesar, you can grant citizen-
> ship to men but not to a word." (Suet. *De grammaticis* 22)

> When Hadrian criticized a word used by Favorinus, the latter yielded. His
> friends then laughingly accused him of conceding to Hadrian over a word used
> by perfectly good authors. His reply was, "You're not giving me good advice
> when you tell me not to believe that anybody who has thirty legions is smarter
> than everyone else." (*Historia Augusta, Hadrian* 15.13)

The two jokes are cut from the same pattern, though one is the mirror image
of the other.[20] When Caligula wanted to kill his brother and suspected him of
taking an antidote against poison, he exclaimed, "What's this? An antidote
against Caesar?" (*Calig.* 29.1). This is the same general topic of imperial
power, and though suspicion about manufactured anecdotes is natural, the
recurrent pattern is consistent with authentic quips since they too follow patterns, all the more so in a society trained to think and speak rhetorically.

In another group of stories reshaping of the facts partly for witty effect
seems clearer.

> Vibullius Agrippa, a Knight, swallowed poison from a ring and died in the
> senate house itself. (Dio 58.21.4)

> People who had been summoned to court opened their veins at home, certain of
> condemnation and eager to avoid bother and humiliation. Others took poison
> before the senate, but they were rushed off to prison quivering and half-alive
> with their wounds bound up. (*Tib.* 61.4)

> Vibullius Agrippa . . . took poison from his clothing and drank it before the
> senate. When he fell dying, the lictors hurriedly hustled him off to prison where
> they tried to execute him by hanging, though he was already dead. (*Ann.*
> 6.40.1)

Dio's version is straightforward; Suetonius' telescopes several incidents, and
the rush to prison imparts a suggestion of oddity which verges on "just so"
absurdity in Tacitus' version about the official execution of a dead man.

In the light of the anecdotes in *Nero* 45.2 popular political wit should not be underestimated, and so a bilingual graffito about the numerous arches built in Rome by Domitian probably did appear (*arci* [arches] = *arkei* [enough!]), though it may have recorded a joke already making the rounds about the emperor's "arches really being quite enough" (*Dom.* 13.3). Dio mentions a "witty" reply to the question, "What is Domitian doing?": "he is all by himself without even a fly for company" (65.9). This is a joke derived from Domitian's habit of stabbing flies, which Dio calls unworthy of history yet records as one of the "ridiculous things" (*geloia*) Domitian continued to do after he became emperor. The story is excellent parody of sadistic aggression ("the emperor assaults everything that moves"), and in fact uncertainty about the seriousness of such reports can affect modern scholarship dealing precisely with that issue. In a careful, sympathetic reassessment of Domitian, K. Waters has suggested that the odd habit was simply an expert bowman's way of keeping his eye sharp (cf. *Dom.* 21) or perhaps was due to dislike of flies as "dirty, disorderly and promiscuous."[21] These startling explanations come close to being as peculiar as the original story, and Niall Rudd understandably wonders whether they are themselves "wholly serious."[22] Since Suetonius actually says that the flies were first caught, then stabbed with a pen (*Dom.* 3.1), Domitian was more probably trying to keep his hand speed up to form. In any case, after a century of emperors a habit of this sort was bound to seem something more than merely quaint, suggesting hostility like that in Commodus' dispatching of an ostrich in Dio (see above, p. 70). And though the joke was perhaps not originally aimed at Domitian's queer violence, which he at first restrained, that would quickly have become its more disturbingly funny point, as it does in the larger context in Suetonius and Dio.

Was it the emperor or quipping critics who said that "a dead enemy smelled best and even better a dead—fellow citizen" (*Vit.* 10.3; cf. *Hist.* 3.39.1)? Did Augustus actually write out private conversations beforehand, including some with his wife, or is that a joke about his habit of putting important things on paper (*Aug.* 84.2)? If those who denied the report (*Ann.* 14.9.1) were right, the story that circulated about Nero admiring his mother's corpse may also have been a joke (*Ner.* 34.4). Perhaps Caligula did force the spectators at a gladiatorial show to sit in the hot sun for no apparent reason (*Calig.* 26.5), but surely it was originally a jest that, since Nero did not permit anyone to leave during his performances, "women gave birth in the theater" and other spectators "pretended to be dead," since you could get out "only as a corpse" (*Ner.* 23.2).[23] It seems more likely that a joke was given dramatic setting than that people actually pretended to quarrel with their slaves in order to be able to cry out safely for an "avenger" (*vindicem* = *Vindicem*) in protest against Nero (*Ner.* 45.2).[24]

In "the well-known affair" (*nota res*) of the man who dozed off at an auction held by Caligula—when the emperor noticed what was happening, he

had the auctioneer count each nod of his head as a bid, until the man woke up
to learn that he had purchased thirteen gladiators (*Calig.* 38.4)—the tenor of
Suetonius' account turns the event into a malicious exercise of power. But
even if it really happened, it might have been nothing more than a royal prank,
part of, in Grant's phrase, Caligula's "continual stream of jokes,"[25] and one
that does seem rather charming. Then again it may be a joke but one about
Caligula. In any event, if some other things mentioned by Suetonius are cases
of Caligula's "irrepressible, bizarre, sense of the ridiculous," it must have been
difficult to tell when he was being witty and when he was being malicious
and, by the same token, when historical accounts should be taken seriously
and when not. If a Knight really was sent to Ptolemy with the sealed message,
"Do nothing to the bearer, good or bad" (*Calig.* 55.1), wit *is* terror, and that is
itself some grounds for wondering whether this is again a joke about Caligula. And if another remark is Caligula's, we still may wonder whether he and
Caesonia (again in Grant's phrase) "no doubt had many a hearty laugh together when he expressed a keen inclination to have her tortured in order to
find out from her why he loved her so devotedly." He lived in incest with all of
his sisters, and when the favorite died, laughter, bathing, or dining with close
friends was declared a capital offense (*Calig.* 24.2). Though public rituals of
mourning were common enough, the *creditur* that introduces one of the other
lurid details of his incestuous relations perhaps again reflects what was
originally witty exaggeration and should be extended to other details like this
one (cf. Suetonius' own hyperbolic "every charge was capital" in *Tib.* 61.3,
creditur in *Claud.* 15.3, and Tacitus' *rebatur* in connection with Tiberius' pride
in dissimulation in *Ann.* 4.71.3).

The account in Suetonius of Caligula's creative fiscal policies is especially
interesting in this connection. The tone is set by such choice details as cancellation of chief centurions' wills on grounds of "ingratitude" if Caligula or
Tiberius was not named heir. Then, having terrified even total strangers into
naming him in their wills, Caligula denounced them as "insincere" when they
kept on living and dealt with the problem by sending them poisoned candy
(*Calig.* 38.2). He imposed a tax on various petty trades, including one on the
income of prostitutes equal to their fee for one visit. A further amendment
made those who had earlier been in prostitution or procuring subject to the
tax and also extended it to marriages (40). These additions are anything but
clear. The first seems to be either a retroactive rule of some sort, or perhaps it
applies the law also at a higher social level to enterprises on a larger scale than
the underground economy represented by prostitution (i.e., to *meretrices*
rather than *prostitutae*). The second provision might seem for a moment to
mean that in his mad zeal for funds Caligula decided to tax connubial sex (*nec
non et matrimonia obnoxia essent*). That would make a fine joke about how
"you have to pay a tax on sex with your spouse." But even in full cry Suetonius
does not go that far. These are actual laws; a tax on prostitution is plausible

enough, and its extension to marriage most likely was intended to block evasion through pro forma ceremonies,[26] or it may have applied to the time when someone, now legally married, had worked as a prostitute or pimp. It is perfectly plausible, too, that prostitution would make some contribution to imperial income and be conected in some loose way with the palace complex (41). But Suetonius is not really interested in fiscal matters, and the overall tone does bring some of these details of "new and unheard-of taxes" close to jokes, in this case about how "the emperor has opened a high-class brothel in the palace with instant credit for those short of cash."[27] Since the laws were not published, they were often violated (Dio says that that was the point). In response to public protest Caligula finally agreed to have them posted—in tiny letters and in an out-of-the-way place so that copies could not be made. Fact, fiction, or something in between (and Dio's version is somewhat different, 59.28.8–11), this amusing situation is thematically close to Tacitus' depiction of senatorial discussion designed *not* to be understood and probably has at least as much witty exaggeration.

A fisherman who breached Tiberius' security system by presenting in person and without clearance a choice catch as a gift for the emperor had his face torn with the fish, but *he* is not likely to have quipped as he was being abused that he was glad he had not offered Tiberius the giant crab he had also landed (*Tib.* 60).[28] Nor is credibility helped when Tiberius immediately takes up the suggestion and uses the crab too on the fisherman. To avoid becoming a party to treason Germanicus threatens suicide, draws his sword, and presses it to his chest. Some restrain him, others urge him on, and a certain Calusidius offers him his own sword with the words, "Here, take mine, it's sharper" (*Ann.* 1.35.5). The rather contrived dialogue suggests at least a partial reworking of an ugly incident into repartee, making use of the familiar *para prosdokian* method of climactic insolence (e.g., Mart. 4.43 and modern cases of people threatening suicide jokingly urged to "jump" by onlookers; Sen. *De ira* 3.23.2: when Philip invited a delegation to tell him what the Athenians would like him to do, Demochares, nicknamed "Frank," told him, "Go hang yourself!"; cf. the odd story in Plut. *Brutus* 39.6). Finally, Tiberius' joke of executing someone to carry a message to Augustus in person has the sound of another amusing "just so" story about the sinister emperor (Dio 57.14.1, cited above, p. 69). The staging in Dio's version seems unlikely, though Suetonius' version is more plausible in that the protest is public (*Tib.* 57.2; there is another joke here when the arrested protester is given "what he has coming" by Tiberius: his share of the largess and—execution).

Though the entertaining wit of Roman historiography carried with it grave problems of credibility, it was at the same time a peculiarly effective tool for bringing out important aspects of political reality that might indeed seem to strain credibility at times. Because wit of this sort is too good to be true, it is too good to be false. That is to say, its point could be thought of as representing genuine axiomatic truth about the Principate so fairly that specific truth was beside the point. In several cases the subject of an anecdote appears in Suetonius as a vague plural instead of the singular used in parallel versions. Since all the versions treat the same incident, this is not proliferation of stories of the same type but an "internal" typology in the sense that typicality is part of the explicit point. Thus under Tiberius "young girls [plural] who could not properly be strangled were raped first" (*Tib.* 61.5; contrast *Ann.* 5.9.2, Dio 58.11.5). Baldwin remarks that "Suetonius breeds plurals from single episodes to the advantage neither of truth nor art. That is, if the rival evidence of Dio is to be preferred. . . . The biographer does not see that the single episode was infinitely more moving than a vague set of such atrocities."[29] There is clearly something to this, but Suetonius' narrative style is also characterized by its "amount of vivid detail,"[30] and the plural's generalizing force does have vividness of its own. If in one way the drama of the situation suffers, it is the plural that brings out its absurdity. For as we have seen, though legal incongruity often takes the form of vividly ludicrous ad hoc procedures, the ultimate absurdity to which they point is lawlessness becoming the *rule* in law. The plural thus has the same force as "every charge was capital" a few lines earlier (*Tib.* 61.3), and in 61.5 itself "death was in Tiberius' view so light a punishment to *those* who wanted to die that when he heard of *one* of the defendants, Carnulus by name . . ." Singular or plural, each in its own way is "funny," the plural in particular by representing what can always be taken as true because it so often is.

If a story is true, the point has been made; if it is not but truly could be, the point has equally been made. Or, to use a rhetorical analogy closer to the intention of the historians, the most effective way of showing that someone is guilty may be to typify him for what he is, even though that is not exactly what he is. The truth then is that of caricature, but it is still that truth. As we have seen (end of chap. 3), some of the most revealing—and implausible—stories make their point through omission. Caligula can find gaming money or a victim with astonishing *suddenness* anywhere and anytime he pleases. The telescoped effect is accentuated by the isolation of each of the stories in Suetonius as a single-sentence anecdote. Not only is this analogous to isolation of formal jokes from a larger context, it also catches a moment of gross slapstick in what is again cartooning or visual aphorism; and one odd feature of aphorism is that even when true it may also be false because it ignores exceptions.[31] Out of sight is out of mind, even if absence makes the heart grow fonder. Historiography, too, is concerned with a larger, typical truth that overrides the facts in specific cases. Perhaps Caligula was often normal, but he cannot be *understood* that way. At the same time, in Tacitus "type" is a concrete not an abstract universal.[32] Annalistic chronicle is transformed into genuine history as patterns—especially of formal contradiction and incoherence—emerge directly in the rhetorical texture of the narrative. The meaning of history is not separate, theoretical, editorial but immanent in events, as speeches are placed in the mouth of those who make history because that is the natural place for them if the historian is confident that his grasp of motive and cause is sound.

V

Wit in Seneca and the Declaimers

I

A point common to almost all theories of wit in ancient rhetoric is the principle that what is funny arises from moral or physical defects.

> The place and region of what we might call "funny" [*ridiculum*]—for that is what we are looking for next—is defined by ugliness and unseemliness [*turpitudo, deformitas*] of some sort; at any rate, we laugh only or mostly at what marks out and points to ugliness in a way which is not itself ugly. (Cic. *De or.* 2.236; cf. 238, 239, 248, 264, 266)

> The witty person wants to denounce [*elengchein*] faults of body and soul. (*Tractatus Coislinianus* VIII)

The ethical perspective comes out clearly in the use of *elengchein,* and this is the deeper level at which historiography overlaps with rhetorical theory. Tacitus observes that candid treatment of recent disgraceful events may arouse resentment in those who detect reproach to themselves (*Ann.* 4.33). He is thinking mainly of content, not witty manner. But that is what in fact often gives his account an offensive edge. In Cicero's language the "place and region of what is funny" includes the ugly absurdity *(ludibrium)* caught in narrative and epigrammatic wit. The story about official dithering over a military reward for fratricide (above, chap. 3, sec. 1) is itself ugly and becomes ridiculous as it is marked out by Tacitus.[1]

Since defects can be detected only in the light of a standard, the theory entails that the ridiculous is derived also from incongruity or violation of expectation. When the witty person denounces a fault, he is asserting one norm to refute another he finds objectionable, and that, as we have seen, is what the historians do when they bring out incongruity through contradiction of one sort or another. Tacitus' antithetic epigrams do so through formal oxymoron that is immediate ("arrogant modesty") or slightly delayed ("Otho acted like a slave to be—master"); or incongruity may be insinuated by comparison ("the Germans provided us more with triumphs than with victories"). Epigrams achieve their witty effect by causing a hitch in our expectation of what should be said in the comparison or contrast, and that can occur on a larger scale as well when an entire situation is seen as contradictory. Tacitus in particular has an eye for the way in which political oxymoron expresses itself through a distinctively amusing, witty, or absurd quality to *events*.

That quality typically appears in connection with such things as bizarre legal procedures or the relationship between senate and emperor, and we can perhaps speak here of a larger epigrammatic conception of events in the sense that the unmasking of truth is played out rather than directly stated.[2] The gap between the lapidary paradox in epigrams proper and the live paradox of unfolding situations is bridged to some exent by anecdotal history and biography, which on the one hand often include epigrams, and on the other are narrative. Plutarch has both epigram and narrative in mind when he couples "minor incidents" with "sayings and jests" (*Alex.* 1.1) as vehicles for historical insight.

In either form wit often depends heavily on anomaly that is specifically macabre and repellent. The taste for that seems to have been a symptom of the times, perhaps because brutal incongruity in the real world became more endurable when it was made into an artifact that could be managed as events could not. The strange institution of bloody gladiatorial or animal games served in part as an outlet and surrogate for violence in Roman society as a whole. Such considerations, of course, are mostly a matter of psychological conjecture, but something of the sort in far more subtle form is plausible also in the case of the often grim historiography of the period. After telling the story of the man who leaves the authorities at a loss when he demands a reward for killing his own brother in battle, Tacitus mentions an earlier case of another brother who killed himself when he learned what he had done. He says that he has included this "as an example of right and solace from wrong" (*Hist.* 3.51.2). Solace in the first instance comes from the appeal to ordinary norms of decency, but in this and many other cases the grotesque violation of normal behavior may itself also have helped some Romans to work through the problem of brutality by offering a measure of relief through schadenfreude of a very sophisticated kind. That is to say, dwelling on just how bad things are may be politically and morally gratifying, and by the same token, it can have the bracing effect of facing up to reality.

Anxiety caused by threats to expectation was, in fact, treated by the philosophic schools with a therapeutic technique in which the threat itself is made real in imagination. The aim, of course, is not to cultivate actual fear of future events (Sen. *Ep.* 74.32–34), but to strip them of much of their power as they are lived through in thought beforehand (18.5–8; 30.13, 76.33–35, 78.29). "This is anticipating the slings of fortune" (18.11), and though the principle applies chiefly to the future, it works with the past as well inasmuch as history exemplifies permanent moral truths. The compulsive, artificial, mannered wittiness of Seneca's style may to some extent be another such method for coming to terms with reality. Though not a historian, Seneca does deal with the same moral and social reality that is the historians' ultimate concern. He is very conscious of writing in a new style for a new age, and Tacitus' remark that his "talent was pleasant and in tune with the ears of his time" (*Ann.* 13.3.1) leaves room for more than literary style. At any rate, taste for anomaly and complexity in literature is epitomized especially by Seneca and also by declamatory rhetoric insofar as it, too, was preoccupied with situations that are notably odd and unsettling.

II

"Seneca's style, well called 'athletic,' incessantly punches, thrusts and parries, mounting climaxes, shifting attacks, always trying for a verbal knock-out."[3] This, of course, also describes the aggressive aspect of wit, whose verbal "knock-out" is more specifically a punch line (for the image cf. *haptesthai* in the sense of witty "touché" in Plut. *Quaest. conv.* 633a, or Sen. *Ep.* 100.8: *subiti ictus sententiarum*). The broad conceptual affinity between the "overstimulated, sensational, nightmarish soap opera" of declamatory rhetoric and Seneca's drama is marked by their use of similar stylistic means to achieve similar ends. Both aim at catching extreme situations in abnormal, arresting language often with a touch of the unreason that goes with joking.[4]

What can a victor fear? What he does not—fear. (*Agamemnon* 799)

If you wish to frighten Andromache, threaten her with—life. (*Troades* 576)

I have one last curse for my husband: that he—live. (*Medea* 19; cf. Suet. *Tib.* 61.5: "those who wanted to die were forced to live")

When the young Astyanax is led unflinching to execution, he "who is wept for, weeps not" (*non flet . . . qui fletur, Troades* 1099; cf. Ovid *Metamorphoses* 13.474 for the conceit). After the spectators had watched him plunge from the walls of Troy (we are intended to think of the moral issue raised by Roman gladiatorial shows), they "wept for the crime they had—committed and turned to another—crime" (1119), which the crowd "hates and—watches" (*odit scelus spectatque*, 1129; cf. Tacitus' *factum esse scelus loquuntur faciuntque*). The technique is provocative *para prosdokian*, and systematic double entendre creates a similar peculiarly witty shock effect. Atreus assures Thyestes that his sons

. . . are in their father's embrace
And will stay there; no part of them will be taken
From you. The faces you wish to see I will give you,
And I will fill the father with his whole family.
Be assured that you will be satisfied.

(*Thyestes* 976–80)

A subsequent exchange (1028–31) is a series of equally grisly puns. When Thyestes asks for his sons' remains, he pleads for "not what I will have but what I will lose" (i.e., bury), and Atreus caps this with "Whatever is left of your sons you have, whatever is not left you also have"—a nasty variant of the riddle put to Homer: "What we caught we don't have, what we didn't catch we have" (i.e., fleas, *Homeric Epigrams* 17).[5]

Several other features of Senecan *sententiae* are in technique as well as purpose pertinent to Tacitus' use of wit. In the first place, words overloaded with reference and dialogue spoken at different levels of intention create multiple frames of meaning.[6] The uses of sytematically ambivalent dialogue are naturally limited in history, but the elaborate evasiveness of political language is, as we have seen, a leitmotiv in Tacitus and the premise for his own use of epigram, parody, and irony. *Sententiae* in drama come for the most part in dialogue; they are especially effective there in revealing character, and that is the function they have also in anecdotal biography or history. They arrest the steady horizontal flow of dialogue with their own multiple levels of meaning and thus serve (so to say) as sudden vertical penetrations extending more deeply into character and situation.

Overload in meaning often comes from clever interplay in sound and sense of key ethical terms,[7] as in this dialogue between Agamemnon and Pyrrhus (*Troades* 332–36):

> Ag. It is proper [*decet*] for a king to prefer country over children.
> Py. No law spares a captive or limits punishment.
> Ag. What law does not forbid [*vetat*], restraint does forbid [*vetat*].
> Py. Whatever the victor wants [*libuit*] to do he rightly [*licet*] does.
> Ag. It is proper [*decet*] for him who has most right [*licet*] to want [*libere*] least.

Or again in this epigram whose peculiar effect comes from a combination of punning and syntactical overload:

Nemo dubitaret quin reus merito damnatus esset, quem is pater damnare potuisset, qui odisse non poterat. (*Clem.* 1.15.2)

[When a son who had plotted his father's death was sent by him into comfortable exile] everyone agreed that he had been justly punished [*damnatus*], whom a father, who could have [*potuisset*] punished [*damnare*, i.e., condemned], could [*poterat*] not [even] hate.

Neither of these passages, of course, is a joke in the narrow sense of the word, yet Seneca's audience had cultivated an extraordinary sensitivity to the texture of language. To take one example, Quintilian's strange (from a modern point of view) remarks about the sexual depravity of an "effeminate" style (*Inst.* 5.12.18) doubtless involve some rhetorical exaggeration of his own, but he and his culture did find such things in language (cf. Tac. *Dial.* 26). They would equally have detected the ethical and verbal banter in Seneca's dialogue or the play on *damnare* and on the ethical and legal meanings of *possum* in his epigram. This is not merely gratuitous verbal jingling since it reflects genuine ambiguity in the situations. Yet it is the very seriousness of the situations that at the same time does after all make the wordplay gratuitous (cf. Heracles "burning to burn" as he accepts his destiny of death by fire, Sen. *Heracles Oetaeus*, 1744). It is hard to say exactly what seems wrong about this kind of thing in Seneca. In part the wit is out of place, though that is why it is there. Events that are not straightforward call for language that is not straightforward either, and the affinity with the rationale of Tacitus' style on this score is clear. The epigrams are amusing in the sense that they create an arresting momentary blur or hitch in comprehension. The violation of expectation is, to be sure, highly refined, but Seneca *is* making his audience notice what the language is doing (*damnatus/damnare/esset/potuisset/odisse/ poterat; decet/vetat/libuit/licet*). Romans were capable of appreciating this dimension of wit in its own right. Atreus does actually pun about cannibalism; Agamemnon and Pyrrhus do engage in clever shuffling of words. On this score the effect is akin to anagrammatic, transformational effects in poetry.[8] Thus while the paradox of killing oneself from fear of dying is not a jest, it is something "funny," and that is the point of Ovid's clever way of *talking* about it: *mortisque timorem morte fugant* (*Met.* 7.604). The momentary suggestion that *mors* and *(ti)mor(s)* are somehow the same word short-circuits the ordinary flow of language and thought to produce a curious quip. It is, of course, difficult to know where the threshold of awareness in such matters lies, but that is always true of anything not wholly transparent, and in the nature of the case this kind of wit is designed to work suddenly and in context.

All of this can be observed in extreme form much earlier in Gorgias' *Encomium of Helen*, where parallelism, antithesis, wordplay, and assonance are used to create a clever haze in thought and expression. If it is not simply dismissed as a joke, the *Encomium* too poses deeper questions about moral reality and was probably intended to do so. For on the one hand, it is clearly a joke. No one really speaks or thinks this way; it is witty to do so and amusing to hear it done, and Gorgias himself at the very end calls the performance a *paignion*.

> For my part, by introducing an account in my account I wish to free the accused of blame and, having reproved her detractors as prevaricators and proved the truth, to free her from their ignorance [2]. . . . It is clear that her mother was Leda, and her father a god, Zeus, but allegedly a mortal, Tyndareus, of whom the former was shown to be her father because he was, and the latter was disproved because he was said to be [3]. . . . Born from such stock, she had godlike beauty, which taking and not mistaking, she kept [4]. . . . But if she was raped by violence and illegally violated and unjustly insulted, it is clear that the raper, as the insulter, did the wronging, and the raped, as the insulted, did the suffering [7]. . . . The persuader, like a constrainer, in speech is wrongly charged [12].[9]

At the same time, the points he makes are reasonable, and in this respect the wit has a serious side. In Seneca the effect is toned down. Blur in expression does not take the extravagant form it has in Gorgias but is a slight doubletake caused by brief epigrammatic tangles of words and of wordplay. Here everything can be sorted out easily enough, but the point is that a moment of sorting is still required.[10]

A set of epigrams on the unfortunate Galba and Piso is a good instance of how this works in Tacitus. Piso's restrained attitude to power suggested that "he was more able [*posset*] than willing [*vellet*] to rule" (*Hist.* 1.17.1) Uncertainty in criteria of leadership is directly embodied in the jingle *posset/vellet*, which is accordingly not simply a neutral statement of fact but also a ruefully amused quip on leadership at a time of crisis. A companion epigram on Piso's equally hapless mentor, Galba, is a somewhat similar pained quip. In this case the hitch in sense comes not from wordplay but from slightly off-center logic to bring out political anomaly: he was "in everyone's opinion capable of power, if he had not possessed it" (*Hist.* 1.49.4; the obverse point is made in an epigram on Classicus, "at his ease, enjoying power as though he already possessed it," *Hist.* 4.70.1). The remark about Piso is set in the *magis quam* formula, which, as we have seen above (chap. 2, sec. 8), insinuates that what is "more than" or "rather than" something else is what we would *not* expect. That is to say, readiness to hold power in time of crisis should be the norm, and though Piso's hesitation was perhaps justified, it was in any event of no more use than anything else in those days, since he was in fact not able to rule either. Galba and Piso are the subjects of a third epigram in the same vein. "Galba said this as though he were making [Piso] emperor, others as though they were speaking with a man already made emperor" (*et Galba quidem haec ac talia tamquam principem faceret, ceteri tamquam cum facto loquebantur, Hist.* 1.16.4). The peculiar jingle between *tamquam faceret* and *tamquam cum facto* again makes what is said into a wry quip about exactly what *was* being "done" at Rome (i.e., nothing). The jingle attracts attention, and its point is not clear until we reflect that, having been duly "made" heir apparent ("as it were"), Piso lasted four days (*Hist.* 1.48.1 has the brutal obituary). The same amusing tangle of words gives *Histories* 2.39.2 its point. "It is not as easy to decide what *should* have been *done* as it is to decide that what *was done* was the very worst thing that *could have been done"* (. . . *quid optimum factu fuerit, quam pessimum fuisse quod factum est*).

Like jokes, *sententiae* take much of their force from sharp economy of structure: philosophic maxims "sink in more easily because they are limited and restricted just as poetry is" (Sen. *Ep.* 33.6). Antithetic form in particular fits neatly into basic metric units, and both help reinforce consciousness of orderliness as such. That is to say, an *orderliness* which helps reinforce consciousness of the moral *disorder* often dealt with by the maxim. Agamemnon and Pyrrhus' debate on the ambivalence of power, a father's unaccountable restraint toward his son, the futility of leadership at Rome are the more noticeable owing to the contrast between disturbing thought and neat form. In drama this transforms epigrams from a character's private reaction into general laws. The speaker is distanced from the particular situation by his clever expression,[11] much as the reader is distanced from immediate historical reality for the purpose of larger moral and political judgment by the formal wit of Tacitus' aphoristic style. "Poppaea had everything else except character" is a general rule rendering her irrelevant in principle. "The *sententia* provides the possibility of going in an instant from the level of statement to the level of meaning."[12]

As we might expect, there is also a larger, specifically philosophic background for Seneca's use of *sententiae* in prose. In *Epistle* 120.8 he comments on the similarity between some virtues and vices: "evil at times has the appearance of good, and what is best shines out from its opposite." This is not a formal methodological statement on the use of paradoxical antithetic epigrams, but it is a general statement about the inverted moral and social reality that Seneca and Tacitus characteristically do deal with epigrammatically.

Seneca is aware that from one point of view the brevity of aphorisms limits the insight they provide. In *Epistle* 33.7 he says that they are appropriate to the restricted attention span of children; more advanced adults will want a much more complete discussion of issues. But aphorism receives its due in the lengthy assessment of the relative merits of "precepts" and "dogma" in *Epistles* 94 and 95. Precepts, of course, are not simply jokes; they are practical philosophical advice applicable to particular cases as general principles are not (94.31). But as brief maxims, they are in fact often witty, and since *exempla* serve the same purpose as precepts do, they are in form a kind of enacted wit, amusing anecdotes that embody ethical rules. Seeing good people in action may be as effective as hearing good precepts (94.40). Seneca is here

conceding that precepts or good stories are needed to make dogma effective
(94.34), and though he is not talking about wit in particular, his analysis
touches on several of its familiar marks. "Admonition does not teach, it
catches attention, excites and focuses the memory" (94.25); it is essentially
persuasive and (like political wit) may be abusive (94.39). Precepts are brief,
being "compacted into prose epigrams" (94.27, 43), and Seneca's example is a
double entendre by Cato on the distinction between want and need: "buy not
what you want but what you need; what you don't need is expensive when it is
cheap" *("emas quod non opus est, sed quod necesse est; quod non opus est,
asse carum est").* The point is instantly clear, yet there is a "point" because
both the idea and its expression are slightly paradoxical. Since precepts work
not by explicit reasoning but by intuitive display of truth (94.25), the sudden
revelation of the point has a shock effect ("they touch the feelings themselves,"
94.28; we hear them "with a shock," 94.43). Some people are content simply
to remember the words of a philosopher, others are moved to action by "a
sharp saying against death or an impertinent remark against fortune." Nature has put in us the seeds of virtue waiting to be aroused, and thus truths
expressed neatly in the theater raise a cheer—even a miser will applaud an
epigram against greed. Seneca then cites Cleanthes' comparison of the pierc-
ing effect of sound forced through the narrow throat of a trumpet to the "tight
restriction of meter" that makes meaning clearer and enables poetic expression to "assault the mind" and to "lead us to admission of the truth"
(108.8–12; cf. 94.29, 38.2). Like Demetrius' definition of brevity (above, p.
27), most of this does admirably as a description of jokes and wit in general as
well as of Tacitus' style in both form and intent.

Philosophic aphorisms are simple, clear, and need no explanation. They
are in that respect an alternative to elaborate Stoic logical subtleties that en-
tertain after a fashion but only because of their fallacies *(fallacia ipsa delec-
tant,* 45.8) and therefore are quite useless. Such "ambiguities and syllogisms"
are much inferior to the bare truth of precepts (108.12 and 35, 45.5, 82.8; *Ben.*
7.1.3). But it is ambiguity, unexpected hitches, or tangles in thought and
language that are marks of wit, too, and Seneca does not mean to exclude
them. Some of the precepts he quotes as good substitutes for logical conceits
are undoubtedly clear, for example, the order of the day given by a Roman
general to his troops on a dangerous mission: "Men, we have to go to a place
from which we don't have to come back" (82.21). But this is also witty because
of the equivocation.

Though Seneca thinks that the cleverness of Stoic paradoxes is ineffective,
his own *sententiae* are themselves not plain maxims but depend on verbal as
well as conceptual paradox. In *Epistle* 55.3, after distinguishing the phases of
Sejanus' career—his startling rise and fall—Seneca telescopes the two in a
quip on the ultimate futility and irrationality of power at Rome: "it was as
dangerous to have been an enemy as to have been a friend of Sejanus." This is

a favorite Senecan theme, turned into a witticism here by initial logical dissonance requiring an instant of amused reflection. The same idea is brought out
elsewhere by neat oxymoron: *(urbes) caesurae stant,* "cities stand to fall"
(91.12; or somewhat differently in English, "it stands to reason that cities
fall"), and several of his epigrams are in technique close to epigrams in
Tacitus. The *para prosdokian* in "Otho played the slave to be—master" (*Hist.*
1.36.3) reappears in "you will be ruler over many men, if reason is your—
ruler" (*Ep.* 37.4). Another Senecan version of a Tacitean epigram ("in the war
between these two you could only be certain that the one who would win
would be the worse," *Hist.* 1.50.3) embodies the uselessness of power politics
in gnarled expression that is witty as well as informative because of the slight
double take it demands: "the better man can win, but the winner cannot help
being the worse" (*potest melior vincere, non potest non peior esse, qui vicerit,*
Ep. 14.13).[13]

On the one hand, then, a good precept (like a good joke) does not require
much discursive explanation. At the same time, (again like a good joke) it is
not by any means always a commonplace. Its force may initially come from
anomaly, and when that is couched in arresting verbal form, epigrammatic
wit delivers a punch that in its cleanness, quickness, and oddness circumvents
ordinary measures of defense—properties of as much value to the historian as
to the philosopher.

III

The declamatory speeches *(controversiae)* that provided an occasion
for recherché fantasy are pertinent to historiography on the same score of
anomaly.[14] It is true that the circumstances envisaged in the speeches are
imaginary and highly artificial, but for that very reason declamation was free
to pursue the same kind of legal and moral absurdity, the same maze of irrationality that appears in the historians' account of the Principate. Rhetorical
"color" was the persuasive complexion given to an argument in declamatory
oratory, and since it was often used to put the best face on farfetched arguments,[15] the result more often than not would be so odd or inadmissible in
the real world as to seem mere jesting. Again like historiography, declamation
dealt with anecdotal material and made extensive use of both epigrams and
jokes. Seneca the Elder touches on the fine line separating epigrams from
overt jokes (*Controv.* 7.3.8–9, 9.4.21), and wit was a factor in declamation on
a deeper level as well. Intense interest in these strange exercises was an intellectual fad, but like all fads, it catered to broader trends of the times and in
particular to the taste for anomaly.[16]

For rhetorician and historian alike the greatest of anomalies at Rome was
lack of freedom. Seneca quotes Latro's remark that rhetorical figures are not

mere decoration but can be used as veiled political expression "so that what might offend the ears if it were said openly can slide in slantwise and secretly" (*Controv.* 1, pref. 24). That is to say, the subtle doubletake or arresting hitch in comprehension that is often the key to wit is prudent as well as amusing in a climate of political repression.[17] Tacitean insinuation is similarly at times also genuinely witty, and even if not motivated in a specific way by prudence, it has the same general background. What is political, what is witty, what is indirect, and what is unexpected all come together.

Addiction to rhetoric as often as not quite divorced from ordinary reality suggests that the appeal of declamation lay precisely in its unreality.[18] In an extraordinarily oral/aural society such as Rome declamation could meet several needs: it could serve as escape from an unhappy present or as an outlet for rhetorical skills increasingly difficult to use for expression of republican ideas. It is true that the surrogate world created by the declaimers was itself usually no less disturbing than the real world, but it could be mastered with words as the other could not. Indeed, it has been suggested that Augustus and some of his successors saw declamation as a safety valve for sentiments better talked out than acted out.[19] It is clear from Tacitus that the senate's business did often become a largely substitute verbal ritual, and at a very much higher level of intensity and sophistication Tacitus' own rhetoric, too, affirms an alternative political and moral reality of his own making, as Seneca's mannerism did.

Seneca the Elder himself touches on the relationship between political repression and the decline of oratory when he complains about various restrictions (including book burning) on free expression. And he does so with an epigram that itself wittily (and prudently?) strikes at imperial repression obliquely through its *victims:* "Thank the gods that persecution of talent began when talent left off!" (*Controv.* 10, pref. 7). Elsewhere he warns (again wittily) against risky political wit: "Some [fools] would rather lose their heads than a good joke" (*Controv.* 2.4.13; cf. Quint. *Inst.* 6.3.28: "losing a friend rather than a good line"). And in yet another touch of sour wit he reminds his son of the dangers of political life, "where even what is hoped for must be feared" (2, pref. 4). Some of his own friends were in fact critical of the Principate, others had been prosecuted.[20]

The appeal of declamation came in good part from its highly stylized and abstract game of wit. Wit often arises from a sense of violated expectation and dislocated logic, and both were a natural by-product of the current vogue in rhetoric of courting "danger" through unusual language.[21]

> The orator should approach the edge; a sheer drop often lies next to high places . . . a runner falls more frequently than a slow walker, but the walker is not praised for not falling, while the runner is, even when he falls. . . . What is most unexpected is most amazing. (Pliny *Epistulae* 9.26.2–4)

This includes a witty epigram about witty epigrams (his non labentibus nulla, illis non nulla laus etiamsi labantur), and Pliny introduces the discussion with another quip: "The only mistake he makes is that he doesn't make mistakes" (9.26.1).

Whatever the declaimers made of them, such ways of talking were more than mere diversion. As we have seen, epigrammatic language and thought of this sort are for Tacitus a fundamental category for understanding the nature of political reality, and as a form of wit can bring out political contradiction. Philosophers and rhetoricians, too, had noticed the possibility of systematic, large-scale incoherence in real society. They knew that its implications were simultaneously serious and absurd and that discussion could itself scarcely avoid becoming in some sense a form of wit. The case of Corax and Tisias (or Protagoras and Euathius) is the most familiar of these amusing, yet serious loop-puzzles (antistrepha or reciproca). Tisias refuses to pay Corax for the lessons in rhetoric he has received and rests his case on the contention that if the court agrees, he need not pay (since he has won his case), and if it does not, he still need not pay, since an adverse decision proves that Corax's lessons are worthless. Corax now advances the same argument by reversing Tisias' claim: if he wins, he collects because he has won; if he loses he still collects, because the loss demonstrates the value of his lessons. This odd situation—at once fail-safe and catch-22—exemplifies the internal incoherence that may lie concealed in the most ordinary rules.

The possibility that law and, on a larger scale, civilization itself include self-refuting loops is treated as an entirely serious matter when Antiphon shows that apparently elementary notions of justice may, in fact, be incoherent (44B, Col. I, Diels/Kranz). It seems obvious that it is just never to harm anyone except in retaliation for prior harm, but if that is so, a third party who testifies truthfully in court in support of a plaintiff is wronging the defendant. And not only is the witness' testimony an act of injustice; he must live in fear of retaliation from the defendant, and if it occurs, it is entirely justified because it avenges prior wrong. The issues raised by this line of thought are formidable, the more so when taken in conjunction with Antiphon's recognition of the "cooperation" (homonoia) on which society depends.[22] He is neither recommending nor criticizing, yet the point he makes is very real in the light of the potential dangers a third party must face, and the self-perpetuating loop connecting fear of retaliation with crime was seen by the historians of the Principate as a key mechanism in the actual working of terror. Of course, those afraid of becoming involved in resistance to official crimes did not rationalize their own intimidation on the theoretical ground that resistance would be "unjust" to the emperor; it was a matter of sheer self-interest. But that is precisely what Antiphon wants to bring out as a factor inherent in law, and what is troublesome about his paradox is that it contains some plain truth. The dilemma in the logic of right and wrong—namely, that it may well be right to do wrong—is dramatized in a scene like the one of Britannicus dying from poison at a dinner party while everyone carefully looks the other way (*Ann.* 13.16). Those who did nothing on this occasion in order to avoid antagonizing the criminal are bitterly said by Tacitus to have had "more understanding" (*altior intellectus*). In the first instance what they understand is what is happening, but Tacitus is also insinuating that they have a healthy measure of prudence about the relation of right to power (cf. *imprudens* in connection with a legal decision that might offend Tiberius in *Ann.* 1.74.5).

The *Dissoi logoi* is an actual handbook of loops in social logic, some of which raise genuine difficulties, such as the larger public utility of vice for those who make a living selling food, drink, or sex (1.3). The Corax and Tisias tale seems to have been a floating *exemplum* of this sort at the border between puzzle and joke. It is of additional interest as an instance of what most probably was an imaginary situation treated as historical fact and attached to specific people. In any case, what matters is the portable idea, and that is true of many of the anecdotes about legal absurdity used by the historians to impart formal craziness to events. Caesonius was "protected by his vices" since as a sexual pervert he would not have committed adultery with Messalina (*Ann.* 11.36.4). It is again lunatic logic (murder legalized through rape and rape through murder) that permits Tacitus' sovereign nastiness to outdo itself in the case of Sejanus' daughter.

> The little girl was so unaware of what was happening that she kept asking what she had done wrong and where she was being taken. "I won't do it again. Why don't you just spank me?" Writers of the time report that since there was no precedent for executing a virgin, she was raped [lying] next to the rope. (*Ann.* 5.9)

This old fascination with amusing yet unsettling incoherence in the order of things is a major factor in both the language and thought of declamation.[23]

> A man has raped two women in one night—one of whom wants marriage, the other execution (the law permits either, Sen. *Controv.* 1.5).

> A man convicted of rape must die unless he wins over his own and the girl's father within thirty days. A rapist who succeeds in winning over the latter but is turned down by his own father takes him to court for insanity. But he now finds himself in a catch-22 situation. His father cannot be accused of having refused mercy until the thirty days are past, since he has the right to change his mind at any time during that period. But when he can be accused of having refused it will be (is) too late (Sen. *Controv.* 2.3.16 and 19). The son thus can act only when he is dead, or—in the more witty and macabre scenario envisaged by one speaker—as he raises the sword, the executioner must keep his eyes glued on the father. Absurd as this all is, the fantasy of sadistic anxiety and perversion of

normal relationships is in principle straight from the pages of Tacitus or Suetonius. In fact, Suetonius credits Domitian with a similar diagnosis of a dilemma
actually faced by the emperor: no one would believe that he had uncovered a
conspiracy until he had been assassinated (*Dom.* 21; cf. "no matter how many
people you kill, you cannot kill your successor," Seneca to Nero, Dio 62.18.3).

A woman has resisted the advances of a wealthy merchant; in admiration of her
virtue he leaves all his property to her in a will that includes the clause, "I found
her chaste." Her husband immediately wants to divorce her on grounds of the
clause (Sen. *Controv.* 2.7). His suspicion is caused by reasonable presumption
of adultery and creates a loop—proof of innocence is proof of guilt—that is
again reminiscent of the climate of paranoia and futility portrayed by Tacitus.[24]

A woman who as a prostitute killed a man in self-defense and is now seeking the
office of priestess finds herself in a similar quandary. In arguing that she did
everything unwillingly she must "defend herself from the charge of unchastity
by pleading murder and from the charge of murder by pleading unchastity"
(Sen. *Controv.* 1.2.12).

   This is the same world in which the truth of charges against the emperor is
the most convincing evidence for showing that they are slanderous (*Ann.*
1.74.3); in which Tiberius defends his good name by bringing up charges
against himself that are true and that no one has made (Dio 57.23.2); and in
which he executes a man, whom he had had mistakenly tortured, on the
ground that the *victim* was too dishonored to live (Dio 58.3.7). It is the contradictory world, too, whose natural language is anecdotal and epigrammatic
wit. Everything is rendered odd or unreal by skewed logic that subverts any
expectation of a normal, sane fit among events. The cases often seem merely
frivolous, but the rhetorical attitude they embody permeated the minds of
many who were active in the politics of the time, and it may have done so to
the extent of coming to be for some a significant part of the shape of social
reality. It is on this deeper level of a rhetorical mind-set that declamation has
points of contact with historiography. The world of pathological conflict it
creates and probes exemplifies the power exercised over the Roman imagination by language that "interests, impresses, moves, startles, shocks"[25]—and,
we might now add, that is "witty." It also exemplifies consciousness of the
potential absurdity of things, and that, too, is a species of wit. This is not to
say that declamation was primarily a product of pressures in Roman society.
On the contrary, many of its favorite themes, its creation of an imaginary
world, and its interest in moral or legal crises go back to Hellenistic times and
earlier. And its pervasive witty coloring in large measure simply reflects the
delight in (verbal) cleverness widespread in the ancient world at all times.[26]
Nonetheless, all of this must have taken on added significance in special
situations, and the early years of the Principate were just such a situation, one
into which the strange world of declamation might well have been felt at times
to be intruding in actual fact.

VI

Wit and Political Irrationality

We have been considering various techniques of wit employed by the Roman historians for bringing political absurdity to light: epigram, irony, *para prosdokian,* anecdote, wordplay. Witty effects come most directly from violation of norms, and since the purpose of norms is to rationalize human affairs, wit was a natural tool also for dealing with absurdity in the special form of paranoid political logic. Critics of the Principate detected many examples of such paranoia, though without fully realizing or admitting that what they saw as mad disorder might in part have been an indispensable aspect of a different, but quite reasonable order which they disapproved. Bias toward moral judgment helped obscure this possibility, though many Romans were aware that objective contradictions inherent in a competitive system had played a role in the fall of the Republic. Tacitus and Dio recognize, too, that the central conundrum in imperial Rome—freedom preserved only when it is lost—is partly a matter of inherent political logic, but they still treat it mainly in terms of moral incoherence.

Irrationality at this level comes out with special clarity in the *form* of the narrative. Events, for example, frequently display a conspicuous circular pattern designed to bring their radical incoherence into focus. In some passages the focus is so precise that it practically "diagrams" the formal contradiction governing situations. This is particularly common in accounts of the relationship between senate and emperor, and the odd logic vitiating official clemency is a special case in point (secs. 1–3 of this chap.). A sense of irrationality is reinforced in another way through the nearly formulaic expressions of futility in Tacitus which often involve carefully placed negation (e.g., Aelius Lamia's status "was enhanced by the province he was not allowed to govern," *Ann.* 6.27.2) and work as a mocking obbligato to the narrative (sec. 4). Futility is again the theme of anecdotes dramatizing peculiarly irrational malice, either utterly empty of any ordinary purpose or utterly extravagant or both at once (sec. 5). Particularly in cases of empty, trivialized irrationality—thoughtless routine, for example, or stupid pranks by the emperor—what is at issue is personal moral incoherence and not something essentially institutional in the modern sense.

›

I

Contradiction in the logic of social systems has received a good deal of attention in connection with game theory, and it has been examined recently by Jon Elster in a series of studies with particular reference to the novels of Soviet dissident Alexander Zinoviev, *The Yawning Heights* and *The Radiant Future*.[1]

> He [Zinoviev] does for Soviet Communism what Marx did for the capitalism of his time. Like Marx, who strove to demonstrate the mechanisms of capitalistic irrationality, Zinoviev has us enter an hallucinatory world that is, however, not a chaotic one but one ruled by principles as irrational as they are intelligible. *Understanding the irrational:* such is the task that Zinoviev proposes. The irrational object is Soviet society; the method used to study it derives in great part from formal logic. . . . Soviet irrationality is not produced, as under capitalism, by the shock of incompatible and uncoordinated intentions; we are reminded, rather, of the snake that bites its own tail, of the right hand that steals from the left, of the dog that chases its shadow, or of the man who verifies the news in a newspaper by buying a second copy of the same newspaper.[2]

A reader of the historians of the Principate might also be reminded of Caligula, who marked a new era of freedom by burning copies of incriminating letters (Dio 59.4.3). The historians, in fact, had much the same task in view as Zinoviev, and Tacitus' antithetic epigrams in particular are often shaped to bring out contradictions in a precise and formal manner. The title "Yawning Heights" is witty refutation of political illusion through internal contradiction on the pattern of Tacitean oxymoron like "wretched peace" or "arrogant modesty." "Radiant Future" parodies official language by simple quotation, much as "liberty" in reported political discourse may in the historians have reverse meaning.

A closely related form of incoherence discussed by Elster is contradictory orders bound to be disobeyed even as they are obeyed: "Don't be so obedient!"; "Remember to forget that . . ."; "Worship me!"[3] The logic of contradictory antithetic epigrams is analogous to such imperatives, and the demand of some emperors for divine status directly illustrates the larger political imperatives carried in grammatical imperatives. The logic of the last injunction was, in fact, turned into a joke by the famous Spartan answer to Alexander's demand for worship: "If Alexander wants to be a god—let him!" This is violation of expectation on two scores: through anticlimax, since we expect outraged refusal or abject compliance, and logically through *reductio ad absurdum,* the technique that lies behind Talking Dog jokes.[4] The response understates and thus accepts rather than rejects an absurd situation. The Spartan joke is a good example of how the technique can be used as a

political tactic of taking something to an extreme in order to show its incoherence.[5] Those who acquiesced in imperial extravagance did not, of course,
generally do so as a gesture of ironic protest, though some may have had that
in mind on occasion.

The first injunction ("Don't be so obedient!") is so obviously odd that it
may seem simply to be a jest. In any case, the mechanism of the wit is close to
that in a well-known quip of Groucho Marx discussed by Elster: "I'd never
belong to a club that would have me as a member."[6] The value of an honor
depends on the worth of the conferring body, and that depends conversely on
the worth of those it honors. Vicious circles of this kind take on considerable
importance in modern game theory concerned with rules—at times self-
defeating—that shape social and political reality. The primary intent of Stoic
paradoxes was, of course, quite different, but when brought to bear on political issues they, too, could expose latent contradiction. Thus Epictetus draws
attention to an analogous double bind implicit in the apparently reasonable
acclamation, "By Caesar's fortune, we are free!" (4.1.14)—a statement whose
potential absurdity reappears in Pliny's salute to Trajan: "You command us to
be free—we will be" (Pan. 66.4).[7] Both of these examples show why insight
into the logic of public language is crucial for the historian. More often than
not its contradictions are hidden, and social illusion of all kinds loses power
when it is made visible.

The most comprehensive application of the notion of a double bind to the
logic of social institutions is Hegel's dialectic of master and slave.[8] The paradox is that master depends on slave, because his status as master is defined by
that of his slave. In Rome senate and emperor were bound to each other under
tacit rules in a similarly elusive circular relationship. Since the emperor held
real power, the senate was cast in the role of subject "recognized" by its master
to secure the victim needed for his own exercise of legitimacy and power. The
report that Nero would occasionally drop clear hints about wiping out the
senate and turning the provinces and armies over to freedmen and Knights is
introduced by Suetonius with a story about his interest in feeding live men to
a monstrous beast of some sort or other (Ner. 37.3). Such ideas "inspired" him
to deeper political reflections, namely, that "no ruler had realized what he
could do" (liquidate the senate, for example). Nero's moral nihilism is, as
usual, the real point of these stories, and his drastic political designs on the
senate may well unfairly exaggerate something that was originally not so very
unreasonable after all. But even if this story was no more than an anxious
exaggeration or joke circulating in senatorial groups, its implications are
nihilistic in the precise sense that emperor and senate depended on each other
systematically.

The notorious "let them hate so long as they fear" is especially interesting
in this connection. In Suetonius' Caligula (30.1) it appears as oderint dum
metuant. Tacitus' version of the idea is "fear and terror are weak bonds of

friendship; when they are removed, those who cease fearing will begin to hate" (*Agr.* 32.1). Seneca (*De ira* 1.20.4) dismisses the principle as monstrous for appealing to sheer fear and proposes "obedience" or "approval" *(probent)* as more tolerable alternatives. Suetonius does in fact have Tiberius use the formula *oderint dum probent* (*Tib.* 59.2). Here the paradoxically positive overtones of "approve" again point to the recognition of sorts provided by the victim, who to that extent creates his master and is part of a relationship he himself legitimizes. When Seneca again quotes *oderint dum metuant* (*Clem.* 1.12.4) to reject it, he explicitly recognizes the loop it creates: "the ruler is driven by conflicting forces into conflicting policies; since he is hated because he is feared, he wants to be feared because he is hated." The power of the ruler (tied to hatred) and the weakness of the ruled (tied to fear) are functions of each other. Seneca detects a similar paradox in the relationship between a good ruler and his subjects. They, too, are mutually dependent, he being their soul and they his body (*Clem.* 1.5.1; 1.19.5: *securitas securitate mutua paciscenda est*). But the master/slave relation in this case is veiled or actually reversed in that the master serves his subjects (1.8.1, 1.19.8).

The good ruler, then, is a slave of his subjects, and according to Suetonius that is how Tiberius spoke of himself and the senators: they were *domini,* he was *servus* (*Tib.* 29). But they refused that role, and Tacitus remarks on the contempt with which Tiberius regarded the senate because of its flattery: "As he left the senate hall he would say in Greek, 'How ready these people are for slavery!' Even he, who did not favor liberty, was disgusted at so open an acceptance of slavery" (*Ann.* 3.65.3; cf. *Ann.* 2.87). This is implicitly the logically odd command, "Don't be so obedient" or "Be free," and we can see a larger political dialectic at work.

Tiberius hesitated to join with the senate in a system that made him princeps. Several motives are advanced by the historians: he was genuinely modest, he feared what he was bound to become (*Tib.* 67; cf. *Ann.* 6.6); he was pretending. The first is for the most part dismissed as false, though perhaps true at the start. The second would match the self-depreciation in Groucho Marx's epigram ("a club that would have me as a member"), but Tiberius is portrayed as, in fact, wanting power though pretending not to and as viewing the senate with contempt for its lack of initiative. Too-ready acquiescence in his authority proved to him that the senate did not merit responsibility. Augustus himself had twice abandoned the idea of restoring the republic (*Aug.* 28.1), and Nero's first speech as emperor again honestly envisaged sharing of authority (*nec defuit fides, Ann.* 13.5.1), but when it did not work out, he thought of eliminating the senate in some way. Tiberius seems in fact to have been motivated by a combination of reluctance or at least caution on the one hand, and ambition on the other. The former made room for a claim to authority by the senate, the latter excluded it, and the senate delegitimized itself by meeting Tiberius' evasions with its own reluctance to put in a responsible claim. That failure made it impossible for him to join with it in governing, for under the circumstances the power thrust on him was honor effectively rendered worthless, since it was conferred by a republican institution fawning on an autocratic leader. What is odd about the situation is that the senate's weakness created and justified the emperor's power while at the same time compromising it, and that is to some extent Tacitus' own view. The emperor faced a vacuum into which he was pulled as much as he rushed, and so in the light of republican political norms he could justify his own position by saying, "I cannot join any (republican) club that can so readily have me as an (autocratic) partner."

At the same time, the genuine efforts of Tiberius and other emperors to enhance the senate's authority reflect dependence on it for their own authority. Roman society was a status system dependent on symbolic gestures to which even the emperor was bound because his own position was ultimately a function of that of others. Augustus ruefully admits as much in an anecdote in Seneca (*Ben.* 3.27). He yields to someone begging forgiveness for an insult who then requests a substantial gift in addition so that people will believe that he really has been pardoned. Augustus yields once more with the quip, "It will pay me not to be angry with you." That is to say, only the emperor has power to pardon, but power dependent on a network of public obligations in which he is himself enmeshed, and so both he and his subjects are both masters and slaves.[9] The remark is a quip because it is unreasonable; it is politically important because it is true.

The dilemma is that of Rome caught between republic and autocracy:

> On the one hand they [the senators] were supposedly exalted, independent leaders of the state; on the other, they were servants of the emperor, totally dependent upon his favor both for individual advancement and for maintaining the position of the corporate body, indeed their class as a whole.[10]

> Far from being a genuine compromise with the Republic, it is now generally held, the Principate was an undiluted monarchy. All Augustus' laborious attempts to persuade his contemporaries that this was not so are of no avail. His "restored Republic" is roundly denounced as a slogan and a pretense.[11]

And yet this does not do full justice to what was a genuinely dyarchic, that is to say, circular aspect of political logic at Rome.[12]

Ambivalence of political intentions and institutions is mirrored in the language that goes with them whenever "tension [arises] between purpose and institutionalization, between substance and form. That tension is essential to their function in language, and is the grammatical source for certain characteristic puzzles about them."[13] A society conceives goals or norms and creates institutions for their realization, but means may become ends, and when they do, conflict between political form and substance, between language and reality develops. Conversely, an institution may come into conflict with goals it was meant to serve and be transformed by them. In the eyes of its critics the Principate had become such an institution, defining its purposes purely for preservation of power and thus destroying republican institutions (e.g., through creation of an imperial bureaucracy).

Suetonius describes Tiberius at first hypocritically hesitating to take the title of power offered by the senate and then, after finally accepting, claiming to exercise it reluctantly (*Tib.* 24). The ambiguous situation invited the sneer that "he was slow to promise what he was already doing, while others were slow to do what they were promising" (24.1). This joke, like Tacitus' "haughty moderation" (*Ann.* 1.8.5), catches verbally the anomaly of events: we are startled and amused to hear the puzzling combination of words, as contemporaries were startled and alarmed to see the course of events and to realize how they had to be spoken of. Tacitus catches the same anomalous situation in a formal quip on Tiberius' ambiguous assumption of power: he "gradually stopped refusing it without admitting that he was taking it" (*Ann.* 1.13.5).[14]

This underlying pattern of internal contradiction is also at work in Tiberius' elaborate incriminating self-defense (above, p. 48) and is described in most startling terms in Dio's general account of his "peculiar" language and behavior (57.1):

> He did not let on to what he wanted, and what he said he wanted he did not; instead, using words opposite to his desire he would deny what he desired and recommend what he opposed. He became angry over things that bothered him hardly at all and remained calm at what enraged him. He would pity those he punished severely and be angry with those he pardoned. He would at times see his worst enemy as a dear friend and deal with his closest friend as a stranger. In general he did not think it wise for a ruler to show what he thought, for from that, he said, many great failures came, while many successes came from the opposite. Now if only this had been true, those who dealt with him could easily have been on their guard. For taking everything backward they could equally have recognized what he did not want by his desire for it and what he did want by his indifference to it. In fact, he became angry if anyone clearly grasped his meaning and executed many on no other ground than that they understood him. So that it was risky not to understand him (many got into trouble by approving what he said instead of what he wanted), yet even more risky to understand him, since he suspected that they had detected and disapproved of his methods. Hence the only persons (and they were very rare) who could survive were those who neither misunderstood his character nor revealed it—then they would be neither deceived by trusting him nor hated for showing that they knew what he was doing. For he was dangerous whether one opposed what he said or agreed with it; wishing one thing actually to happen but to appear to wish something else, he always had opponents on each side and therefore hated the one in truth, the others in appearance.

This very odd and in some ways genuinely amusing state of affairs is in principle akin in its logic to Orwell's doublethink, "the power of holding two contradictory beliefs in one's mind simultaneously and accepting both of them," or to the Ibanskian rule that "if the leadership allows something it does not wish to allow, that is the most stringent form of ban."[15] And each, in turn, is also akin to the radical incoherence of some of the most elegant jokes.

> Two Jews met in a railway carriage at a station in Galicia. "Where are you going?" asked one.
> "To Cracow," was the answer.
> "What a liar you are!" broke out the other. "If you say you are going to Cracow, you want me to believe you are going to Lemberg. But I know in fact that you're going to Cracow. So why are you lying to me?"[16]

This is a joke because it is isolated from a real context and can be taken safely in the abstract. But such wit gets its force from its paranoid implications for real life. The picture of Tiberius' equally arresting paranoia may go back to an early hostile portrayal of his character which decisively influenced the historical tradition at Rome. In fact, it may go back even further, to conventional descriptions of the tyrant:

> A tyrant is most incoherent: if you admire him moderately, he is angered because he is not getting enough recognition, and if you give him a lot of recognition, he is angered at your flattery. (Herodotus 3.80)

In Dio the theme has undergone considerable inflation through its connection with the supreme ruler of the Roman empire and its sustained suggestion of an Alice-in-Wonderland maze of irrationality. The immediate source for Dio or Tacitus is likely to have been not a single work but a more fluid, anonymous tradition that rose in the course of the early Principate, "the talk and opinions of a large group—the upper classes."[17] Such talk and opinion would have included a great deal of hostile wit, and the theme of Tiberius' two-facedness must have been a rich source of jesting on the formal absurdity of imperial politics. Dio's version, to be sure, does not itself have much formal wit. "It lacks bite and is antithetic but not epigrammatical."[18] But his elaborate account does unfold the complex political dialectic from which epigrammatic wit springs.

Tiberius' policy repeatedly falls into this pattern. He responded to the senate's hasty execution of Clutorius Priscus for treason with typical ambiguity by "praising Lepidus [who had opposed the action] and not blaming Agrippa [who had favored it]" (*Ann.* 3.51.1). The situation was perhaps genuinely difficult, and that not entirely through Tiberius' doing, but quite apart from the legal facts of the case, the sour wit of Tacitus' epigram neatly catches absurd but serious emptiness in policy. All the more so since he adds that a decree was passed calling for a nine-day waiting period in the future, "but the senate had no freedom to change its mind and Tiberius would not do so either." That is to say, he neither approves nor disapproves or both approves and disapproves one policy, which is then improved on by another policy that itself neither has nor can have effect. Put in these terms, his attitude has the form and sound of a self-canceling joke much like Martial's quip about coy women who don't say "yes" but don't say "no" either.[19]

Tiberius' "remarkable" *(thaumaston)* technique for destroying Sejanus as it is described by Dio is contradiction put to more sinister ends—"one moment Tiberius would praise him highly, at another he would denounce him bitterly" (58.6.3)—and it reaches its climax in a set of events that taken together are pure contradiction: "he was escorted to the senate house in honor at dawn and later dragged to prison in contempt" (58.11.1). Seneca puts the paradox in even starker terms: on the very same day Sejanus was granted an escort by the senate and torn apart by a mob *(Tranq.* 11.11), much like the man in Tacitus who began the day by celebrating his birthday without the slightest concern, to be then "dragged off to the senate for summary conviction and execution." The rhythm of the Latin has a certain derisive jauntiness: *raptus in curiam pariterque damnatus interfectusque (Ann.* 6.18.1). Still another victim of Tiberius had a similar and again "wholly unexpected" *(paradoxotaton)*) experience of dining in honor with the emperor on the very day he was being condemned in the senate.[20]

II

Self-contradictory language and behavior, then, are traits of the devious Tiberius. Tacitus remarks that his *verba suspensa* were "ambiguous, uncertain, and complicated" even when he was trying to be frank *(Ann.* 1.11.2). Aside from the tactical value of baffling opposition by depriving it of a clear target, to some extent this must also have been a natural expression of the circular logic binding emperor to senate. The peculiar seriocomic effect of loops in social logic has attracted the attention of modern political science and satire. It is enshrined in the original catch-22 of Joseph Heller's novel. (A) If a pilot wants to fly combat missions (B) he is regarded as crazy and (C) therefore eligible for medical exemption but only on request, and (D) a request proves his sanity.[21] The loop formed when one part of a policy serves in this way as a frame of reference reducing other parts to nonsense is close to logical puzzles like "This sentence is false" and "All Cretans are liars" or to subversive rhetorical arguments (above, p. 100). The perpetual oscillation brings about "a feeling of vertigo no doubt analogous to the vague feelings of guilt that hover permanently over many citizens of Ibansk" (Zinoviev's Soviet Union).[22]

Though we might prefer to speak of terror rather than guilt in connection with Roman society, and though the historians usually link episodes of irrationality with individual emperors, in ancient and modern satire alike irrationality regularly accompanies violence. The key to its witty effect lies in an odd formal elegance increasing with the degree of unreason. Dio draws attention to an intricate catch-22 pattern in the proscriptions. He is aware of the irrational logic at work in escalating violence, observing that because the Romans had earlier experience with terror, the triumvirs could carry it to "paradoxical" lengths to create "many complicated situations" (47.3–15). Some, in fact, resemble scenarios found in the declaimers (10.2). Under Sulla, at least the friends of those in power were safe, though Dio notes that already his terror showed signs of mad contradiction (33, frag. 109.15–20). But now the political system of temporary personal alliances had made almost anyone who supported one triumvir an enemy of the other two, and so everyone was an enemy of the three as a group. Conversely, each enemy of any triumvir would be a friend of the other two and could be proscribed only at the price of one of the proscriber's own friends. The logic of the situation thus guaranteed that friends would suffer the same fate as enemies or that some died at the hands of their dearest friends, while others were saved by their bitterest enemies.

Livia's analysis of the security problem keeping Augustus awake at night involves a similar, if more familiar crazy, inverted logic imposed by ineradicable human untrustworthiness. He confesses bafflement at the thought that friends are a greater threat than enemies are, though they still have to be called friends. Conveniently forgetting Julius Caesar, she concludes that the only way out of the vicious circle is to make real friends from real enemies by simply treating them as friends through clemency (55.14–21). Though this exercise in incipient game theory is written in Dio's customarily bland style, move and countermove between self-defense and threat do have cumulative force and add yet another twist to the dialectic of clemency (sec. 3, below), which in the light of her argument may be an admission of weakness as well as genuine mercy or a veiled gesture of power.

Patterns of this sort hold special interest for Zinoviev, himself a logician by profession. The Ibanskian government (A) imposes exile and (B) denies emigration while (C) treating requests to emigrate as crimes punishable by (D) exile.[23] Another situation closely reproduces the original catch-22. A man essential for carrying out a dangerous attack is in the stockade. He agrees to lead the attack if his court-martial is cancelled, but that is contrary to regulations, though it is also contrary to regulations to release him, so he is promised that if he dies, his family will not be told about the court-martial, which therefore has lost its purpose, since he is bound to die, and for the same reason might just as well be carried out anyway.[24] Then again, when someone complains that his fur cap has been stolen, the police charge him with slandering the Soviet people. They do so because they have vowed to reduce unsolved crime, and crimes that have not been committed count as crimes that have been solved.[25] A dialectic explanation of a wave of robberies is equally efficient: as the state withers by becoming all-powerful, so robbery diminishes as it becomes more widespread and will completely vanish when everything has been stolen.[26] Such anecdotes have a special mad elegance imparted to them by the full-blown ideology they satirize, but the general pattern recurs in the *hysteron/proteron* inversion of legal procedure by some emperors, for example, Gaius' practice of first setting the amount he wanted to raise from fines, then staying in court until he got it (*Calig.* 38.3).[27] An even more effective measure for combating crime on such principles is liquidating criminals before they manage to commit their crimes,[28] a measure not unlike Nero's policy of informing defendants of charges against them only after they have learned of the penalties (*Ann.* 15.71.5; above, p. 65).

What was perhaps a genuine legal puzzle came up when Sejanus sent agents to court to complain that Cremutius Cordus, one of his prospective victims, was starving himself to death (Sen. *Ad Marciam* 22.7). The issue apparently was whether a defendant on a capital charge had a right to die at will. The passage is a typical instance of Senecan dialectic, setting "necessity imposed" against "permission denied" to show that death may be desirable. Cordus now finds himself in a trap: "if he wanted to live, he had to ask Sejanus, if he wanted to die, he had to ask his daughter. Both were inexorable." The actual details are unclear. He may have been about to escape trial on a capital charge through perfectly normal legal procedures, for example, because he had not yet actually been indicted. But Seneca is not interested in legal details; the wry remark that by entering the complaint about Cordus' death the authorities wanted "to prevent him from doing what they had forced him to do" *(queruntur mori Cordum ut interpellent quod coegerant)* brings out the irrationality of the situation. Trying to stop someone from doing what you have forced him to do is roughly the inverse of punishment to prevent what has not been done.

Another variation of this curious situation could arise because the property of those who committed suicide might escape confiscation. Thus when Vibullius Agrippa took poison in the senate he was rushed off to prison to be formally hanged but proved to be dead on arrival (*Ann.* 6.40.1). Dio says nothing about the emergency trip to deliver a dead man for execution (58.21.4), and that touch of burlesque may be the product of political jesting about official procedures for prolonging life in order to take it or trying to take it when it is gone (cf. *Tib.* 61.5: "those who wanted to die were forced to live"). Zinoviev has a story about a young Ibanskian who tries to burn himself to death in protest and has difficulty keeping the fire lit because the gasoline is (typically) watered. He is saved by heroic action on the part of the police, who then take him to the nearest station and nearly beat him to death for his offense.[29]

Another case of formal legal irrationality comes up in *Histories* 1.77.3. Some who had been convicted of bribery under Claudius and Nero were later acquitted "by having 'bribery' changed to 'treason,' for that was so hated that even good laws were made useless by it." Treason, that is to say, had been so overworked as a false charge that it had practically come to be a warrant of innocence, even for those who were plainly guilty.[30] The logic at work in the issue of Tiberius' bodyguard is even more intricate (Dio 57.2.2–3). Dio remarks that Tiberius was running everything while saying that he had no desire to do anything. Though he already had a bodyguard he requested one from the senate for protection from violence at Augustus' funeral, and so a senator "facetiously" proposed that it be granted. Tiberius perceived the sour wit and protested that "those soldiers [which he had] are not mine but the state's." The joke is in the legislative charade dramatizing the extralegality of the emperor's power (much as the Spartan's proposal that Alexander be *granted* divine honors is witty because it denies the honor by rendering it fraudulent). Since what one has cannot be asked for and a fortiori not granted, Tiberius is compelled to acknowledge what he in fact has but immediately tries to undo the admission and denies that he has it in order to exercise power which he has by demanding that it be granted officially. (The Parthians similarly "ridicule" the Romans by "asking for what they had already taken from them," *Ann.* 15.25.2). To have its amusing effect the account ignores reasonable questions of legitimacy, and Tacitus, too, makes a point of the public ridicule occasioned by the strong military presence at Augustus' funeral (*Ann.* 1.8.6). Its purpose was to serve as both honor guard and security force, but by emphasis on the latter, Tiberius' anxiety about danger to a government obviously in control is made to seem absurd.

Dio immediately goes on to another equally futile exercise in political logic (57.2.4–7). At the start of his reign Tiberius wanted to reduce the burden of power by dividing government into three spheres. When he began to press the senate on the issue, some senators insisted that he retain unified power in his own hands, but Asinius Gallus accepted the proposal and demanded that he choose one sphere for himself. Tiberius refused on the ground that "the same person cannot both choose and divide." Gallus, seeing that he had gotten himself into serious trouble by taking Tiberius at his word, tried to smooth things over by assuring the emperor that he had meant him to choose undivided power, that is, not to divide and therefore not really to choose either. Whatever the true motives may have been, what matters is not simply the fact of servility and hypocrisy but its queer ritual logic. Tacitus, too, confesses that he is baffled by procedures for consular elections under Tiberius, though he is certain that they were "false in word, in reality empty and dishonest" (*speciosa verbis, re inania aut subdola, Ann.* 1.81).

Dio mentions another incident of the kind (which he calls "even more ri-

diculous"). The senate voted Tiberius an armed guard from its own member-
ship, but since senators were the only threat to the emperor inside the senate
house, they would be guarding him against themselves (58.17.4). The
situation is, as Dio says, ridiculous because it plays out the paradox of
Juvenal's *quis custodiat ipsos custodes* (6.031). Tacitus' version also focuses
on the absurdity of the situation. Trogonius Gallus' effort to "push his way
among the famous" by proposing that Tiberius choose twenty senators to
serve as an armed bodyguard in the senate house was received "with much
merriment" *(per deridiculum)*. The honor was declined by Tiberius "with his
wonted mixture of farce and seriousness" *(Ann. 6.2.2)*.

Dio's characterization of Gaius' contradictory attitudes uses the same intricate involutions used for Tiberius but is perhaps more effective for being
written with some measure of epigrammatic compression.

> Gaius was the first to denounce Tiberius and so others did the same; but then he
> also praised Tiberius and denounced others for their denunciation of him and
> hated both those who denounced Tiberius and those who praised him. (59.4.2)

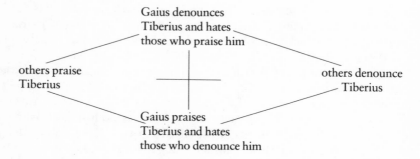

Gaius was both annoyed and pleased at both those who flattered and those who
were frank. Hence no one knew what to do or say to him, and those who did the
right thing, did so only by chance. (59.4.5)

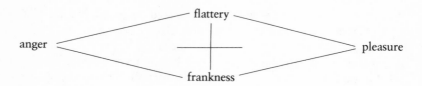

Gaius was angered at small honors (he regarded them as slights) and also at
large ones (he regarded them as precluding still larger honors). He was reluctant
to accept honors from the senate since doing so made him feel inferior to it, yet
he also resented its failure to grant him honors. (59.23.3)

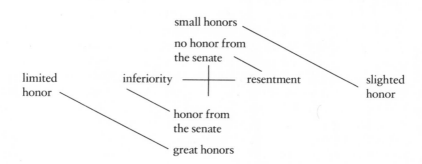

The inner, horizontal axis in the last passage is the emperor's paranoid perception of offense forever askew with whatever gestures the senate made.[31] His reluctance to accept honors because of the dependence they imply is again an aspect of the master/slave loop.

It is worth calling to mind once more at this point Freud's joke about the gourmand (chap. 5, n. 10) or the trip to Cracow (sec. 1 above) as well as the preposterous situations in declamatory oratory, all of which involve a mad point-counterpoint rivaled by this picture of political paranoia at Rome. Tacitus outlines the following version (which he rejects) of Drusus' death.[32] Sejanus forewarned Tiberius that Drusus would try to poison him. So when Tiberius was offered a cup (poisoned by Sejanus) at a banquet, he passed it on to Drusus, whose subsequent death was taken as proof of his guilt (not of his innocence) on the ground that he had drunk it to commit suicide because Tiberius' refusal to drink showed that his attempt at murder had been detected (*Ann.* 4.10). That is to say: Tiberius is induced to misunderstand the offer of the cup and to attempt unnecessary self-defense, which, in fact, becomes the apparently unintended murder of Drusus mistakenly seen as suicide for a failed attempt to murder Tiberius by Drusus himself, who is in fact murdered by Sejanus.

We have considered the case from *Annals* 1.74.3 of a quaestor who accused his praetor of slandering Tiberius and who rendered the charge "inescapable" by selecting the emperor's worst features to make the charges plausible, since they were known to be true (see chap. 2, sec. 7). The already considerably involuted situation becomes worse when the story continues with an enraged Tiberius insisting on casting his own vote in the case. The effect of this would be to force each senator to support or oppose the emperor publicly. Prudence dictated the customary dishonest vote for conviction, and that painful issue was brought out in a gesture of "dying liberty" by an apparently innocent procedural question put to the emperor: when did he intend to cast his vote, for if he went first, others would have a guide; if last, they might make a foolish mistake (*Ann.* 1.74.5). This was too much even for the devious Tiberius, who retired in confusion.

In yet another case "it was not easy to see into the emperor's mind, so mixed were the signals of clemency and anger" (*Ann.* 3.22.2). Tacitus proceeds to trace the baffling crosscurrents of motivation. Tiberius asked the senate not to deal with certain charges of treason but induced witnesses to reveal what he had wanted concealed and then prevented the consul designate (his own son) from being the first to express an opinion—a move that some regarded as equitable (*civile*) because the senate would not be under pressure of an official position on the matter. Others thought it malicious on the ground that Tiberius had waived control of the first vote not to invite acquittal but only because he intended the decision to be for conviction and was therefore shielding his son from resentment for starting the process.

At the end of the *Agricola* (42.2) we pass from the bracing atmosphere of honest and vigorous service in Britain to suffocating intrigue at Rome. Domitian, who wants to get rid of Agricola, after forcing him to request retirement "agrees to the request," but to cover any suggestion of dismissal then "permits expression of thanks" without so much as a blush at what had become a "hateful favor" (his ruddy complexion, in any case, made a show of shame impossible, *Agr.* 45.2). What is more, he withholds the customary proconsular salary either because he is offended that Agricola did not request it or because he wants to avoid the appearance of buying what he had in fact refused. The absurd charade unfolding at the surface of this bewildering narrative plays out a deeper logic of paranoia switching back and forth between official facade and truth behind the facade.[33]

Agricola should have the right to choose his own future, ———→	but is forced to request retirement as an apparent "favor" from Domitian, ↓
instead of simply granting him his due, ←———	who also expects him to request a salary,
↓	
since that would mean that Agricola has a claim on him, ———→	and Domitian might then appear to have offered a salary in order to
when in fact he had refused to retain him. ←———	induce (bribe) Agricola to leave service and choose retirement,

Contradictory injunctions, attitudes, or policies, then, are—at a much higher level of complexity—akin to epigrams and jokes in that all alike embody political irrationality in dislocated thought sequences that are at once amusing as well as alarming. In their traplike involution passages like these are large-scale *griphoi* (above, p. 60) or loops on which cause and effect run in two directions at once.

Augustus occasionally left the senate in anger at awkward attempts by senators at free speech (*Aug.* 54) and was not averse to intricate deception of his own. On one occasion he had announced in the senate his intention of abandoning power; his true purpose was to win for the regime an appearance of popular approval, and Dio's paragraph tracing the layers of intention and pretense is a tour de force of its kind.

> While Augustus was reading his speech the senators had varied feelings. A few knew his real intention and applauded him loudly. Of the rest, some were suspicious of his words, others believed them, and both were surprised equally, the one group at his cleverness, the other at his decision. And both were displeased, the former at his scheming, the latter at his change of mind. For there were some who hated the democratic constitution as a cause of strife, were pleased at the new government, and took delight in Caesar. Hence, though they were variously affected by his announcement, their views were the same. On the one hand, those who believed what he said could not show their pleasure—those who wished to do so being restrained by their fear, the others by their hope—and those, on the other hand, who did not believe what he said did not dare accuse him or expose his insincerity—some because they were afraid, others because they did not want to do so. Hence all the doubters either were compelled or pretended to believe him. As for praising him, some had no courage, others no desire to do that. On the contrary, both as he was reading and afterward they kept shouting out for monarchy, until they forced him, of course, to take absolute power. (53.11)

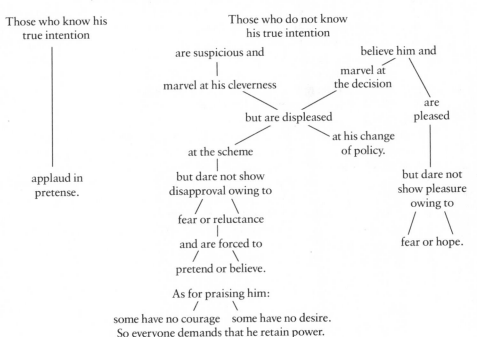

III

Formal contradiction was seen by the historians as a specific symptom of repression, and they detected yet another instance of it in an important political ritual that had in fact been created by the anomaly of the emperor's position while at the same time helping to veil it. The situation was again a classic catch-22: the emperor expressed his supremacy through *clementia* and received the title *civilis* for it.[34] Suetonius concedes that the language of Tiberius could be *percivilis* (*Tib.* 26.1, 28); he despised flattery and insisted that his authority be spoken of only in modest terms (27). Yet the complicated dialectic of power turns genuine forebearance also into hypocrisy. For though he patiently endured ugly rumors or abuse because (he said) in a free state speech and thought should be free (28), when Suetonius characterizes the liberty he encouraged as a "semblance" (30), even restraint is seen to be an assertion of power after all, since its premise is the princeps' absolute authority, always present and revealing "little by little the despot" (33).[35]

By the same token, claims to free speech on the part of his subjects are acts of submission. Tacitus can accordingly see public talk about candor as "the last form of flattery." Thus when Tiberius asked whether a decree honoring him had been proposed freely, its author assured him that it had and that he would act boldly even at the risk of offending the emperor (*Ann.* 1.8.4). In *Annals* 2.35.2 Gallus urges a policy that defers ostentatiously to the emperor's authority, "because Piso had gotten in first with a proposal for pretended independence." Tiberius listened in silence as the debate raged. By reverse logic the servility lies precisely in the boldness, as the emperor's power makes clemency an equivalent of repression. Tacitus is prepared to use this as material for broad farce. Claudius, Messalina, and Vitellius are all moved by the eloquent self-defense of Asiaticus. "Wiping away her tears," Messalina urged Vitellius not to allow him to escape; Vitellius, too, "weeping copiously" suggested that in the light of Asiaticus' service and friendship he be allowed free choice of the mode of death, and Claudius' official decision "reflected just that clemency" (*Ann.* 11.2.2–3).

Seneca's reiteration of the connection between clemency and great power (*Clem.* 1.1.2–3; 3.3; 5; 7.3; 11.2; 17.3; 20.3) seems in part to be an anxious effort to prevent a virtue from turning nasty in the hands of someone like Nero. Tacitus notes that Nero's own talk about clemency was the work of Seneca (*Ann.* 13.11.2). Though Seneca envisages an idealized bond of affection and trust between ruler and ruled, considerations of realpolitik come into view as well. For one thing, clemency keeps the ruler safer because the hatred caused by outright terror is dangerous (*Clem.* 1.8.6, 12.3; 13; 26). Yet leniency should not be taken too far either; a measure of fear helps safeguard the ruler's authority (1.12.4), and since it does so by calling his power to mind, we are again made aware of the complex crosscurrents at work and the potential for deception. When Seneca tells Nero *tibi enim parcis cum videris alteri parcere* (1.5.1) he is saying "when you *are seen* to be merciful to another you are merciful to yourself" and not "when you *seem* to be merciful . . ." That is to say, he is not recommending pretense, though clemency is ultimately useful for the ruler's own security because of the sobering exercise of power it implies whether sincere or not. "A ruler's power is so evident that he does not need to prove it by harming another" (1.21.1); he exercises it by "mercy," and in the same section Seneca gives the game away by treating clemency as a form of revenge and contempt at the expense of one's enemies. It may be true that armed force is a mere "ornament for a mild ruler because he needs none" (1.13.5)—yet that is true because he *has* armed force; "both king and tyrant are protected by arms, the one to preserve peace [through the implicit threat], the other to create [open] fear" (1.12.3).

Subsequent events bore out any fears Seneca may have had, for Nero and the senate did turn clemency into a species of brutality (*Ann.* 14.48–49). When a praetor was accused of insulting the emperor and faced death by scourging, Thrasea Paetus successfully argued for exile, pointing out (ironically?) that such a demonstration of official mercy would force its beneficiary to live out a more wretched life. When Nero was then consulted he complained that the harsher penalty was proper, but had it been assessed by the senate he would have exercised clemency. As it was, he would not interfere and the senate was free to acquit the criminal. The link in political logic between clemency and threat is brought out by both parties' treatment of the latter as a premise for the former. The absurdity to which this could lead comes out again in cases in which—after the victim's death—the emperor professes that he had intended all along to offer clemency (*Ann.* 15.35.3, 3.50.2, 2.31.3; Dio 62.14). The actual identity of clemency and sentence of death is again the point of an anecdote about Vitellius. He had a moneylender who was paying him a morning call suddenly condemned, then as he was being led away called him back and amid general praise for clemency ordered him executed on the spot (*Vit.* 14.2; cf. *Dom.* 11; Plut. *Sulla* 10.1).

The larger political fact to which the logic of clemency points is that once legal restraints have been removed by absolute power, anything less than absolute brutality can be construed as a humane favor to the victim, who as a result is implicitly put in the wrong as the recipient of mercy, even when it is posthumous. In this rationalization of implicit terror as an act of kindness (most recently familiar as a factor in the so-called Stockholm Syndrome) the victim cooperates, "understands," or sympathizes with whoever wields power. The principle of praising people for the vices they do not have (e.g., violence they graciously do not use; see also n. 38 below) is a more general form of the same thing. In the historians it is connected especially with the flattery elicited by threats from the emperor. The senate responded to Gaius' harsh words ("Tiberius told me not to be a friend of any of you and not to spare any of you," Dio 59.16.5) with fawning decrees and expressions of gratitude. "Panic about internal events had taken over the minds [of the senators], and they tried to find a remedy for it in flattery" (*Ann.* 4.74.1). A most striking case is Tiberius' report that Agrippina had killed herself on the second anniversary of Sejanus' fall. When he boasted that he had not had her hooked and thrown on the Gemonian Stairs, "the senate thanked him and voted to make an offering to Jupiter on the anniversary" (*Ann.* 6.25.1). Tiberius' report is a *statement* implicitly *commanding* and getting servile flattery (see n. 34), the flattery being itself again a stellar instance of praise for vices one does not have. Power veiled as restraint and servility veiled as assent interlock.

IV

This queerness in the way things work, these various guises taken by formal incoherence in political logic all contribute to the atmosphere of a society permeated finally as much by futility as by fear. The impression, of course, is a good deal exaggerated. Only a very small portion of Roman society was caught up in baffling contradictions, though at that level they were often real enough, even discounting the historians' bias. Tacitus draws attention to the peculiarly futile political climate with occasional direct apologies for the "tedium and depression" created by his story of "endless deaths" (*Ann.* 16.16; cf. 6.7.5, 4.32 and 33) or for the "same wrath of the gods, the same human insanity, the same excuses for crime" (*Hist.* 2.38.2).

The theme of futility takes added force from Tacitus' generally pessimistic view of human nature, in particular its capacity for wholly empty illusion: "as often happens with great lies, some swore that they were eyewitnesses [to what had never happened]" (*Hist.* 1.34.2). This is halfway between mendacity and illusion, and Tacitus detects the same quality again in the exploits of the false Agrippa, which in any case have the ingredients of a good story (*Ann.* 2.39–40). As rumors began to spread ("Agrippa lives!"), the imposter (actually a slave of the real Agrippa) was careful to be seen only at dusk, never close up or for any length of time. "But because truth is supported by direct evidence and by time to think, while lies feed on haste and doubt, he would always vanish after or appear before word spread that he was present [*sed quia veritas visu et mora, falsa festinatione et incertis valescunt, relinquebat famam aut praeveniebat*]." The tactic of avoiding close scrutiny is ordinary enough, but the snap of Tacitus' Latin makes this a political quip of a high order: "Agrippa" is never *here* but always *there,* somewhere *else,* managing to be on both sides of his own fame, going and coming (as the word order wittily suggests), but never really anywhere and thus always a faintly absurd empty presence. When excitement spread from Ostia to Rome, "Tiberius was worried about what to do: whether to crush the slave with military force or permit empty credulity to vanish in time." He is faced by political unreality real enough to worry about, and though the farcical side of the situation relates principally to human gullibility in general, it is tied as well directly to imperial politics. After the imposter had been captured, Tiberius asked him how he had become Agrippa, and his answer "is said to have been, 'The same way you became Caesar.'" The question is an obvious straight line, and the joke was perhaps current in Tiberius' day (and reused for the robber Bulla, Dio 77.10).

Someone who takes his political reality from not being present is an emblem of emptiness rather like the good plans "whose time is always past" (*Hist.* 1.39.1). Again, emperor and slave both in fraudulent roles are emblems of political vacuity much like Otho confessing that his treason makes it hard to say whether he is emperor or chief public enemy (*Hist.* 1.37.1). All of these cases bring out a peculiar dead space lying between opposites: serious/ludicrous, emperor/slave, legitimate/false. Tacitus had a keen eye for such neither-nor gaps and finds them elsewhere, for example, between war and peace or virtue and vice. The pattern is so pervasive that its effect is largely subliminal. Thus his report of a passing event like the death of Poppaea's infant is not notably compassionate or cruel, but simply bleak: the senate had voted elaborate celebrations for the birth of her daughter—"all in vain; she died in four months" (*Ann.* 15.23.3). After recording public thanksgiving, this time to celebrate the death of Octavia (a pathetic bride of death, *Ann.* 14.63.3), Tacitus again pauses in dismay at the monstrous aimlessness of political violence: "what finally is the point of mentioning such things?" (*Ann.* 14.64.3, 16.16).

But such general reflections do not come to anything like a formal theory about history. Tacitus' concern is with specifics of political life, and futility emerges as something we are aware of as a by-product of events that time and time again work at cross-purposes: self-defeating policies and strategies, institutionalized pretense, useless behavior. Either things seem empty of political or moral substance or they end in the paralysis so marked in Tiberius' political manner that it could be the subject of a popular joke. Because of his habit of announcing formal tours to the provinces and armies, making large-scale preparations nearly every year, permitting vows for his return but never in fact going anywhere, he was called "Callippides" after a Greek athlete who ran furiously in place without moving an inch (*Tib.* 38). Tacitus, too, picks up this theme of mad aimlessness: "Tiberius was uncertain about entering Rome or, because he had decided not to, he was pretending that he would" (*Ann.* 6.1.1). Dio remarks that under the circumstances people "did not know whether he was about to die or about to return to Rome" (58.6.5).

Aimlessness is a leitmotiv again in the lynching of Vitellius (*Hist.* 3.84.5). The tone is set as the emperor of Rome is paired dramatically with an unknown German soldier, who suddenly rushes into the mob and cuts off the ear of a tribune only to be killed himself on the spot. But despite this burst of furious activity, "whether he was attacking Vitellius, trying to end his torture, or assaulting the tribune—that was not clear." The remark that Vitellius' fate was so shocking that it precluded sympathy is not true if the soldier intended an act of mercy, and that makes a further depressing point about "pity": it could only take the form of attempted murder (cf. the implication of assassination as a "favor" to Nero, *Ner.* 36.2, *Ann.* 15.68.1, and of violence as an act of despairing kindness, *Agr.* 38.1, *Ann.* 12.51.3). The times are such that no one can say what things mean, and when Agrippina fell from power, she too was instantly deserted "except by a few women, it [again] not being clear whether they came out of friendship or hatred" (*Ann.* 13.19.1). *Annals* 6.50.3 is another case of the wry emptiness of this pattern. Proof that Tiberius *had* noticed unwanted medical attention was that he pretended *not* to have noticed, "it being uncertain whether he *didn't* show anger because he *did* feel it" (*incertum an offensus tantoque magis iram premens;* cf. Sall. *Historiae* 4.1: *perincertum stolidior an vanior,* with the twist that uncertainty here is between two bad possibilities).

The frequency of such patterns and their almost formulaic repertory of variations are a fair index of the importance Tacitus attached to them. The little catalogs assembled in the following pages can preserve in concentrated form the large-scale effect, though the timing in each case is lost and that is often a good part of the effect.

During the civil war Flavian troops arrested Julius Gratus on suspicion of dealing with his brother, who was serving with Otho and had himself been arrested by Othonian troops on suspicion of dealing with *his* brother (*Hist.* 2.26.1). (This has a striking parallel in Zinoviev, who tells of the leaders of two factions in Ibansk preparing dossiers on each other only to be *both* arrested.[36]) Things have a way of losing track of themselves, of making no difference, of finally coming to the same thing or to nothing at all. "The troops wanted to kill their leaders equally in success or in failure" (*Hist.* 4.36.1; 1.72; *Ann.* 2.2.4, 16.33.1); "whether he spoke or kept silent he was accused for what he said and for what he did not say" (*Ann.* 4.60.2); "he was destroyed not from friendship with Sejanus but by the equally dangerous hatred of Macro" (*Ann.* 6.29.3); "adulation is equally dangerous when it is too little and too much" (*Ann.* 4.17.1); Dolabella's honor increased as it was denied (*Ann.* 4.26.1); powerful lackeys of the emperor "never seem servile enough to their masters or free enough to us" (*Dialog.* 13.4). Tacitus has an especially keen eye for the uselessness of censorship. Once books are legal to possess, everyone forgets them (*Ann.* 14.50.2); "because discussion of the war was forbidden in Rome, those who would have spoken the truth had more— and less accurate—things to say about it" (*Hist.* 3.54.1; cf. 2.96.2; *Ann.* 4.35.5).

The pattern is especially useful for bringing out the muddle of sedition, a special sore point with Tacitus. Vocula faced the irrationality of a "double mutiny: some wanted him to return to camp, others refused to go back themselves" (*Hist.* 4.35.4). Unruly troops "made requests, but ones which it was impossible to refuse" (*Hist.* 4.46.4, imperative requests are the logical companions of unobeyable commands; cf. *Ann.* 14.14.4: "gifts from those who can order have the force of necessity"; the reverse logic of clemency belongs here too). Mobs act in the same way, "with equal fervor and on the very same day shouting demands for exactly opposite courses of action" (*Hist.* 1.32.1). Or, by the same token, when they all shout the same thing on cue they all do so with equal ignorance,[37] and *Annals* 1.25.2 brings out the absence of logical mediation between a mob's contradictory impulses: *murmur incertum, atrox clamor et repente quies; diversis animorum motibus pavebant terrebantque.*

The futility to which fear reduces its victims by doubling back on itself is the point of several formal antithetic epigrams: "the more they tried to hide their fear, the more obviously fearful they were" (*Hist.* 1.88.2); "they were afraid of having been afraid" (*Ann.* 4.70.2); "when Otho was afraid, he was feared" (*Hist.* 1.81.1). Absence of elementary ethical standards is a major motif in Tacitus' near burlesque account of the remarkable affair of Messalina's marriage to Silius. The commander of the praetorians could not be trusted since he was "equally ready for noble or base action" (*Ann.* 11.33), and in accordance with Messalina's "simultaneous feelings of desire and disdain" one of her lovers "had been taken in and kicked out in one and the same night" (36.3). Sejanus was a victim of the same dialectic (above, p. 110).

Not only does futility rise, as in these cases, from a gridlock of contradictory forces. It may also come from a vacuum of forces, an absence of any effective claim, decision, action, or policy. That effect is achieved in language through nicely placed negatives yielding wittily empty sentences. The technique was a familiar one. For example, seen from the perspective of the nobility, it was "an age when great loyalty [*pietas*] was to do *nothing* disloyal" (Sen. *Ad Marciam* 1.2); a slave "wanted to die for his master at a time when it was rare loyalty *not* to want one's master to die" (Sen. *Ben.* 3.25). Amid the images displayed at a funeral, "those of Cassius and Brutus were conspicuous for *not* being visible" (*Ann.* 3.76.2). "Galba did *not* so much possess virtues as *lack* vices" (*Hist.* 1.49.2);[38] Vitellius was reduced to "declining offers of help that were *not* being made" (*Hist.* 3.58.4); Caligula "would have all of Sulla's vices *without* any of his virtues" (*Ann.* 6.46.4); Poppaeus Sabinus' political successes were "*not* due to outstanding skill but to his adequacy—*nothing* more—to the job" (*Ann.* 6.39.3). Tiberius' policy was to select nonentities, "looking *neither* for outstanding virtue yet hating vice . . . and because of his hesitation finally assigning provinces to which he *never* intended to permit the nominees to go" (*Ann.* 1.80.2). So it was that "a province Aelius Lamia was *not* allowed to govern [*non permissa provincia*] increased his stature" (*Ann.* 6.27.2). Piso "can be called *neither* a private citizen since he has been proclaimed princeps *nor* can he be princeps if somebody else is" (*Hist.* 1.37.1). Acilia, Lucan's mother, "was ignored [by Nero]—*not* acquitted, *not* condemned" (*Ann.* 15.71.5). When Suetonius' Nero (47.3) can find at the end no one even to kill him, he realizes "that he has *neither* friend *nor* enemy" (a variant of "if one did not have an enemy, he would be killed by a friend," *Hist.* 1.2.3). After various measures were advanced for dealing with the flooding of the Tiber at last "Piso's proposal was accepted—that *nothing* be done" (*Ann.* 1.79.4); "the only remedy for treachery is to *ignore* it" (*Ann.* 14.6.1); "it is *not* as easy to decide what should have been done as it is to decide that what was done was the very *worst* that could have been done" (*Hist.* 2.39.2). Everyone went to meet Vitellius, "some from fear, many for flattery, others and soon everyone [only] so they would *not* be left behind when others were going" (*Hist.* 2.87.2). In the ambiguities of civil strife, "though they were *not* at war, they tried everything to attain peace" (*Hist.* 1.63.2) and "they did *not* even ask for peace when they had given up war" (*Hist.* 3.31.2; cf. 4.1.1; *Ann.* 1.50.4).

Piso's ill-starred reign ("he was an exile for a long time, Caesar for four days, and his hasty adoption gave him one advantage over his elder brother— he was killed first," *Hist.* 1.48.1) is the backdrop for some precepts of statecraft by Galba, ending with an epigram that catches the futility of power at Rome on a deeper level: "you are going to rule over men who can endure *neither* total slavery *nor* total freedom" (*Hist.* 1.16.4). This is meant to be a cool assessment of Roman politics along with a recommendation for balance and moderation, but it also unintentionally touches in a sly way on the senate's futility.

It is reasonable enough to make decisions from negative motives, but since Laco and Icelus have no alternative candidate, they have no policy: "Laco and Icelus agreed in supporting *not* so much anyone as anyone else [than Otho]" (*Hist.* 1.13.2). In his dullness the same Laco "*failed* to notice equally what was obvious and what was hidden" (*Hist.* 1.24.2); Vitellius was forced by false public adulation "to assume the title [of Augustus] as *uselessly* as he had earlier refused it," because as his modesty then was unreal, his authority now was false (*Hist.* 2.90.2); in the midst of a crisis "most men could do *nothing* but object to the suggestions of others" (*Hist.* 1.39.1); "as happens in that situation, all offered advice, *none* accepted danger" (*Hist.* 3.69.2); "*no* one knew, everyone was sure" (*Hist.* 1.35.1). When two proposals for vigorous action were presented to Valens, he rejected both "and by following a middle course was *neither* daring *nor* cautious" (*Hist.* 3.40.2); Claudius Apollinaris was a man "*neither* constant in loyalty *nor* firm in treason" (*Hist.* 3.57.1); one of Tiberius' victims found himself under house arrest for years, "*not* to prevent escape but to prevent death" (Dio 58.3.5). Octavia "was taken from life by fear of coming evils but was *not* yet at rest in death" (*Ann.* 14.64.1); military awards had become so common that "there was greater distinction in preserving peace" (*not* fighting) (*Ann.* 13.53.1); Tiberius was "feelingless and closed to the defendant, with *no* pity, *no* anger" (*Ann.* 3.15.2). There would be "*no* trouble from Claudius, who felt *neither* strong like *nor* dislike for anything that had *not* been ordered" (*Ann.* 12.3.2) and who "favored whatever prospective wife had been proposed last" (*Ann.* 12.1.2); he "gave *no* sign of human feeling—pleasure or hatred—at Messalina's death, *neither* when he saw those who rejoiced *nor* those who grieved" (*Ann.* 11.38.3). Agrippina "could give her son power but could *not* tolerate his having it" (*Ann.* 12.64.3).

At times the motif conditions the narrative on a larger scale, as it does notably in the implicit moral judgment running through Tacitus' portrayal of the absurdity and futility of the battles at Bedriacum (*Hist.* 2 and 3).

> Everything will shortly start again at the same place and will lead to disaster again. The future does not belong to either of the two antagonists, and whatever happens during this period is, in the final analysis, completely useless. . . . One sees then that civil wars are absurd wars in which things lose their sense; they breed each other and in this way are always their own negation.[39]

That is true again of Tacitus' brief and decidely jaundiced sketch of events on Corsica. The place was almost ruined by the rashness of its procurator, whose effort to help Vitellius simply out of hatred for Otho would not have been of any use even if it had succeeded. When he had executed a few opponents of his policy, the populace went over to Vitellius, but then realized the dangers of war, suddenly had a change of heart, assassinated the procurator along with his supporters, and took their heads to Otho—"who did *not* reward them, as Vitellius did *not* punish them, caught up as the Corsicans were in the brutal crimes of the time" (*Hist.* 2.16).

Many of the thumbnail sketches of politicians and generals (patterned on those of Sallust) are again written so as to leave a sense of great possibilities habitually coming to nothing (*Ann.* 4.52.4, 4.1.3). Otho's reputation, when all was said and done, was "as good as it was bad" (*Hist.* 2.50.1). The battle during which the Capitol was destroyed was "the most foul crime in Roman history," and one of the commanders who took part in the action was himself a veritable embodiment of the futility of it all: so sluggish that he seemed paralyzed in mind, "unable to speak or hear, unable to follow his own or others' plans, . . . vetoing what he had ordered, ordering what he had vetoed; soon, as happens in disaster, everyone gave orders, no one obeyed" (*Hist.* 3.73.1). The more formidable Mucianus was "notable [or just as well "notorious"] in success and in failure . . . once as near to exile as he was later to imperial power, a blend of luxury and industry, good nature and arrogance, good and evil methods; when at ease excessively self-indulgent, in the field highly self-disciplined, with a fine public and a bad private reputation . . . a man for whom it was easier to pass on than to hold power" (*Hist.* 1.10).

"Depending on mood, Titus Vinius was an evil or a good man with equal force"(*Hist.* 1.48.4). Petronius "slept through the day and lived at night . . . was carried to fame by idleness as others are by industry . . . after showing vigor as consul he reverted to vices or perhaps to imitations of them" (*Ann.* 16.18.2). The abrupt antitheses suggest talent that is self-defeating rather than versatile, and waste of potential is further underscored when such sketches are used as obituaries.

Everything is drawn into the overpowering master pattern. Even opposition to the prevailing order becomes in its own way a mirror image of fruitless action. Thrasea's withdrawal from political life was seen by the imperial court as systematic negation: "he regards public places as deserts, threatens his own exile" (*Ann.* 16.28.3), and "everywhere the public journal is carefully read to see what he has *not* done," (*Ann.* 16.22.3; cf. the senators who aimed at *not* understanding or *not* being understood or pretended *not* to know: *Ann.* 1.11.2–3, 6.50.5; *Hist.* 1.85.3). And Tacitus for his part concedes that there is something to this assessment, for while Thrasea's silent departure from the senate chamber "was dangerous to him, to others it was *not* the beginning of liberty" (*Ann.* 14.12.1). Dio puts the dilemma into an antithetic epigram: he left the senate because "he could *not* say what he would, and would *not* say what he could" (61.15.2). The peculiar fatuity of Roman society comes out best of all in the hint that at the highest levels even vice might not amount to anything: after effective public service Petronius "returned to a life of vice or—an imitation of it" (*Ann.* 16.18.2; fake virtue is less startling: "famous for virtue or—the appearance of virtue," *Ann.* 15.48.2; "fearing nothing or—pretending not to," *Ann.* 15.69.2). The vignette of Sallustius Crispus (*Ann.* 3.30) is a subtle variation. He was a mixture of luxury and vigor, "capable of great deeds, yet the more intense he was, the more sleepiness and sloth he displayed." His self-indulgence is evidently real enough, but when it is correlated to virtue not inversely but directly in this way, he too becomes a man famous for inertia—or its appearance. Both here and in the case of Petronius, pretended vice was perhaps a shrewd tactic for furthering aims (cf. *Ann.* 14.57.3). But though Tacitus appreciates this *virtus* for what it is, the final point of the paradoxical formula is lack of moral and political substance.

V

Roman politics thus dies the death of a thousand stabs, relentlessly punctured by each epigram or anecdote of negation cumulatively deflating coherence and integrity. The effect of the gradual rhetorical conditioning is akin to the effect of wit that works by anticlimax: "Why did the chicken cross the road? / To get to the other side"—that is to say, to no (particular) end at all. The amusing point is the pointlessness, the disparity between expectation set up by witty form and vacuous content which can be of great importance for historical insight. The technique has been given the somewhat pretentious but convenient name of "metajoking," a notion also recognized in ancient rhetorical theory as "suspension" followed by either climax or anticlimax (Quint. *Inst.* 9.2.22–23).[40] The prize case is Martial 1.32, where anticlimax is reinforced by a formally precise loop:

> No amo te, Sabidi, nec possum dicere quare:
> Hoc tantum possum dicere: non amo te.[41]

Pliny opens one of his letters with the same trick: "You haven't written to me for a long time. You say that you have nothing to write—well, then, write that: that you have nothing to write" (*Ep.* 1.11).

Deflationary banality of this kind is the politically serious point of a joke about Claudius handing down a decision in one case: "I decide for those who told the truth" (*Claud.* 15.3). Jesting is ordinarily set apart from serious talk precisely by the absurd implications it would have if it were taken seriously. Real life thus provides the norm which makes the exception amusing, and so when Claudius' decision is treated as fact, its genial emptiness represents a specifically deflated political reality.

Suetonius has another example of political metajoking. A Knight who had annoyed Caligula was sent by him to Ptolemy carrying this message: "Don't do anything good or bad to the man I have sent to you with this message" (*Calig.* 55.1). Banality is coupled to expectation of violence which transforms the anticlimax into queer climax after all. Metajoking thus becomes a sinister exercise of what we might now call "metacruelty." For what is interesting about this again is the implicit logic: cruelty is an expected norm that makes (stories of) metacruelty possible, as routine wit is the presupposition of metawit. The norm in this case is set by Dio's report that Nero would send official dispatches consisting of brief instructions like "Kill this man" or "This man is dead" (62.11). The underlying logic is illustrated by R. Smullgan.[42] If I promise to fool somone on 1 April and never carry out my threat, I have nevertheless carried it out because he has been fooled into doubly painful expectation of being fooled. Dio mentions another, still more striking example. Domitian gave a dinner party in a room set up as a tomb, his guests were attended by waiters painted demonic black, and when they returned home their already considerable anxiety became panic when imperial messengers arrived—to deliver prizes (67.9). When Nero and Gaius called urgent meetings at night, the senators apparently did not themselves feel threatened, but if they were not unpleasantly relieved they must have been unpleasantly surprised to learn that Nero had found a way to improve the water organ (Dio 63.26.4) and that Gaius wanted to dance (59.5.5; cf. *Ann.* 15.69.3)

These silly situations depend in a fairly precise way on logic common to aimless power and pointless wit. In the absence of any normal purpose, form becomes its own empty content or doubles back on itself as its own end. Like Petronius' shameful sham vices substituting for real ones, such practical jokes make something doubly cruel after all happen because nothing happens. And insofar as linking expected brutality with unexpected restraint has close formal affinities to the rhetorical pair climax/anticlimax, the distinctively banal wit of the anecdotes is another instance of rhetorical technique furnishing categories for insight into (and perhaps invention of) history.

Real climax and real extravagance are naturally much more prominent in the portrayal of irrationality. Excess, in fact, was a major motif in the literature of the time, connected by Erich Burck with the extreme violence that had become a factor in the recurrent crises of political legitimacy at Rome.[43] His essay on Roman mannerism opens with a nightmarish account of the firebombing of Hamburg during World War II, and actual exercise of "total" power in the modern world may well resemble ancient rhetorical inflation of political reality into absolute evil.[44] Thus a remark of David Rousset's on the implications of absolute power in connection with concentration camps ("normal men don't know that everything is possible") has striking Roman echoes.[45] "Remember, I can do anything I want and to anybody" (*Calig.* 29.1); "no emperor has yet realized what he could do" (*Ner.* 37.3). "This is why savagery [*saevitia*] is most abominable: first it goes beyond customary limits, then beyond human limits . . . to reach insanity" (Sen. *Clem.* 1.25.2), and aggression is most dangerous when it has full power to realize itself (*De ira* 3.16.2).[46] Nero's dictum is embedded in some highly charged rhetoric of Suetonius' own about how he was "neither selective nor restrained in executing anybody for anything," how he thought about feeding live victims to some kind of Egyptian "monster" and about wiping out what was left of the senatorial class. Boggling rhetorical surfeit of violence is a common theme: Vitellius enjoying the stench of corpses (*Vit.* 10.3), Hannibal gazing with delight into a pit full of blood (Sen. *De ira* 2.5.4), or Caesar taking dinner in full view of a carpet of rotting bodies (Lucan 7.792–94) and picking his way over the battlefield, personally applying first aid to those in danger of hemorrhaging to death (565–67; since he apparently does this to get the last bit of violence out of his men, the moral effect is like that of the combats between physically handicapped contestants staged by Caligula).

Hannah Arendt has suggested that the sheer scale of crimes may be designed to "render all punishments provided by the legal system inadequate and absurd," and shatter normal reality so that protest or resistance is impossible.[47] It is doubtful whether anything quite so subtle is often a specific reason for atrocity even in modern politics. But rhetorical hyperbole does help the Roman historians draw attention to a similar effect from overloading the legal system through crime. Nero's crimes finally "went beyond protest" (*Ann.* 14.11.30), and *Histories* 3.84.5 is a psychological version of the insight that terror de-moralizes men by destroying the moral standards binding them together: Vitellius' fate was so shocking that it excluded sympathy.

The historians' own narrative frequently courts unbelievability as a political phenomenon in its own right. *Feritas* in Seneca's *De ira* approaches the concept of brutality without aim beyond itself and verging on nihilism (victims are typically innocent).[48] An anecdote at 1.18.3 is a fine example of how this is tied to wit. A soldier returning from leave without his comrade is instantly sentenced to death by Piso on suspicion of murder. (Piso is "free from many vices but perverse in taking ruthlessness for toughness"). No time is permitted for investigation of the facts, and as execution is about to be carried out, the missing soldier appears. The centurion naturally halts proceedings to spread the good news, but Piso orders execution "both of the one who hadn't killed and of the one who wasn't dead. . . . Because one man proved to be innocent, two were to die. And then Piso added a third by ordering the centurion's execution too, so that three were to die on the spot because one was—innocent." The mad logic of the situation is brought out by the crazy wittiness of Seneca's own telling of what is in fact a good story as well as an extravagant moral lesson.

Spectacular frightfulness of this kind establishes the general proportions of irrationality which make cases of banal malice all the more disconcerting by anticlimax. Arendt has connected the notion of the banality of evil chiefly with routine bureaucracy,[49] and so the cruelty of the emperors' viciously harmless practical joking does not exactly fit her use of the term. But distinct species may belong to one larger genus. Anecdotes especially about Caligula's casual, domesticated brutality come very close to Arendt's banality (e.g., his good day at the office condemning forty defendants on various charges with one efficient sentence). Elaborate official pranks, on the other hand, and Nero's cool assessment of his mother's corpse fit less well. Still, all such stories do fall under a broader category of "monstrous insensitivity," whether the accent is on the banality of the terror or on the extravagance in the banality. Arendt's term, too, is understated overstatement—the banality is beyond comprehension—and Veyne's notion of "expressivity" (above, chap. 4, n. 15) unites the two extremes of blasé indifference and ostentatious brutality.

Caligula's own word for his behavior (*adiatrepsia,* translated with *verecundia* as "shamelessness" by Suetonius, *Calig.* 29.1) was probably a deliberately tough term, "shameless" in the sense of "cold-blooded, hard-nosed." But Claudius' ineptitude, pedantry, absentmindedness, and blindness (*ablepsia, Claud.* 39.1) made him a special case for the historians on this score. Some of Arendt's remarks on the casual *irrelevance* rather than frightfulness typical of Adolph Eichmann's thinking are curiously appropriate to Claudius as well.

> He was not stupid. It was sheer thoughtlessness—something by no means identical with stupidity—that predisposed him to become one of the greatest

criminals of that period. And if this is "banal" and even funny, if with the best
will in the world one cannot extract any diabolical or demonic profundity from
Eichmann, that is still far from calling it commonplace. It surely cannot be so
common that a man facing death, and, moreover, standing beneath the gallows,
should be able to think of nothing but what he has heard at funerals all his
life.[50]

The reference is to the "grotesque silliness" of Eichmann's last words: after
declaring that he did not believe in life after death he assured the witnesses
that "they would all meet again."[51] In Arendt's words, "he forgot that this was
his own funeral"—an admirably Tacitean or Suetonian scene, and one that in
its absurd heedlessness of what is at stake is in a way analogous to the unintended galgenhumor in the anecdote about Claudius making official appointments with people he had condemned to death on the previous day and
wondering why they were sleeping late when they did not appear (*Claud.*
39.1).

The connection between Claudius and Eichmann is, of course, historically
remote, to say the least, and the value of large-scale comparisons in any case
lies in establishing differences. Though at this level similarities are too imprecise to be of much use, the parallel between the two anecdotes can furnish a
larger context for seeing what is distinctive about irrationality and about funniness more generally as categories in ancient historiography.

The banality of Eichmann's last words is that of a man so conditioned to
unthinking routine that he cannot see even his own death as out of the ordinary. Two of his traits in particular—mendacious detachment from normal
reality and astonishingly inconsequential thinking—are traced by Arendt to
the broader political climate, specifically the high value placed on performing
duty imposed by an all-encompassing political system. That, in fact, was the
core of Eichmann's defense: "What is there to 'admit'?"[52] Hence, though
(again exactly like Claudius) he can be made out to be both monster and
clown, he represents norms no longer moral in an ordinary sense but political
or ideological and, more specifically, "totalitarian."

Needless to say, these distinctions are not clean, totalitarianism in particular being a notably imprecise term,[53] but for our purposes one feature often
associated with it is of some use: absorption of ordinary moral norms in political norms resting on theoretical considerations. When this takes extreme
form, it tends to invade the private sphere and destroy its distinctive values.
Tension between the two is, of course, in one degree or another a factor in all
societies. In the ancient world, too, morality was politicized in that the com-
munity was regarded as the natural setting for virtue. Romans in particular
had a strong sense of institutional values and commonly enough were prepared to subordinate other obligations to them. But morality was not thought

of in any rigorous way as a mere aspect of the political system, and philosophy reinforced the distinction. The Stoics saw the threat posed by official norms to individual integrity and exploited the difference between them in opposing the emperor. The overlap comes out again in a political point being made through moral resistance, still, the political point lies precisely in the moral resistance. And imperial policy for its part was not made in the light of the kind of abstract, secular laws governing social life that in recent centuries have given support to the notion of autonomous, omnicompetent political reality (Hobbes' concept of the mighty Leviathan, Adam Smith's invisible hand, Hegelian and Marxist laws of history).

Irrationality in the eyes of the Roman historians, accordingly, is an occasion for fairly direct, uncomplicated moral indignation. Claudius' matter-of-fact demeanor seems odd because it is so manifestly wrong in a personal way as well as inept. Eichmann's seems odd because it is so normal—eccentric, but in the light of all-encompassing political principles, not wrong.

Caligula's "I can do anything I want and to anybody" *(omnia mihi et in omnes licere)* is another case in point. It is not a principle of value-free totalitarian politics nor is it a general Hobbesian behavioral axiom about "wanting everything to be allowed to oneself alone" *(omnia licere sibi soli vult,* Hobbes *De cive* I.4). The formal similarities in both cases are striking enough, but what they bring out is the difference of Suetonius' view: Caligula's claim is an ethically revealing remark made to his grandmother about what he is capable of doing with power as an individual moral agent, not as an embodiment of political theory. By the same token, Sallust's epigram on Catiline as *appetens alieni et sui profusus (Cat.* 5.5) marks incongruity in one man's character pointing to wider moral confusion. In the eighteenth century, on the other hand, Mandeville cites this passage from Sallust to show how the coexistence of avarice and prodigality exemplifies the theoretical axiom that "the best of Virtues want the Assistance of the Worst of Vices." Here incoherence is not an obvious moral problem; instead, contradictory qualities are normal corollaries of each other and indispensable to a social order in which public benefits are fostered by private vices.

Tacitus' "arrogant modesty" differs from Mandeville's "noble Sin" of prodigality in the same way, disorder deplored by the first oxymoron being described as higher level order by the second.[54] What Tacitus objects to is Tiberius' politely excusing senators from doing what he can forbid or order them to do. Indicative is imperative, and so Tacitus again detects absurdity in the use of imperial power. But if the arrogance is exercise of power on which political order in general depends, the paradox comes closer to Mandeville's "noble Sin" and is then not a matter of mere hypocrisy but a political imperative, though Tacitus "cannot resist the temptation [wittily] to pervert by his [moral] interpretation a [political] virtue to which Tiberius could and did lay claim."[55]

This contrast is what accounts for the unmistakably different bearing of
the anecdotes on Claudius and Eichmann as well. On the one side is a paradigm of individual irrationality as measured by moral criteria that seem self-
evident. On the other is a paradigm of irrationality as abstract political procedure to which moral criteria seem irrelevant.

> There are crimes of passion and crimes of logic. The boundary between them is
> not clearly defined . . . We are living in the era of premeditation and the perfect
> crime. . . . This is not the place for indignation. . . . One might think that a
> period which, in a space of fifty years, uproots, enslaves, or kills seventy million
> human beings, should be condemned out of hand. But its culpability must still
> be understood. In more ingenuous times, when the tyrant razed cities for his
> own greater glory, when the slave chained to the conqueror's chariot was
> dragged through the rejoicing streets, when enemies were thrown to the wild
> beasts in front of the assmbled people, the mind did not reel before such una-
> bashed crimes, and judgment remained unclouded. But slave camps under the
> flag of freedom, massacres justified by philanthropy or by a taste for the super-
> human, in one sense cripple judgment.[56]

Camus's crimes of passion could be judged uncloudedly because they still fell
within the orbit of commonsense moral norms, as crimes of logic do not. And
it is their "ingenuous" measurability that is embodied in the tendency of the
historians of the early Roman empire to think more biographically and morally in terms of queer people than ideologically in terms of queer systems.[57]

NOTES

SELECTED BIBLIOGRAPHY

INDEX

INDEX OF PASSAGES CITED

Notes

Introduction

1. F. R. D. Goodyear, *The Annals of Tacitus, Books 1–6* (Cambridge, 1981), vol. 2, ad loc. E. Koestermann, *Annalen I, Buch 1–3* (Heidelberg, 1963), ad loc. For a general discussion of insinuation see R. Devlin, "Tacitus and Techniques of Insidious Suggestion," *Antichthon* 17 (1983): 64–95.

2. W. Booth, *A Rhetoric of Irony* (Chicago and London, 1974), 47–86.

3. "The Historian Servilius Nonianus," *Hermes* 92 (1964): 421.

4. R. Saller, "Anecdotes as Historical Evidence for the Principate," *Greece and Rome* 27 (1980): 69–83.

5. *Semantic Mechanisms of Humor* (Dordrecht, Boston, and Lancaster, 1985), 102.

6. M. Griffin, *Seneca, a Philosopher in Politics* (Oxford, 1976), 416.

7. T. Jerome, *Aspects of the Study of Roman History* (New York and London, 1923), 54, italics added.

8. H. Willrich, "Caligula," *Klio* 3 (1903): 461.

9. E.g., a set of stories told about Caligula. According to Suetonius he matched scruffy animals against overage gladiators and had respectable citizens with conspicuous handicaps stage "playful" combat which the spectators were forced to watch in the broiling sun (*Calig.* 26.5). He cut costs by feeding convicts in place of cattle to animals used in the arena (27.1). In Dio (59.10) he forces many people of relatively high status who have squandered their property to fight and die in gladiatorial combats. Moreover, during a shortage of criminals sentenced to the beasts, he orders spectators of the lower class near the stands to be used instead. To prevent any outcry he has their tongues cut out first. The special handicap games, which begin to look tame in comparison with these incidents, are probably not sheer fiction, but the distinction between fact and witty invention is breaking down. On another occasion Gaius made unsuccessful contestants literally eat their words (*Calig.* 20), and later Domitian matched women and dwarfs in combat (Dio 67.8.4; cf. *Dom.* 4.1). Insofar as these stories of brutality are linked in the taste of the time to entertainment, they in effect serve as enacted "sick humor" (*Calig.* 26.5 corresponds exactly to a joke current some years ago: "Hire the handicapped, they're fun to watch"). Grim humor is a species recognized by the rhetoricians (Demetrius *On Style* 130, 152). Suetonius remarks that Gaius did match savage language with savage deeds (29.1, 32.1), and the opposition reciprocated with ferocious jokes overlapping with his actual deeds.

10. See below, chap. 4, n. 13; B. Baldwin, "Nero and His Mother's Corpse," *Mnemosyne* 32 (1979): 380. For the principle of "a search for ambiguity between the imaginary and the real" in spectacles at Rome, see R. Auguet, *Cruelty and Civilization: The Roman Games* (Woking and London, 1972), 103–6. Actual deaths during

dramatic performances, for example, turned theater back into real life while still remaining theater. Such "reality in the second degree" is implicit also in Tacitus' concept of sham as a major political phenomenon, e.g., in Petronius' "life of vice—or an imitation of it" (*Ann.* 16.18.2). Rhetoric naturally has a key role in such a house of mirrors, and a modern reader will inevitably think of problems of political reality currently much discussed in connection with the "media"—a mechanized equivalent of both rhetoric and spectacle.

11. For a recent discussion, B. Manuwald, *Cassius Dio und Augustus,* Palingenesia 14 (Wiesbaden, 1979).

12. P. Gay, *The Enlightenment: An Interpretation,* vol. 1 (New York, 1966), 16.

13. *Politics, Language and Time* (New York, 1971), 19.

14. Cf. Pöschl's remarks on "das irrationale Moment" and "die Dämonie der politischen Welt" in "Der historiker Tacitus," in *Tacitus,* ed. V. Pöschl, Wege der Forschung (Darmstadt, 1969), 167, 174–75. Political irrationality, of course, is in the eye of the beholder. In the Roman historians it is whatever seems politically foolish or morally improper by (roughly) republican standards.

Chapter I. Ludibrium *and Political Wit*

1. An anecdote in Plutarch (*Comparison of Demosthenes and Cicero* 1.5) hinges on the same dual sense of "funny." When Cicero (consul at the time) aroused laughter at Stoic paradoxes in court against Cato, Cato's retort was, "How funny a consul we have!" i.e., *geloios* = "clever/amusing" and "silly/unseemly." Cf. "consular buffoon" *(consularis scurra)* in Macrobius *Saturnalia* 2.1.12.

2. Cf. O. Seel, *Römertum und Latinität* (Stuttgart, 1964), 211–45 (chap. entitled "Römische Antithetik"); and 245–82 for pervasive tension between opposites and awareness of incongruity as part of the "Morphologie des Römertums." "Preservation of what is contradictory and opposed, rejection of systematic, conceptual simplifications and single meanings and, instead of that, desire to endure tension . . . a combination of pride and irony directed at oneself, of strong belief and sarcasm, of pomp and satire [all of this] was part of the intellectual household of Roman culture from the beginning. The unclear situation and ambiguity of the dying Republic and of the Principate greatly increased this state of affairs because of their conceptual and programmatic vagueness" (260, my translation). H. Peter, "Die Literatur der Witzworte in Rom und die geflügelten Worte im Munde Caesars," *Neue Jahrbücher für Philologie und Paedagogik* 155 (1897): 853–60, treats the role of wit in Roman politics and the problems of historical authenticity that go with it.

3. A. Wallace-Hadrill, *Suetonius* (London, 1983), 166.

4. Ibid., 10.

5. For climactic anecdotes that bare the character of an emperor cf. E. Cizek, *Structures et idéologies dans "Les vies des douz Césars" de Suétone* (Paris, 1977), 40–41, 124, 198; W. Steidle, *Sueton und die antike biographie,* Zetemata, 1, (Munich, 1951), 84.

6. B. Baldwin, *Suetonius* (Amsterdam, 1983), 325–78, esp. 337 on Suetonius' political views; for possible criticism of Hadrian, 51. Baldwin notes that Tacitus' decision to postpone treatment of Nerva and Trajan until his old age may "without utter cynicism" be taken to ensure that he would have an old age. "Suetonius Tranquillus might have

felt the same way." See Baldwin, 511, on Suetonius' wit. For his political views and the relationship of biography to history see J. Gascou, *Suétone historien,* Bibliotheque des écoles françaises d'Athènes et de Rome, 255 (Rome, 1984), 343–800. For a favorable assessment of Suetonius' style see R. Lounsbury, *The Arts of Suetonius,* American University Studies, Series XVII, Classical Languages and Literature, vol. 3 (New York, 1987).

7. J. Vogt, "Tacitus und die Unparteilichkeit des Historikers," in *Prinzipat und Freiheit,* ed. R. Klein, Wege der Forschung (Darmstadt, 1969), 373.

8. A. Lintott, *Violence in Republican Rome* (Oxford, 1968), 6; for the censoriousness and frankness of ancient societies see P. Veyne, "Le folklore à Rome," *Latomus* 42 (1983): 3–30; for public cruelty *(ludibrium)* as a form of popular sarcasm, ibid., 16.

9. For the shifting application of these stages to literary history, R. Janko, *Aristotle on Comedy* (London, 1984), 244.

10. *Prolegomena de comoedia,* fasc. 1A, ed. W. J. W. Koster, (Groningen, 1975), 40; cf. 11, 26, 27.

11. C. Mendell, "Martial and the Satiric Epigram," *Classical Philology* 17 (1922): 18. Cf. Plut. *Cato Minor* 21.5 for Cicero's use of Stoic paradoxes as an occasion for joking to raise a laugh in court. In *De finibus* 4.74 Cicero dismisses the paradoxes as mere *verborum praestigiae;* Seneca (*De beneficiis* 7.4.7 and *Epistulae* 48.7) discusses Stoic dialectic as joking.

12. Janko, *Aristotle on Comedy,* 36. For a collection of passages on the etiquette of wit, M. Grant, *The Ancient Rhetorical Theories of the Laughable,* University of Wisconsin Studies in Language and Literature, 21 (Madison, 1924), 76.

13. K. Heldmann, *Antike Theorien über Entwicklung und Verfall der Redekunst,* Zetemata, 77 (Munich, 1982), 179.

14. Ibid., 195.

15. "[There was a] decline of political philosophy from assassination of a dictator to mere gasconade, for after the Ides of March it was not philosophers who slew autocrats, but soldiers, palace flunkeys, even women" (Baldwin, *Suetonius,* 334).

16. Cf. the discussion in Koestermann, *Annalen I, Buch 1–3,* ad loc. On a first reading, as part of the first sentence in the section, *dissimulatio* is naturally taken in a bad sense. As the account proceeds it also takes on a positive sense.

17. Seel, *Römertum und Latinität,* 230, notes a similar effect in a speech of Catiline's that represents *Sallust's* own view: "Precisely this diabolical distortion of truth—so that between truth and lie a difference can no longer be detected—lends Sallust's style its peculiar inner vibration."

18. R. Syme, *Tacitus* (Oxford, 1958), 2:563.

19. Gibbon's celebrated Tacitean tricolon on religion is similarly imprecise in fact, amusing in form, and literally true only at a higher order of political logic where public consensus may well be the sum of gullibility, skepticism, and cynicism: "The various modes of worship which prevailed in the Roman world were all considered by the people as equally true, by the philosopher as equally false, and by the magistrate as equally useful" (*The History of the Decline and Fall of the Roman Empire,* ed. J. B. Bury [New York, 1914], vol. 1, chap. 2, 29). Absurd absentmindedness is again a theme in Messalina's fall. When Silius has almost made off with Claudius' wife (and throne), Narcissus asks the emperor in exasperation, "Haven't you heard about your

divorce? Everybody else has!" (*Ann.* 11.30.2). "It is said," Tacitus adds, that "in panic he kept asking whether he was [still] emperor and Silius a private citizen" (31.1). In view of current methods of succession the question is not unreasonable, but "Am I emperor or is he?" does have the sound of an unsympathetic jest.

20. D. Flach, *Tacitus in der Tradition der antiken Geschichtsschreibung,* Hypomnemata, 39 (Göttingen, 1973), 52–68; 180.

Chapter II. Antithetic Epigrams

1. G. Kennedy, *New Testament Interpretation through Rhetorical Criticism* (Chapel Hill, N.C., and London, 1984), 3.

2. R. Syme, *Ten Studies in Tacitus* (Oxford, 1970), 10, 18, 137: Tacitus is "fierce, gloomy . . . penetrating, ferocious . . . austere." See B. R. Voss, *Der pointierte Stil des Tacitus* (Münster, 1963), 12, for the aggressive tone of the pointed style. For the large component of violent language in Tacitus' vocabulary see B. Walker, *The Annals of Tacitus,* 2d ed., (Manchester, 1960), 62.

3. For the psychological dynamics that create solidarity between joke teller and audience against the butt of a tendentious joke see A. Richlin, *The Garden of Priapus* (New Haven, Conn., and London, 1983), 60. For the technique of "hidden co-optation" in political rhetoric (e.g., using "we") see R. Goodin, *Manipulatory Politics* (New Haven, Conn., and London, 1980), 105. Plutarch (*Quaestiones convivales* 2.631e) observes the same phenomenon: when a joke is told at the expense of one member of a group, those who laugh ally themselves with the teller hubristically against the victim. Cf. Cic. *De or.* 2.236: "It is clearly part of a speaker's job to raise a laugh . . . because amusement itself wins the jester good will [*benevolentiam*]." Demetrius *On Style* 222 quotes Theophrastus' advice to "leave some things for the hearer to work out. When he gets what you have not said, he will be not only your hearer but your witness and more sympathetic. He is flattered by having a chance to use his brain." Cf. Plut. *Quaest. conv.* 631e (also quoting Theophrastus): "a joke is concealed criticism of a fault, hence the hearer adds to the innuendo by himself what is missing, since he knows it and believes it." Booth, *Rhetoric of Irony,* 28, makes the same point about irony: "The author I infer behind the false words is my kind of man, because he enjoys playing with irony, because he assumes *my* capacity for dealing with it, and—most important—because he grants me a kind of wisdom."

4. Ch. Wirszubski, *Libertas as a Political Idea at Rome* (Cambridge, 1950), 160. For the conservatism of Tacitus' political ideals, J. Vogt, "Tacitus und die Unparteilichkeit des Historikers," in *Prinzipat und Freiheit,* ed. Klein, 379. His concept of liberty is nuanced because liberty is a vehicle for virtue and subject to its conditions (see also W. Jens, "Libertas bei Tacitus," ibid., 391–420).

For a Marxist evaluation of Tacitus' overtly "ruling class" code of *libertas* see G. de Ste. Croix, *The Class Struggle in the Ancient Greek World* (London, 1981), 366 (on *Ann.* 2.75.2: when Tiberius was present in court, decisions were not influenced by bribery or power, and this led to "concern for honesty but destruction of liberty"; cf. Tac. *Dial.* 381: the new oratory under the Principate is "better for the truth, the old oratory was better for eloquence"). At times Tacitus does permit imperialism to unmask itself. The Roman general Vocula calls for ruthless suppression of unrest; gentle measures simply lead to more trouble, for "now they are enemies because their slavery is light; when they are robbed and stripped they will be our friends" (*Hist.* 4.57.2). Tacitus himself endorses imperialism but also displays a certain ambivalence, and here "slavery" undercuts the integrity of "friendship." Tension between *libertas* and *servitium* is especially noticeable in the *Agricola* (e.g., cf. *Agr.* 13.1 to 14.1 on "slavery"). Agricola entertains an exiled Irish leader "under the guise of friendship for later use" and believes that if Ireland were occupied, Britain could be held more securely because "liberty would disappear from sight" (*Agr.* 24.3). It is difficult to suppose that Tacitus would put false language in the mouth of Agricola, but it is equally difficult to imagine that he was wholly insensitive to the cynical overtones of this, even if "liberty" simply means "independence" for Agricola and is therefore obviously undesirable from a Roman point of view. For some reflections on this issue in Tacitus see Syme, *Tacitus,* 2:527; and Seel, *Römertum und Latinität,* 270, for Roman political consciousness generally.

5. See F. Klinger "Beobachtungen über Sprache und Stil des Tacitus am Anfang des 13. Annalenbuches" in *Tacitus,* ed. Pöschl, 547, for the connection specifically between Tacitus' violation of expectation through disjointed syntax and the reader's awareness that history itself is unpredictable. Syme, *Tacitus:* "the Sallustian manner [used by Tacitus] corresponds to an organic necessity in Roman historiography (1:197) . . . verbal disharmonies reflect the complexities of history and all that is ambiguous in the behaviour of men (1:347)." On the relation of syntax to content see also Walker, *Annals of Tacitus,* 56; R. Martin, *Tacitus* (Berkeley and Los Angeles, 1981), 221. Peter Gay has an excellent general discussion of style in the writing of history with some reference to Tacitus in *Style in History* (New York, 1974), 3ff., 185ff.

6. Raskin, *Semantic Mechanisms of Humor,* 113, quotes a version of this as a joke ("She seems to have the best of everything, except manners") which he oddly ranks low in wit owing to absence of tension between codes ("scripts" in his terms). Sallust's judgment on Aurelia Orestilla makes the same point the other way around ("no good man ever praised anything about her except her beauty," *Catiline* 15.2). The idea that those with power may in fact be slaves is in the first instance a conceptual paradox (e.g., "Is there doubt about the slavery of those who accept the worst servitude through desire for money?" Cic. *Paradoxa stoicorum* 39), but its full force and truth come out when it is made into a epigram to violate expectation formally: "Otho acted like a slave to be—master" (*Hist.* 1.36.3). Sallust's judgment of Pompey has the same epigrammatic edge to it: "Pompey was moderate about everything else but—power" (*Hist.* 2, frag. 17), i.e., in a sense he was not moderate at all, since under the (implicit) code of authentic values genuine moderation is effective where it is needed most. Gay, *Style in History,* 4, touches on the three levels of rhetoric, fact, and judgment when he remarks that "style may be, for [the historian], an object of gratification, a vehicle of knowledge, or an instrument of diagnosis." S. Bastomsky, "Tacitus, *Agricola,* 5.3: More than an Epigram?" *Philologus* 126 (1982): 151–53, comments on the way in which the very form of epigrams can suggest the perversity of society by placing good and evil on the same level or by treating good as the cause of disaster, and he cites Syme's remark that a political work of the empire "should not carry its meaning on its face." For a connection between paradoxical modes of expression in general and perverted political reality see E. Lefèvre, "Die Bedeutung des Paradoxen in der römischen Literatur der frühen Kaiserzeit," *Poetica* 3 (1970): 82. H. Heubner, "Sprache, Stil und Sache bei Tacitus," *Gymnasium,* Beiheft 4 (1964): 136, discusses another case of tension

between two standards in the epigram at *Hist.* 1.5.2: *accessit Galbae vox pro re publica honesta, ipsi anceps.*

7. Pocock, *Politics, Language and Time,* 17. For the appropriateness of language analysis to historiography see 201: "[philosophy] is only one of the specialized intellectual activities which can be generated by discussion and exploration of the language in which the articulation of politics is carried on. Historiography is another."

8. I take this example from J. Whitfield, *Machiavelli* (New York, 1965), 98; and H. Pitkin, *Wittgenstein and Justice* (Berkeley, Los Angeles, and London, 1972), 308. The latter examines the logic of political language and ideas in terms of Wittgenstein's theory of language games.

9. M. Rose, *Parody//Meta-Fiction* (London, 1979), 171. For the other aspects of this analysis of parody see 21ff., 44, 109. Irony displays a similar structure: "The term irony generally describes a statement of an ambiguous character, which includes a code containing two (or more) messages, one of which is the message of the ironist to his 'initiated' audience, and the other the 'ironically meant' decoy message. In the parody the complex function of the dual meaning is sometimes matched by that of the dual text—and while the ironist may use parody to confuse his meaning, the parodist may also use various forms of irony. . . . Verbal irony may, however, be more cryptic, and dissimulative, than parody, which—through the quotation of another text—may create two distinct codes, in comparison to the usual combination of messages in the single code of the ironist. . . . The more specifically individual the preformed language used in the parodic work is, and the closer it can be identified with a certain person or group, the greater is the possibility of satirical criticism of its public" (51).

10. Ibid., 34, 115.

11. Ibid., 93. Reverse language or antilanguage as a tool for subverting norms is discussed by R. Fowler, "Anti-language in Fiction," in *Literature as Social Discourse* (London, 1981), 149. "Reversing the normal meanings of the words, the users of antilanguage address the norm society dialectically. The rogues' *law* only works, semantically, if the original meaning is not completely erased; that which is refused legitimation by your society is precisely that which receives honour and legitimation in ours. There are similar modern slang usages, e.g., *bad* = 'eminently appropriate or suitable; excellent, wonderful.' Such words become the sites of dialogue between society and anti-society." Fowler goes on to illustrate "dialogue between antithetical ideologies" with newspaper accounts of trials staged by the kidnappers of Aldo Moro. In the headline "MORO 'TRIAL'" the false use of "trial" is formally marked by quotation marks (i.e., "They make desolation and call it 'peace'" as opposed to "They call it a crime and do it"). "Language, as well as the courtroom, becomes the locus within which the norm society and the deviant group confront and negotiate. . . . Language here is working dialogically, each participant using language ironically and with acute consciousness of the alien character of the other. The essential feature is the antithetic logic of the relationship between an official and an unofficial voice: an unresolved, unmediated antithesis which preserves critical, dialogic openness." (158). For a more general discussion of antilanguage see M. Halliday, *Language as Social Semiotic* (London, 1978), 164–82.

12. Parody is thus another method for creating the contradiction that gives bite to epigrams and to wit generally. Kierkegaard is one of many who have traced wit to contradiction, and he cites an example directly pertinent to the structure of these two

epigrams of Tacitus. "When a woman seeks permission to establish herself as a public prostitute, this is comical. . . . To be refused permission to become something despicable is a contradiction. To be sure, if she receives permission, it is also comical, but the contradiction is different, namely, that the legal authority shows its impotence precisely when it shows its power: its power by giving permission, its impotence by not being able to make it permissible" (*Concluding Unscientific Postscript,* tran. D. Swanson and W. Lowrie [Princeton, 1941], 460). Denial of permission for what is not reasonably requested is the equivalent of Tacitus' irony about authority for what is not rightly authorized. And granting permission for what is not rightly allowed is incoherent for the same reason, i.e., the permission is an exercise of power that is in fact impotence, since power that allows the unallowable is sham even when official. Cf. the irony of *concessae voluptates* in *Ann.* 13.2.1, 12.2, 14.14.2, 14.21.3. Many of these features of irony and parody are discussed in Booth, *Rhetoric of Irony* chap. 1; for the framing effect, 238.

The underlying logic of epigrammatic irony has points of contact with the Marxist concept of contradiction as an effect of ideology and mystification on language (e.g., D. Turner, *Marxism and Christianity* [Oxford, 1983], 25–51). Turner stresses that ideological language is false in a subtle sense because in its own terms it is actually true. The occasional ambivalence of Tacitus' own talk about Roman imperialism fits the model nicely. "Where they make desolation, they speak of peace" (*Agr.* 30.4) is one statement within another: justification as well as rejection of Roman authority placed in the mouth of an anti-Roman by the Roman Tacitus. The contradiction in the statement itself is like that in a line from *Felix Holt* discussed by Turner: "You're told not to rail at your betters, if they be the devil himself." The first half sets terms in one frame ("betters"), the second in another, incompatible frame ("devil"). That is to say, "Those [in fact morally] worse [e.g., the devil] are nevertheless better [i.e., socially dominant]" = "[disorder] desolation is nevertheless [order] peace." As "desolation" subverts "peace," it unmasks the disorder behind Roman order. The subtle interplay among truth, lie, and illusion, then, lies in the way Roman talk of peace might well have been to a degree false consciousness (to stay with Marxist terms), i.e., genuine political unconsciousness of the consequences of pacification, much as the devil—as a figure of social authority—*is* a "better" for social inferiors. Hence, though what is unmasked by political epigrams in Roman historiography is generally treated as mere hypocrisy (propaganda), it also points to something that at a deeper level is ideology in a Marxist sense. "When read as a whole which encapsulates both readings, with the two interpretations allowed to oscillate within the phrase 'one's betters' . . . the sentence pulls off a certain kind of plausibility." (Turner, 44). What is more, it could also be a joke, and as a joke it would unmask the sense of "betters" as witty, antithetic epigrams do (see below, chap. 6, n. 16 for circular, self-referential wit). The witty social irony (contradiction) implicit in the English "betters" reappears in the Latin *boni,* which is overtly demystified when the blur in meaning caused by oscillation is resolved in plainer talk, e.g., *Hist.* 2.10.1: "in money, power, and character Vibius Crispus belonged more to the notable [*claros*] than to the good [*bonos*]," i.e., "social worth is nevertheless not true worth." "It is, then, the capacity of ideological language to sustain contradictory elements in this precarious tension with one another which represents its defeat of logic and its capacity, in spite of the internal contradictions which it sustains, to 'represent reality,' to 'normalize the irrational' (Turner, 44) . . .

the language of domination is a language which *exhibits* a dominative situation in the course of *obscuring* the dominative character of the situation from which it arises" (48). This second point was noticed by Epictetus in respect to imperial *grants* of *freedom* (see below, p. 105).

13. Heldmann, *Antike Theorien,* 280; A. Köhnken, "Das Problem der Ironie bei Tacitus," *Museum helveticum* 30 (1973): 32-50; Flach, *Tacitus in der Tradition,* 201-24.

14. The following discussion draws heavily on J. L. Austin, *Philosophical Papers* (Oxford, 1961), 220-39; Austin, *How to Do Things with Words* (Oxford, 1962); I. Berlin et al., *Essays on J. L. Austin* (Oxford, 1973), 69; 141; 160; Pitkin, *Wittgenstein and Justice,* 37; and J. Searle and D. Vanderveken, *Foundations of Illocutionary Logic* (Cambridge, 1985). Alternative ways of making a similar distinction between levels of political discourse are discussed by E. Vedung, *Political Reasoning,* tran. D. McCune (Beverly Hills, Calif., London, and New Dehli, 1982): function oriented analysis/content oriented analysis (41,113); intentionalist explanation/rational assessment (55); analytic language/object language (60). Analytic language provides a frame of reference that does with object language what the epigram permits Tacitus to do with official language: "They [the schemes embodied in analytic language] help us to order and clarify claims and reasons into more comprehensive patterns and to compare them and confront them with each other" (60). The antithetic epigram *is* itself an analytic technique in this sense.

15. Austin, *Do Things with Words,* 144.

16. B. Barry, *Political Argument* (London, 1965), 23.

17. Austin, *Do Things with Words,* 121.

18. L. W. Ferguson, "Locutionary and Illocutionary Acts," in Berlin et al., *Essays on Austin,* 172.

19. Austin, *Philosophical Papers,* 225.

20. Austin, *Do Things with Words,* 27.

21. Cf. *tamen* in *Ann.* 14.47.1. It is nonlinguistic expression that is pointless in Domitian's kiss of friendship for Agricola (*Agr.* 40.3) and Nero's kiss for Seneca (*Ann.* 14.56.3).

22. Austin, *Philosophical Papers,* 235.

23. Austin, *Do Things with Words,* 51, 136: it is like a null and void contract. "A speaker cannot both recommend that the hearer carry out a certain course of action and simultaneously complain under the same aspects that he will carry it out." (Searle and Vanderveken, *Illocutionary Logic,* 150). The rhetorical effect of Dio's characterization of Gaius' attitude (quoted below) is to make him do just that. For the logic of "I order you to disobey all orders" see ibid., 151, and below, pp. 104-7.

24. Austin, *Philosophical Papers,* 237. The two phases correspond to our two levels of fact and norm discussed above. Pocock, *Politics, Language and Time,* 18: "[political speech] invokes values, it summarizes information, it suppresses the inconvenient, it makes many kinds of statement and does so by means of formulations which can often convey several kinds of statement at once, while simultaneously diverting attention from others."

A. Danto's penetrating discussion of the nature of historical knowledge deals with the same issues from an epistemological point of view (*Narration and Knowledge* [New York, 1985], 160-81). To use his own example, "This man is putting a seed in a hole" is a strictly literal account of an event that we are more likely to describe by saying, "This man is planting a rose," though that is true only in the light of subsequent events (e.g., the seed actually comes up). In this sense the future affects (if it does not precisely cause) the past. The later appearance of roses makes the gardener actually to have planted roses and not merely to have put seeds in a hole, and it is the special function of narrative to bring out the larger temporal structures whose coherence gives events their significance. (The argument is in effect an open-ended version of Herodotus' "count no man happy until he is dead.") Locution thus answers to "literal account," illocution to "narrative" embodying large-scale patterns that may or may not correspond to the actor's intentions but do reflect the historian's. Tacitus' bias then would be his fusing of "literal" with "narrative" modes. More particularly he would be viewing events in terms of larger moral intentions as well as of actual consequences, as he does for example when his lurid narrative about the earlier Principate is colored by the ethical as well as political problem of despotism in his own time under Domitian. It is not only possible but necessary for him to see the earlier career of (say) Tiberius in the light of later events and to conclude that he was autocratic even then, since the actions and intentions that Tacitus selects take their meaning as history from the narrative perspective of his own time. To the extent that the present in this sense makes things about the past true, "bias" is a function of historical knowledge itself. "To be alive to the historical significance of events as they happen, one has to know to which later events these will be related, in narrative sentences, by historians of the future. It will then be not enough simply to be able to predict future events. It will be necessary to know *which* future events are relevant, and this requires predicting the *interests* of future historians" (Danto, 169). Thus as a matter of epistemological necessity the interests of Tacitus or Suetonius—who are "future historians" relative to the early Principate—later define the substance of historical reality. "The Thirty Years War began in 1618" is, so far as human knowledge goes, true only many years after 1618; the conviction that Tiberius was autocratic and his policy hypocritical from the very start (Suet. *Tib.* 42.1) is by the same token bound to be hindsight. Dating of the Thirty Years War, of course, is true in an obvious way that assessment of Tiberius' character is not, yet if history is to be more than chronicle it must employ narrative judgment of one sort or another, and as it does the inevitable tension among possible perspectives is transformed (in the case of the ancient historians) into rhetoric. The methodological pitfalls that multiple norms or "frames" of intention can lead to are discussed by D. Fischer, *Historians' Fallacies* (New York, 1970), 8 (the "fallacy of question framing"). The fallacy called "false dichotomous questions" by Fischer (9) and stigmatized as often "encouraging simple-minded moralizing" has some points of contact with the technique of polemical antithetic epigrams.

25. Austin, *Do Things with Words,* 51. For the "preparatory conditions" or "world of utterance" in which statements take on meaning see Searle and Vanderveken, *Illocutionary Logic,* 17, 18; for the various kinds of fit or lack of fit between language and reality, ibid., 53, 92.

26. Pocock, *Politics, Language and Time,* 25.

27. On bipolarity in Tacitus, H. Bardon, "A propos des *Histoires:* Tacite et la tentation de la rhétorique," *Collection Latomus* 44 (1960): 146; Heubner, "Sprache, Stil und Sache," 133–48; J. Lucas, *Les obsessions de Tacite* (Leiden, 1974), 8–12 (an explanation in terms not of rhetoric or moralism but of Tacitus' obsessional character). For

the blending of *sententiae* and antithesis as a stylistic device, E. Courbaud, *Les procédés d'art de Tacite* (Paris, 1918), 263. Antithetic expression and its relation to Tacitus' thought is dealt with extensively by E. Aubrion, *Rhétorique et histoire chez Tacite* (Metz, 1985), though without particular reference to wit (esp. 407–90, with a summary on 485–90; 695). I saw this study only after my manuscript was well along in editing.

28. F. R. D. Goodyear, *The Cambridge History of Classical Literature* (Cambridge, 1982), 653.

29. Gibbon, *Decline and Fall,* vol. 1, chap. 3, 91. For Tacitus' attention to titles and names: *Ann.* 1.1.1, 1.2.1, 1.3.1 and 7, 1.9.5, 2.87, 3.56.2, 11.25.4; *Hist.* 1.57.1, 2.39.1, 3.58.3, 4.11.1, 2.62.2. Cf. Lucan 5.385–86.

30. "Tacitus has an acute sensitivity for the disparity between men's professions and their actions, and still more between their professed and their real motives," Martin, *Tacitus,* 215; cf. 235. On creation of political reality through language cf. Thucydides *History* 3.82.4; Plato *Republic* 560; Aristotle *Politics* 1261b16. C. Mueller (*The Politics of Communication,* [New York, 1973], 25) cites some striking examples from editions of a German lexicon published successively during the Weimar Republic and the Third Reich. In the latter *fanatisch* and *hart* have positive connotations; *rücksichtslos* is "inconsiderate" in the former, in the latter "a term that has a positive meaning denoting resoluteness and energy. Describing the enemy it preserves its old connotation." *Haß* becomes a virtue when applied to the proper side, e.g., "the heroic hatred of the Nordic race." For unmasking of appearance through epigrammatic antithesis see Voss, *Der pointierte Stil,* 118. When Vitellius offers a choice between war necessary to crush mutiny on the one hand, peace attainable simply by making him emperor on the other (*Hist.* 1.56.3), all intermediate alternatives are suppressed and "the irony shows to perfection Tacitus' understanding of revolutionary slogans" (G. E. F. Chilver, *A Historical Commentary on Tacitus' Histories I and II* [Oxford, 1979], ad loc.). Vitellius' loaded choice is a textbook example of Fischer's (*Historians' Fallacies* 9) "fallacy of false dichotomous questions" (e.g., "Plato: Totalitarian or Democrat?" "What Is History—Fact or Fancy?").

The ultimate perversion of language is its suppression, e.g., *Hist.* 3.54: "strange silence" about the war against Vespasian was observed in the presence of Vitellius, with the result that those who would have spoken the truth if they had been allowed to do so now gave even more disturbing reports. Those who came with firsthand knowledge of the enemy were questioned and then executed by Vitellius. Finally a centurion whom he had refused to believe and accused of treason committed suicide to demonstrate the disinterestedness of his report. (Tacitus adds that other reports tell of his execution.) Silence is either denial of reality or ominous in some other way: Tiberius' silence (*Ann.* 4.52.3, 2.35.2) or the senate's (*Ann.* 5.3.2; cf. *Agr.* 3.2); "whispered expression and suspicious silence" (*Ann.* 3.11.); a speech "received in silence or with quiet murmurs" (*Ann.* 2.38.4); denial of free exchange "of speaking and hearing" (*Agr.* 2.3); none had to fear Agricola's silence (*Agr.* 22.4); silencing of political activity (*Agr.* 39.2); Tiberius refuses to attend the senate so as not to hear criticism (*Ann.* 4.42.1) and lives in sinister secrecy (3.37.2); the sign that a man is marked for condemnation is refusal of others to speak with him, and his own silence or statements are taken as equally guilty (*Ann.* 4.60.2). Paetus' resistance first takes the form of few or no remarks at all in the senate (*Ann.* 14.12.1). "To speak at all is to give some other [person] power over us, and some assert their own power by refusing to speak at all [e.g., Paetus], to speak intelligibly [e.g., senators, see below] or (so far as this is possible) within any frame of reference they cannot unilaterally prescribe" (Pocock, *Politics, Language and Time,* 24). For various limited forms of protest possible to the general populace at Rome, Z. Yavetz, *Plebs and Princeps* (Oxford, 1969), chap. 2: silence, rumor, grumbling, joking.

31. R. Häussler, *Tacitus und das historische Bewußtsein* (Heidelberg, 1965), 280, 291 for the ambivalence of virtues; H. Drexler, *Tacitus: Grundzüge einer politischen Pathologie* (Frankfurt, 1939), 132, 178. Ambivalent language was not always deliberate; Pöschl notes that conservatism allowed emperors—as well as Tacitus himself—to use the language of the Republic without cynicism ("Der Historiker Tacitus," in *Tacitus,* 164). Stoicism, too, employed sharp antitheses that in extreme form led to what was at least an unusual use of words (e.g., that everyone not wholly *sapiens* is wholly *stultus*): T. Jerome, "The Tacitean Tiberius, a Study in Historiographic Method," *Classical Philology* 7 (1912): 271. *Prinzipat und Freiheit,* ed. Klein, 2, 68, 94: "ahistoric thinking" permitted Romans in different eras to use the same political vocabulary and ignore its ambivalent, changed meaning.

32. Martin, *Tacitus,* 232.

33. Occasionally Tacitus reveals his own judgment by replacing one word with a more candid equivalent, e.g., *patentia/servitus* in *Agr.* 2.3; see also Voss, *Der pointierte Stil,* 111. The frequency of allusions to specious, ambivalent, or misunderstood language is a measure of its importance for Tacitus. "After the empty words 'peace' and 'concord' had been used, he got down to the business of terrorizing the town" (*Hist.* 2.20.2); *Ann.* 1.52.2, 1.81.4, 2.33.4, 2.36.4, 3.70.3, 4.44.3, 6.5.2, 11.17.2, 12.4.1, 14.21.1, 14.39.3; *Hist.* 1.35.1, 1.51.3, 1.57.1, 1.71.1, 1.77.3, 1.90.2, 3.58.1, 4.6.2, 4.15.3, 4.17.2; *Agr.* 21.2; *Dial.* 40.2.

"Where issues are settled by strength, 'moderation' and 'honor' are words of the stronger; thus the Cherusci, who once were called 'good' and 'fair' now are 'lazy' and 'stupid,' while the luck of the victorious Chatti now is 'wisdom'" (*Germ.* 36). Tacitus is saying more than that only the stronger can afford actually to practice virtue; "words" (*nomina*) suggests that reality is created by how people speak of themselves and are spoken of. For political distortion of language see n. 11 above, and Sall. *Cat.* 38.3, 52.11; the remark in 12.5 *proinde quasi iniuriam facere id demum esset imperio uti* (cf. 12.1) applies in the first instance to ideas but can easily include language. For the cynical reversal of conventional terms see also Syme, *Tacitus,* 196, 344, 412; Walker *Annals of Tacitus,* 241.

34. See J. Cousin, "Rhetorik und Psychologie bei Tacitus," in *Tacitus,* ed. Pöschl, 113, on the role of outward emotional expression and its relation to the theme of enforced concealment of truth. For facial expression and body language generally (esp. Tiberius'): *Ann.* 1.7.7, 2.28.2, 2.29.2, 2.34.3, 3.3.1, 3.15.2, 3.44.3, 4.12.1, 4.34.2, 4.60.2, 6.24.1, 16.24.2; *Hist.* 2.52.1, 4.8.2, 4.11.1; *Agr.* 43.3, 44.2. Rhetoricians specified the facial expression that should go with various types of wit (W. B. Stanford, *Ambiguity in Greek Literature* [Oxford, 1939], 63). For physical appearance as a political statement see chap. 4, sec. 3.

35. Cf. Vitellius' *verba suspensa,* his pretense of ignorance, and Claudius' silence (*Ann.* 11.34). For an ironic complaint by Claudius about vacuous senatorial debate see the papyrus quoted by A. Momigliano, *Claudius,* tran. D. W. Hogarth (Oxford,

1934), 39. *Ann.* 1.7.1 is an elegant, balanced sentence conveying empty senatorial expression through antithetic pairs brought together in jumbled asyndeton at the end to cancel each other. "*Quanto* quis inlustrior, *tanto* magis *falsi ac festinantes,* vultuque composito ne *laeti excessu* principis neu *tristiores primordio, lacrimas gaudium, questus adulationem* miscebant" (The *more* notable they were, the *more false* and *forward,* and with expression set lest they seem *happy* at *one* emperor's death, *sad* at *another's* accession, they mixed *tears, joy, regrets, praise*).

36. Tiberius' ambiguity was as a rule deliberate (*Ann.* 13.3.2). Tacitus hints at an interesting psychological diagnosis of his elusive language when he says that "his speeches were ordinarily carefully written and delivered with difficulty, but when he was supporting someone he spoke more fluently" (*Ann.* 4.31.1). This goes with his taking Tiberius' confession of speechlessness on one occasion as an expression of guilt (*Ann.* 6.6).

37. D. Shotter, "Ea Simulacra Libertatis," *Latomus* 25 (1966): 267. When the dying Tiberius suddenly is rumored to have recovered, those who made premature gestures of power "pretend not to know anything" (*Ann.* 6.50.5).

38. For a full discussion of the logic of metaphor, J. Soskice, *Metaphor and Religious Language* (Oxford, 1985); for the idea that the conceptual dissonance in metaphors works like a "bump on the head," 29. Soskice's own view emphasizes the connection between metaphor and *model:* "Theories of metaphor which see metaphor as the consequence simply of verbal tension (an oddity of predication) fail to see that while the reader may be alerted to the fact that a metaphorical construal is required by an odd conjunction of terms (say, 'giddy brink') [or "merchant pirates," "free slavery," "peaceful desolation"], his construal of this oddity as metaphor depends upon his ability to see it as suggesting a model or models which enable him to go on extending the significance of what he has read or heard" (51). Odd predication, then, though not the core of metaphor may well be the witty "bump on the head" (incongruity) by which an alternative model is called up.

39. Halliday, *Language as Social Semiotic,* 175–76, on antilanguage: "the antisociety is, in its structure, a metaphor for the society; the two come together at the level of the social system . . . we should *expect* in antilanguage metaphorical compounding, metathesis, rhyming alternatives. . . ."

40. For *tego* in the sense of "mask" see *Ann.* 6.20.1, 6.24.3; *Hist.* 4.11.1. Walker, *Annals of Tacitus,* 196: "The impulse of his inquiry, then, was probably never simply to discover *what happened.* It was rather to answer the question, 'How did we reach this degraded world, in which the evil may expect honour and the good can hope at best to be inconspicuous?'" *Hist.* 4.3.2 is an example of good and evil exchanging positions. "It is easier to repay an injury than a favor, because the latter is felt to be a burden, the former a gain." Tacitus presumably means that repaying an injury should not be regarded as a gain (though vengeance was ordinarily thought of as a good thing), and so this is a general observation unmasking the inversion of values in human nature itself. Cf. Häussler, *Tacitus,* 267. For pessimism about the tendency of human nature to reverse values see also *Ann.* 4.18.3 (the hatred created by feelings of *obligation*); *Ann.* 1.33.1 (hatred is more bitter when it is *unjustified*). The remark that during a military disturbance "the chief spur for the worst troublemakers was the distress felt by good men" (*Hist.* 1.38.3) has no real basis in the events described by Tacitus and is added gratuitously to mark inversion of values.

41. Goodyear, *Cambridge History of Classical Literature*, 652.

42. There are other examples of false language. Liberality: men are deceived by "luxury" in the guise of "liberality" (*Hist.* 1.30.1); communities forced by a governor to pay for extravagant entertainment suffer from such "liberality no less than from rapacity" (*Ann.* 13.31.3). Friendship: "the worst kind of enemies are those who praise you" (*Agr.* 41.1); "the lowest of the poor and the worst slaves betrayed rich masters, while others were betrayed by friends" (*Hist.* 4.1.2; R. Seager, "Amicitia in Tacitus and Juvenal," *American Journal of Ancient History*, 2 [1977]: 40–50, deals with perversion of friendship). Law: "as the country once suffered from crimes it now suffered from laws" (*Ann.* 3.25.1), i.e., the law encouraged informing as a civic virtue. Sympathy: none bewailed the fate of Germanicus more openly than those who were most happy (*Ann.* 2.77.3).

43. In doing so they are at least partially unmasking their own inversion of values, but popular insight is rarely reliable. Thus when Vitellius lauds his own "industry" and "temperance," although his audience and all of Italy know his crimes well, since they are unable to distinguish between true and false, they praise him loudly (*Hist.* 2.90.1). Unmasking is perhaps unconscious in the case of a speech defending indulgence as "relaxation" and characterized by Tacitus as "confession of vice under honorable words" (*Ann.* 2.33.4). Seneca's defense of Nero is similarly a "confession"; because of the enormity of his crimes they are "beyond complaint" (*Ann.* 14.11.3), hence any defense is (unwitting) confession. For "crime beyond remedy" as a rhetorical topos, Arist. *Rh.* 1374b30. For confusion of virtue and crime during civil war in Lucan, Lefèvre, "Bedeutung des Paradoxen," 75.

44. Suetonius' report that nothing so convinced Gaius of his daughter's legitimacy as her savagery (she attacked the face and eyes of her playmates with her fingers, *Calig.* 25.4) is another case of unwitting self-degradation. Cf. the great "amusement" felt by people at Nero's punishing others for the kind of crimes of which he himself was guilty (Dio 61.7.6; cf. Sen. *De ira* 2.7.3). A somewhat similar self-condemnation occurs when Otho and Vitellius exchange letters that at first are "unseemly" only because of their pretended civility, then degenerate into a brawling exchange of insults—"neither side being wrong" (*Hist.* 1.74.1). Plutarch makes the same point, though less wittily: the insults were exchanged "not falsely, but stupidly and absurdly" (*Otho* 4). Tacitus slyly suggests that faults and the ridicule they rightly invite are the primary source of morale when he speaks of troops mutually denouncing their leaders and "working themselves into a passion more with rich abuse than with praise" (i.e., than with praise for their own equally worthless leadership) (*Hist.* 2.21.4). For self-incrimination as a formal comic technique in Aristophanes, R. Harriott, *Aristophanes, Poet and Dramatist* (Baltimore, 1986), 153.

45. His hypocrisy becomes doubly clear in view of the parallel between the "thanks" Seneca offers to Nero and that offered to Domitian by Agricola (*Agr.* 40.3). Griffin, *Seneca,* 442.

46. Sallust's epigram on Cato is a fine example (*Cat.* 54.6): "he wanted to be *rather than* to seem a good man, and so [*ita*] the *less* he pursued fame the *more* it pursued him." The first clause states the proper though not the usual state of affairs. The second hints at the absurd corollary which that brings for attainment of true fame at Rome: (pursuit of glory is bound to be dishonest at Rome) and so he gained fame by *not* trying to win it. Cf. *Ann.* 14.22.1.

47. For a brief discussion of *magis quam* see Voss, *Der pointierte Stil,* 26; a full collection of comparative expressions is on 126-28. *Magis quam* is a special case of the category Greater/Less Than discussed at length in Arist. *Rh.* 1363b. The obverse formula—*(nec) minus . . . quam*—has the same range of uses: neutral statement of fact ("He trusted no less in the enemy's mistakes than in the bravery of his own men," *Hist.* 4.34.3; 1.2.3, 2.31.1; *Ann.* 4.69.1); a touch of ironic wit ("Lepida and Poppaea contested no less in vices than in the advantages they had from fortune," *Ann.* 12.64.3; *Germ.* 23; *Hist.* 3.59.2, 4.2.2; *Ann.* 2.70.1); absurdity ("Owing to misgovernment peace was no less feared than war," *Agr.* 20.1; *Hist.* 1.5.2, 4.8.3; *Ann.* 12.64.3, 13.31.3). *Agr.* 5.3 has special polish: *nec minus periculum ex magna fama quam ex mala (minus/magna//magna[= bona]/mala).* Implicit cancellation of expectation by negation is discussed in G. Dillon, *Language Processing and the Reading of Literature* (Bloomington, Ind., and London, 1978), 142: "Perhaps the first point about a negative is that it negates an expectation. Although something is said not to be the case, it might have been: to comprehend it, then, we must see the expectation that is negated as a plausible one, an outgrowth of possibilities inherent in the world at that point."

For *tamquam* (as though . . . , in the misguided belief that . . .): *Hist.* 1.16.4, 2.12.2, 2.90.1, 4.44.1; *Ann.* 1.7.3, 14.4.3; *tam . . . quam: Hist.* 1.13.2, 2.86.3, 2.90.2; *proinde . . . quam: Hist.* 2.39.2; *malle . . . quam:* "the barbarians prefer to get rather than have kings from Rome," *Ann.* 12.14.1; *Ann.* 13.42.1; Corbulo "preferred to be at war rather than to wage it," *Ann.* 15.3.1.

48. Sen. *Ep.* 114.11: "Some [rhetoricians] cut the meaning short and hope that it will be pleasing if the *sententia* is suspended [*pependerit*] and makes the hearer doubt his ears" (i.e., amuses him with momentary incoherence). In 114.17, with Sallust in mind, Seneca speaks of words that "fall before we expect them to" *(verba ante expectatum cadentia).* For the compact, oracular, and suggestive effect achieved by emphasis and *deinotēs,* F. Ahl, *Metaformations,* (Ithaca, N.Y., and London, 1985), 298.

49. For the relation of style and substance in Tacitus, Voss, *Der pointierte Stil,* 22, 35, 81, 112. See also E. Norden, *Die antike Kunstprosa,* 5th ed. (Stuttgart, 1958), 1:321; both Tacitus and Sallust have "pessimistically earnest world views (329) . . . and a sovereign striving for the unusual." Their aim (as was that of Thucydides) was not to please but to "grip and seize the reader and share with him the same powerful movement which rushes through history" (330). Voss comments on the way in which the abstract nouns favored by Tacitus contribute to a sense of insight into the principles at work in events (51, 92). See A. Bergener, *Die führende Senatorenschicht im frühen Prinzipat* (Bonn, 1965), 218, for Tacitus' resignation.

50. F. R. D. Goodyear, "Cyclic Development in History: A Note on Tacitus *Annales* 3.55.5," *Institute of Classical Studies University of London,* 17 (1970): 101-6; Häussler, *Tacitus,* 49, 292. For a similar pattern in Thucydides see V. Hunter, *Past and Process in Herodotus and Thucydides* (Princeton, N.J., 1982), 167.

51. W. Jens, "Libertas bei Tacitus," in *Prinzipat und Freiheit,* ed. Klein, 391-420, holds that Tacitus became increasingly pessimistic about a balance between liberty and repression at Rome.

52. Political reality undergoes inversion along with values and language. Greed, envy, and especially hatred are manifestations of the underlying desire for power that often distorts the very reality it seeks to master. Thus Piso was sent to the camp "either because he was Vinius' enemy or because those who hated Vinius wanted him to be,"

Hist. 1.34.1 (cf. *Hist.* 1.41.2 for creation of false reality by political passion: Galba's last words vary depending on whether one likes or hates him).

Chapter III. Techniques of Wit

1. Patricia Cox, *Biography in Late Antiquity* (Berkeley, Los Angeles, and London, 1983), xi. The primacy of moral principles in history is implicit in Tacitus' disgusted epigram *magis alii homines quam alii mores* (*Hist.* 2.95.3: "new players, same rules"). People generally connect the character of a regime with that of its leader (*Ann.* 15.48.3), hence the emphasis on moral character in brief biographical sketches.

2. A. Wardman, *Plutarch's Lives* (London, 1974), 8.

3. For violation of expectation, Demetrius *On Style* 152–53; *Tractatus Coislinianus* VI (in Janko, *Aristotle on Comedy,* 36); and P. Plass, "An Aspect of Epigrammatic Wit in Martial and Tacitus," *Arethusa* 18 (1985): 189. The part played by expectation in the act of thinking attracted Aristotle's attention and figures in his discussion of the logic of metaphor in the *Rhetoric.* He observes that touches of "strangeness" in style are pleasureable because they cause "wonder" at learning something new (1404\u200b11). The same explanation applies to metaphors, which connect two things by revealing an unexpected likeness between them.

4. P. Berger and T. Luckmann, *The Social Construction of Reality: A Treatise in the Sociology of Knowledge* (New York, 1966), 172.

5. *Remedium* is again euphemistic in *Hist.* 1.37.4. Tacitus also draws attention to the use of "liberty" as a buzzword by all sides (*Ann.* 11.17.2; *Hist.* 4.73.3), and "capture" became an issue of political conscience and propaganda in civil war: "they should not want to capture rather than save Rome" (*Hist.* 3.60.3). On the "capture" of home territory, *Hist.* 1.82.2, 2.12.2, 2.89.1, 2.90.1, 3.49.1, 4.1.3, 2.6.2. See E. Keitel, "Principate and Civil War in the *Annals* of Tacitus," *American Journal of Philology* 105 (1984): 306–25.

6. M. L. W. Laistner, *The Greater Roman Historians* (Berkeley, Los Angeles, and London, 1947), 119, remarks on the ironic point of this passage. Cf. Dio 61.59.2 on civil war: "they recognized their opponents and—wounded them; they called them by name and—killed them; they knew their native cities and—sacked them." Cato in Lucan 9.213: "I don't mind being held for Caesar so long as I am held without—a head"; 10.369: "who of us is not regarded as guilty by Cleopatra if he is—innocent? [of an affair with her]"; Juvenal 10.285 (on Pompey): "his own and Rome's fortune preserved him in order to—take his head off." Laco thought of killing Vinius "either to appease the angry troops or for treason or finally because he—hated him" (*Hist.* 1.39.2); by hiding in the temple of Vesta, Piso delayed death not because of the killers' "sense of religion or propriety but because they—couldn't find him" (*Hist.* 1.43.2); "so that no one would usurp their place with Vitellius it seems that they destroyed—Vitellius himself" (*Hist.* 2.101.1). After describing various reports of Galba's last words Tacitus abruptly adds, "the killers didn't care *what* he said" (*Hist.* 1.41.2), a gratuitously deflationary remark disturbing the tone of the narrative to bring out the brutal reality behind conventional Last Words of Famous Men. Such epigrams with their strong ending have on a small scale and within themselves the same effect epigrams have within the larger context of the narrative, where they come at the end of larger sections and "obviously provide the cue for applause" (Walker, *Annals of Tac-*

itus, 57, n. 1). The practice of allowing time for applause after short punch lines in declamation (Norden, *Antike Kunstprosa,* 1:275, 1:295) resembles the timing essential for the modern comic delivering one-liners.

7. S. Freud, *Jokes and Their Relation to the Unconscious,* vol. 8 of the Standard Edition (London, 1960), 69. Freud defines unification as "stringing things together" though one member of the series is incongruous (e.g., Heine's "speaking generally, the inhabitants of Göttingen are divided into students, professors, philistines, and donkeys"). Cf. L. Carlson, *Dialogue Games* (Dordrecht, Boston, and London, 1983), 152, for a discussion of logical and grammatical subtleties in the syntax of "but," "and," and "or." Even in ordinary usage "but" marks something that is contrary to expectation ("My name is Sue, *but* I am a boy"), and when its adversative force reaches a certain level ("Who are you, *but* who is he?") it produces incoherence or amusing *para prosdokian.* Antony's joke about the Megarian senate house is a good example: "it is small, *but* shabby." A statement like "two plus two are four, but Hitler was Austrian" is again incoherent except when heard in a proper context, e.g., as the statement of a teacher acknowledging one correct answer while pointing out another erroneous one. "And" signals that what follows is "the same topic treated in the same manner," whereas "but" signals a "coordinate but contradictory topic," and so Antony's remark is a joke because it introduces the same topic with the signal for a contradictory topic (we expect something like ". . . *but* elegant"). Many of Tacitus' epigrams employ the reverse sequence to achieve their surprise: an assumption of same topic/same manner set up by "and" is instantly knocked down by a contradictory topic. To use Carlson's example: "My name is Sue, *and* I am a boy" is a subtle grammatical witticism insofar as the abnormality marked by "but" is replaced with an initial denial of abnormality in "and" to accentuate further the unexpectedness of "I am a boy." Cf. "astrologers are a race of men, untrustworthy to the powerful and deceitful to the ambitious, which in our city will always be both banned *and* consulted" (*Hist.* 1.22.1). The correlative form *(et vetabitur semper et retinebitur)* makes the incongruous second *et* the more unavoidable. Nero's justice leaves its victims "still living *and* about to die (*Ann.* 16.11.2; see also sec. 4 below). Several epigrams leave it to the hearer to supply the conjunction: "speech was restricted and dangerous under a ruler who feared liberty, [and/but] hated flattery" (*libertatem metuabat, adulationem oderat, Ann.* 2.87); "where they make desolation, [there] they [also/nevertheless] call it peace" (*ubi solitudinem faciunt, pacem appellant, Agr.* 30.4). Cf. the force of *et* in *Ann.* 6.38.3 (quoted above, p. 48), and below, n. 14.

8. Freud, *Jokes and the Unconscious,* 26. For some excellent remarks on the wry wit of Tacitus' epigram see K. Quinn, *Latin Explorations* (London, 1963), 112: "It was being emperor that made him a fool. The words make us feel the ludicrousness of the situation. . . . We first smile, then ponder." For a similar twist in thought see *Hist.* 3.39.1: "the best proposals seemed to be those whose time had passed." For the syntax cf. *Ann.* 11.34.3: as Claudius was entering Rome, his and Messalina's children "were brought forward [and would have met him], had Narcissus not ordered them removed." H. Nutting, "Subjunctive Conditions," *University of California Publications in Classical Philology* 7 (1923): 166–79; and Nutting, "The Latin Conditional Sentence," ibid. 8 (1925): 89, prefers to see anacoluthon or a "corrective conditional clause" rather than an ellipse in such sentences. Many sentences in Tacitus are formally incomplete, e.g., "Germanicus pointed his sword at his own chest [and would have

struck] if those near him had not seized his right arm" (*Ann.* 1.35.4). *Ann.* 16.13.2 is a striking example: they were wept for by wives and children, "who as they attended and mourned [were suffering from the plague, then died and] were often burned on the very same pyres." Though the ellipse may not have been strongly felt, it can create a foreshortening or syntactical flicker. Many of the constructions occur in the *Annals,* and Nutting concludes that "this would seem to show rather conclusively that the anacoluthic type marks Tacitus' mature choice of a distinctive method of handling the crises in affairs, which his subject matter often calls upon him to describe" (176). That is to say, the grammatical jolt matches the jolt caused by unexpected events, and Nutting notes the potential comic effect.

9. *Julius* 49.3, 50.2; *Aug.* 12.1; *Ner.* 39.2, 45.2, 46.3. See Richlin, *Garden of Priapus,* 81, on political invective.

10. Dillon, *Language Processing,* xvii-xxxi, discusses the various "frames" that determine how language is processed. Thus the absurd sentence "John dressed and had a bath" is naturally corrected into "John had a bath and dressed" under the influence of what ought to have been said. In the same way, epigrammatic violation of expectation or cases of legal *hysteron/proteron* are transformed into epigrammatic wit from mere nonsense as they are corrected by appropriate frames of meaning. Cf. Booth, *Rhetoric of Irony,* 35.

11. Demetrius (*On Style* 24) discusses the technique used in this epigram (false appearance of antithesis) and cites as an example of his own some "deceptive words probably said in jest" by Epicharmus: "At one time I was among them, at another I was with them."

12. For subversion of law as an attack on the basis of Roman society see Walker, *Annals of Tacitus,* 59.

13. For legal *hysteron/proteron* see *Ann.* 16.14.3: people were regarded as "condemned rather than as defendants." In *Ann.* 11.20.3 a legion asks that generals be given triumphs in advance of their appointment so that they have no need to wear out the troops in an effort to earn them; and Corbulo in fact was "granted the emblems of triumph, though he had been denied the war" because the emperor feared him (*Ann.* 11.20.2).

14. Köhnken's analysis in "Das Problem der Ironie bei Tacitus," 35, brings out the mad logic of the entire scene. In *maerens Burrus ac laudans* or in Juvenal's *probitas laudatur et alget* (1.74) *ac* or *et* is both "and" and "though," the latter representing normal disjunctive logic, the former the conjunctive illogic of corrupt political reality.

15. For Tacitus' omission of information in accounts of trials see R. S. Rogers, "The Emperor's Displeasure," *Transactions of the American Philological Association* 90 (1959): 224-37; and Rogers, "A Tacitean Pattern in Narrating Treason Trials," ibid. 83 (1952): 279-311. Also A. R. Hands, "The Timing of Suicide," *Proceedings of the African Classical Associations* 5 (1962): 27-31. F. Klinger, "Tacitus über Augustus und Tiberius," in *Tacitus,* ed. Pöschl, 528, comments on deformation of events in Tacitus' narrative. For other political jokes by omission see Sen. *De ira* 2.33; Suet. *Dom.* 10.2. Nero's famous "mushrooms are the food of the gods" works the same way, and Seneca's brother was using omission "when he said a great deal in a short space by remarking that Claudius had been raised to heaven on a hook" (Dio 60.35.3). For narrative "fragmentation" in Suetonius see Gascou, *Suétone historien,* 373, 389.

Chapter IV. Enacted Wit

1. H. Parke and D. Wormell, *The Delphic Oracle* (Oxford, 1956), 2:309, for the white raven oracle. On omens generally, Wallace-Hadrill, *Suetonius,* 19; H. Gugel, *Studien zur biographischen Technik Suetons,* Wiener Studien Beiheft 7 (Vienna, Cologne, and Graz, 1977), 24. For ambiguous oracles not as commands but statements that are part of political debate, P. Vidal-Naquet, *Black Hunter,* tran. A. Szegedy-Maszak (Baltimore and London, 1986), 257.

2. E. Segal, "Tacitus and Poetic History," *Ramus* 2 (1973): 107–26, treats the wider symbolism of omens in Tacitus. Caligula's display of his wife (*Calig.* 25.3) recalls the ominous import of Candaules' behavior in Herodotus. *Ner.* 40.3 has another allusion to Herodotus.

3. For the theme of religious/political "prodigy" in Juvenal 4 see C. Deroux, "Domitian, the Kingfish and the Prodigies," in *Collection Latomus,* vol. 180, Studies in Latin Literature and Roman History, 3 (Brussels, 1983), 283–98.

4. Baldwin remarks on the occasional "hilarity" of omens, e.g., the hand given to Vespasian or the woman killed by a bolt of lightning during intercourse (Baldwin, *Suetonius,* 359).

5. Cf. Goodyear, *Annals of Tacitus,* vol. 1, on 1.39.6. Tacitus' references to the gods, though, are not so much "totally devoid of serious meaning" as devoid of literal reference; their political meaning could not be more serious.

6. Freud, *Jokes and the Unconscious,* 51, 151, 205.

7. See Cic. *De or.* 2.266 on caricature. Plutarch's discussion of the distinction between acceptable and unacceptable joking about deformity illustrates the sensitivity about physical vulnerability which makes caricature effective. A snub nose or baldness is fair game, bad breath or loss of an eye is not (*Quaest. conv.* 2.633b). Cicero cites Appius' joke at the expense of a one-eyed man as an instance of provocative wit: "I'll dine at your place, since I see that you have room for one more" (*De or.* 2.246).

8. Cox, *Biography in Late Antiquity,* 13; Cizek, *Structures et idéologies,* 139; A. E. Wardman, "Description of Personal Appearance in Plutarch and Suetonius," *Classical Quarterly,* n.s., 17 (1967): 414. Gascou, *Suétone historien,* denies close correspondence with physiognomic details and prefers to speak of impressionistic portraits rather than caricature (592–616).

9. E. Evans, "Roman Descriptions of Personal Appearance in History and Biography," *Harvard Studies in Classical Philology* 46 (1935): 67.

10. For protest by actors through lines taken to refer to the emperor see *Aug.* 68, *Tib.* 45, *Calig.* 27.4, *Ner.* 39.2; cf. *Vesp.* 19.2. For vulgar comedy in particular as a means of degrading authority see J. Winkler, *Auctor et Actor* (Berkeley, Los Angeles, and London, 1985), 279.

11. Cf. Baldwin, *Suetonius,* 501. Tiberius' effort to hide his depravity toward the end of his life is loosely linked in Tacitus to his sensitivity about his appearance: tall but stooped, bald, and an ulcerated face dotted with plasters (*Ann.* 4.57).

12. *Iul.* 80.3, *Aug.* 70.2, *Ner.* 45.2, *Galb.* 1, *Vit.* 9. Caligula threw down statues of famous men indiscriminately (*Calig.* 34.1). Sejanus' statues were torn down "as though he were himself being assaulted and witnessing what he was to suffer" (Dio 58.11.3). As Vitellius was dragged out to real death he was also forced to watch his statues fall (*Hist.* 3.85.1), and statues of Piso were taken to the Gemonian Stairs, the place of

exposure for bodies of executed criminals (*Ann.* 3.14.4). In other cases the substitute target is a name (*Ann.* 3.17.4; *Tib.* 42.1, 75.1).

13. A. Dawson, "Whatever Happened to Lady Agrippina?" *Classical Journal* 64 (1968): 253–67. For the comic effect see B. Baldwin, "Tacitean Humour," *Wiener Studien* 90 (1977): 128–34.

14. P. Bicknell, "The Emperor Gaius' Military Activity in A.D. 40," *Historia* 17 (1968): 499–500, discusses various explanations of the seashell episode, e.g., that it was a misunderstood military order concerning *musculi* ("sappers' huts" as well as "mussels").

15. Among what Suetonius calls Caligula's "jokes" was his remark when he kissed his wife's or mistress's neck: "So pretty a head comes off whenever I say so!" (*Calig.* 33). At the same time, radical irresponsibility can be a facet of what P. Veyne calls "expressivity," i.e., the principle that authority is enhanced by power exercised wholly without external restraint. Expressivity aims not so much at display of superiority as at automony, superiority being only a by-product (and in fact the more impressive for that very reason). Insofar as anecdotes about megalomanic behavior are not mere exaggerations or fabrications they represent a type of political narcissism in which communication for such normal purposes as informing or influencing is irrelevant (*Le pain et le cirque* [Paris, 1976], 94, 101, 569, 658, 675).

Veyne's conception of expressivity is a psychological and historical model on a very high level of generality; it does not work everywhere, but if not pressed too far it fits emperors like Caligula and Nero fairly well, or at least the picture of them drawn by ancient historiography, whatever the idea's explanatory power for actual Roman history may be. Nero was at once popular for generosity and notorious for extravagance (J. P. Sullivan, *Literature and Politics in the Age of Nero* [Ithaca, N.Y., and London, 1985], 40), and like the "insensitivity" of Caligula discussed by Suetonius (*Calig.* 29), sovereign indifference to some sections of public opinion seems to have been at work in his immense expenditures on entertainment and building. It is, in any event, at work in the story of his assessment of the Golden House: he could at last live like a human being (*Ner.* 31.2; Vitellius outdoes even this when he complains of its meanness, Dio 64.4.1). His extravagant brutalizing of Christians evidently offended public opinion, and if Tacitus' account is at all accurate, the incident can hardly be explained entirely as calculated terror or as a failed attempt to curry public favor. On a more theoretical level Maecenas' statement of the ideology of benign despotism in Dio again touches on expressivity. When he advises Augustus against responding to some charges, true or false, and against accepting any notable honors from his subjects, since only he can give himself recognition (52.31.7; 35.1), he is cutting the emperor's position off from public opinion to a considerable degree.

Tacitus does not, of course, for a moment allow that the emperors possessed any such special expressive right, but he does believe that a similar principle is a factor in genuine virtue. Agricola is a case in point: "by his very dissimulation of reputation, his reputation was increased [*ipsa dissimulatione famae famam auxit,* with the jingle underscoring the oddity], since the scale of his hopes for the future could be inferred from the scale of what he concealed" (*Agr.* 18.6). It is not clear whether this is an inference on Tacitus' part from the tone of Agricola's official reports or whether it was Agricola's own intention; in either case it is a variation of the paradox that success may come from not trying. Tacitus makes similar remarks on reputation enhanced by retirement from political life, and the idea is a major theme in the *Agr*. "He did not even seek reputation [*famam*]—which even good men are often intent on—by display of virtue or through craftiness; he was far from competing with colleagues, far from arguing with government officials, since he thought it inglorious to succeed in such matters and debasing to lose" (*Agr*. 9.4). Indifference to appearances is thus in its own way a form of the old ideal of being rather than seeming. The emperor should be free to be exactly and only what he is, and as that was rejected by critics of the Principate as insolence, so the "expressive" indifference to official values which they cultivated was in turn rejected as self-centered insolence by the court. Indifference commonly took the form of withdrawal *(secessio)* from active politics. The difficulty with Veyne's notion of expressivity is that it depends crucially on motivation, but very few actions can be a matter of pure self-realization.

16. Several anecdotes in Suetonius do appear as formal jokes in the late jokebook *Philogelos* (62 corresponds to *Vit*. 2.5 and 77 to *Claud*. 15.3; *Philogelos: The Philogelos or Laughter-Lover*, tran. B. Baldwin, London Studies in Classical Philology, 10 [Amsterdam, 1983]). In the latter (77) a man who has just buried a son meets the boy's teacher and says, "I'm sorry he has been absent, but he's dead." In *Claud*. 15.3, after hesitating for a long time to explain why his client was not present though he had been summoned by Claudius, an advocate finally said, "He's dead—I think that's a valid reason." As a joke *about* Claudius, the story is absurd because it is absurd that such a remark should not be too absurd to be the kind of thing one might say to him. In *Philogelos* 62 a man consoles an athlete defeated at the Millennial Games of Rome by saying, "Cheer up! You'll do better next time." For *Vit*. 2.5 see above, p. 10.

17. Hermogenes in L. Spengel, *Rhetores graeci* (Leipzig, 1854), 2.441.26. Cf. Swift's remark in "The Art of Political Lying," quoted by R. Goodin, *Manipulatory Politics* (New Haven, Conn., and London, 1980), 45: "The right of inventing and spreading political lies is partly in the people . . . as ministers do sometimes use tools to support their power, it is but reasonable that the people should employ the same weapon to defend themselves, and pull them down."

18. Plut. *Sayings of Kings* 176b is a variation of this. Tacitus (*Ann*. 1.10.7) has Augustus make himself look better already during life by excusing Tiberius in a speech in such a way as to condemn him. Dio has the same report (introduced by "some suspected," 56.45.3) and mentions a similar rumor about Tiberius: "they say that he was glad to have Gaius succeed him because his own deeds would be dwarfed by Gaius'" (58.23.3). See *Calig*. 25.1 for two versions of what "others report" about the emperor's fantastic behavior at a wedding. When Antonius complained about lack of hot water in a bathhouse where he had gone after the battle of Cremona to wash off some blood, the remark was made (by an attendant?) that "things would soon be hot," and in connection with the subsequent burning of the city it was transformed into a slanderous joke (*Hist*. 3.32.3). When asked by Tiberius how he had become Agrippa, an arrested imposter "is said" to have replied, "Just as you became Caesar" (*Ann*. 2.40.3).

Several other anecdotes look very much like jokes originally based on well-known character traits. When the tribune Subrius Flavus was taken out to execution, the detail assigned to dig his grave so offended his sense of professional competence that he could not forgo a last complaint ("They can't do even this right!": *ne hoc quidem ex disciplina*, *Ann*. 15.67.4). Pallas refuted a charge of conspiracy by pointing out that he rarely deigned to speak with his servants, limiting himself instead to nods, gestures, or writing ("Why won't Pallas ever be implicated in a plot? / He couldn't bring himself to speak with agents," *Ann.* 13.23.2). The defiant obscenity against Tigellinus by a slave under torture was perhaps actually a jest made in less dramatic circumstances by one of his enemies (*Ann.* 14.60.3). See also J. Balsdon, *The Emperor Gaius* (Oxford, 1934), 216, for the growth of "good stories" about Caligula. R. Saller, "Anecdotes as Historical Evidence," discusses the doubtful historical value of anecdotes along with aspects of their typology; cf. R. Hock and E. O'Neil, *The Chreia in Ancient Rhetoric, Texts and Translations,* 27, Graeco-Roman Religion Series, 9 (Atlanta, Ga., 1986), 1:43. Jokes would come from the "clubs and circles where talk against the government was ever the fashionable pastime" and was spread through "the rancour of senators, muttered or petulant in the curia but ferocious and indignant when they met privately together for talk" (Syme, *Tacitus,* 1:23, 435; for wit in the emperor's own circle see Syme, *The Augustan Aristocracy* [Oxford, 1986], 366). For *conviviis et circulis* see *Ann.* 3.54.1; Baldwin, *Suetonius,* 114, 154, for written political wit. Sullivan, *Age of Nero,* 153, discusses the highly sophisticated social setting for wit and (177) possible allusions to "poisoned jokes" spread against Seneca, whose own colloquial style reproduces clever talk at court. H. Willrich, "Caligula," *Klio* 3 (1903), has interesting suggestions for the origin of anecdotes about Caligula in jokes, especially his own (461–62), though *Dienstbotenklatsch* or *Stallwitze* suggests the wrong social setting. He holds that Caligula's absurd cruelty was often simply a harshly literal sense of law (438).

19. Poetry is more philosophic than history since it deals with what "could or would" be true and therefore is concerned with universals (*Poet.* 1451b). By the same token, the point of wit in historiography is not its literal truth but its revelation of what would and could be true in fact because it is true in principle. In *Rh.* 1394a2, on the other hand, Aristotle emphasizes the persuasive power of empirical truth. It is easy to invent stories that illustrate a point, but historical examples are better since they are at least in the long run likely to be literally true.

Dio (61.8.5) remarks that almost everything that happened in the palace spread as a rumor or story. "For in view of the depravity and licentiousness, what could happen was talked of as having happened and what sounded at all plausible was taken as truth." He himself is unsure whether the story of the incest between Nero and his mother was true "or invented to fit their characters," and so he contents himself with observing that Nero's mistress was very much like Agrippina in appearance and that Nero made jokes about "making love to his mother" (61.11.4; Suet. *Ner.* 28.2 says nothing about the joke). Cf. Dio 53.19.4 for the connection between secrecy in the imperial system and the spread of false stories. Historiography was often shaped not by the criterion of truth but by that of rhetorical effect (T. P. Wiseman, *Clio's Cosmetics* [Old Woking, 1979], 27). This is especially true of anecdotes, which could quickly be accepted as sober history, though in fact invented in rhetorical schools to provide *exempla.* "Just as the criteria that apply to historical narrative are contaminated by those that apply to rhetorical *narratio,* so the *exempla* that help the individual to form his moral judgments become fatally confused with the *exempla* that help the orator to make his case persuasive" (Wiseman, 35). Rhetorical invention, joke, and historical fact tended to overlap, since the Romans took their rhetorical mentality from the schools into actual life, and the rhetorical schools thus became a major source of political humor. Biographies of philosophers were affected by the same process; stories told about Pyrrho are jokes about the kind of thing that might happen to an extreme skeptic (e.g., Why bother to avoid a cliff, since it might not be real? Diog. Laert. 9.62).

20. Baldwin, *Suetonius*, 18.

21. "The Character of Domitian," *Phoenix* 18 (1964): 53, n. 9.

22. *Themes in Roman Satire* (Norman, Okla., and London, 1986), 72, n. 2.

23. Suetonius' *morte simulata* seems to exaggerate the "dead faint" *(ekthnēskein)* described by Dio (62.15.3). A. Athanassakis sees in the account of Claudius' "breathing out his last anima" systematic scatological wit connected perhaps with the mention in Suet. *Claud.* 32 of a proposed edict allowing flatulence at dinner parties ("Some Thoughts on *Double-Entendres* in Seneca *Apocolocyntosis* 3 and 4," *Classical Philology* 68 [1973]: 292–94). But the story of the edict may itself be a joke or, if authentic, a joke by Claudius himself.

24. In Zinoviev's *Yawning Heights* (see chap. 6), 57, a man shouts, "Arrogant blockhead!" and is arrested on the spot for insulting the leader. He insists that he meant a fellow worker, but the police say, "Come on! Everyone knows who the blockhead is."

25. M. Grant, *The Twelve Caesars* (London, 1975), 113–14.

26. H. Willrich, "Caligula," 425.

27. Ibid.: "This tax created a target for Caligula's witty enemies, who claimed that the emperor had established a bordello on the Palatine" (my translation).

28. For the story see J. Gagé, "Tibère à Capri," *Revue des études italiennes*, n.s., 8 (1961): 22.

29. *Suetonius*, 256.

30. G. Townend, "Suetonius and His Influence," in *Latin Biography*, ed. T. A. Dorey (London, 1967), 95.

31. Grotesque anecdotes in the historians thus have the same serious purpose as rhetorical exaggeration in Seneca; both are a means of getting at general truths about evil as a principle. C. J. Herington, "Senecan Tragedy," *Arion* 5 (1966): 448; "the *idea*, as so often in Seneca, overrides the demands of the factual realism and even of individual characterization" (455). For touches of slapstick humor in Suetonius see Gascou, *Suétone historien*, 422. For the universalizing force of epigrams and anecdotes see Drexler, *Tacitus*, 121. A revealing moment is caught by surreal imagery in the quasi-detached "angry faces and voices of sedition" (*Ann.* 1.31.5, 1.57.2, with Goodyear's notes in his edition of *Annals*).

32. T. E. Luce, "Tacitus' Conception of Historical Change: The Problem of Discovering the Historian's Opinion," in *Past Perspectives*, ed. I. S. Moxon, J. D. Smart, A. J. Woodman (Cambridge, 1986), 149–51. The combination in Tacitus of sensitivity to political ambiguity and strong moralistic judgment perhaps reflects his own uneasy consciousness of compromising.

Chapter V. Wit in Seneca and the Declaimers

1. Ugliness thus extends in historiography to wholly serious subjects arousing powerful moral feeling excluded from joking by Cicero, who limits the laughable to relatively minor matters and stresses moderation. Still, laughable remarks may formally be identical with serious ones (*De or.* 2.248, 2.262), and his example of political

wit dealing with *subturpia* (2.264) could easily express strong disgust. Defining the laughable in terms of moderate emotion goes back to Plato's and Aristotle's concern about aggression in Old Comedy, and Cicero warns against wit "substituting for hatred of crime" (*Orat.* 88). In the first case wit is too strong, in the second too weak. Tacitus can see his own as a proper mean between the two.

2. The distinction between witty epigrams and witty events is roughly parallel to the distinction drawn by Cicero between specific wordplay *(dicacitas)* and a general attitude of wittiness *(cavillatio, De or.* 2.218). The former is *peracutum* and *breve,* the latter is *aequabiliter omni sermone perfusum* and a *perpetua felicitas.* For the distinction in Ovid see K. Galinsky, *Ovid's Metamorphoses* (Berkeley and Los Angeles, 1975), 159. In Tacitus, of course, pervasive large-scale wit is not *perpetua felicitas* but a darker *perpetua acerbitas.* For gradual replacing of *sententiae* by a narrative "formule piquante" see Aubrion, *Rhétorique et histoire chez Tacite,* 205–8.

3. N. Pratt, *Seneca's Drama* (Chapel Hill, N.C., and London, 1983), 154.

4. Ibid., 141. "He could not be caught himself if he did not want to—catch me," *Thyestes* 288; "this one evil was lacking to the ruined Trojans—to rejoice," *Troades* 888; "whoever is guilty for you is for you—guiltless," *Medea* 503; *De providentia* 4.3: "I judge you wretched because you have never been—wretched"; *Tranq.* 16.4: "Cato wounds his—wounds."

5. Similar paradoxes in Ovid's *Metamorphoses* include 2.704: Mercury "laughs at being betrayed to—himself"; 2.796: Envy "can hardly keep from lamenting because she sees nothing to—lament"; 2.430; 781; 4.461; 7.339 *(ne sit scelerata, facit scelus).* See Galinsky, *Ovid's Metamorphoses,* 161, 179; 196, for wit derived from self-deception and incongruity in general. Paradoxes are especially effective in describing relationships (e.g., a daughter becoming "wife" or "mistress" of her father; cf. above, p. 61). The story of Narcissus ("an ingenious exercise in paradox," B. Otis, *Ovid as Epic Poet* [Cambridge, 1966], 158) is a paradigm of this, and Ovid takes full advantage of the possibilities offered by Narcissus' encounter with himself (3.424–26; cf. 6.537, 9.488). For riddling epigrams in the story of Myrrha's passion for her father cf. 10.314–18; 10.339: "because he is my father he cannot be mine." See also Ahl, *Metaformations,* 214.

6. B. Seidensticker, *Die Gesprächsverdichtung in den Tragödien Senecas* (Heidelberg, 1969), 86, 99, 141.

7. Ibid., 184. Examples include *Octavia* 45–54; Luc. 8.523: "Do you wonder why I *must* kill you when I *may [liceat]*?"; Juv. 10.96: "Even those who don't *want [nolunt]* to kill *want [volunt]* to be *able* to kill"; Sen. *Thyestes* 212: "Let men wish *[velint]* what they don't want *[nolunt]*"; *Ep.* 9.14: "the philosopher wants *[egere]* nothing, though he needs *[opus esse]* much." *De Prov.* 4.16: "it is useful to endure things that are not bad *[mala]* except for one who takes them badly *[male]*"; *Ep.* 120.18: "the last day of life takes *[carpit]* but does not steal *[corripit]* us," i.e., death is the natural end of life ("when our last day comes we have it coming"); cf. *Ep.* 66.30, 78.24. For a brief assessment of this facet of Seneca's style see Griffin, *Seneca,* 14; on his fondness for wit, 133.

8. For a fascinating study of this as a pervasive quality of Latin literature see Ahl, *Metaformations.* "Ovid's anagrams and etymological word plays enable him . . . to subvert, reshape, and redirect his reader's thoughts, as every important poet or other master of rhetoric does. It is not that he is changing the reality; he is, rather, trying to change our perspectives on reality" (302). Ahl argues that, although by traditional

standards of criticism what is "plural, latent, paradoxical or contradictory" is dismissed as nonclassical (18), complexity, multiplicity, chaos, and incoherence are often norms for classical poetry and reflect its feeling for reality (271–95). It is fair to add that the force of these qualities, in turn, comes largely from their contrast with the opposite qualities of order and reason, which must to that extent also be normative. My example from Ovid in the text is taken from Ahl (54).

9. G. Kennedy's translation (modified) in *The Older Sophists,* ed. R. Sprague (Columbia, S.C., 1972), 50.

10. Cf. R. Moss, "The Case for Sophistry," in *Rhetoric Revalued,* ed. B. Vickers (Binghamton, N.Y., 1982), 216. Gorgias' *Encomium* is close to an "antilanguage" (above, chap. 2, n. 11) and has a similar effect; see Halliday, *Language as Social Semiotic,* 181: "The modes of expression of the anti-language, when seen from the standpoint of the established language, appear oblique, diffuse, metaphorical." Freud has a joke that illustrates the potential comic effect of this:

> An impoverished individual borrowed 25 florins from a prosperous acquaintance, with many asservations of his necessitous circumstances. The very same day his benefactor met him again in a restaurant with a plate of salmon mayonnaise in front of him. The benefactor reproached him: "What? You borrow money from me and then order yourself salmon mayonnaise? Is *that* what you've used my money for?" "I don't understand you," replied the object of the attack: "if I *haven't* any money I *can't* eat salmon mayonnaise, and if I *have* some money I *mustn't* eat salmon mayonnaise. Well, then, when *am* I to eat salmon mayonnaise?" (*Jokes and the Unconscious,* 49–50)

The insouciant gourmand's baffling play with language (have/haven't/can't/mustn't/am to) is a facade to rationalize manifest repudiation of ordinary standards of responsibility. In form the joke is very close to epigrammatic *chreiai* exploiting parallel syntax: to someone who asked when lunch should be eaten, Diogenes said, "If you are rich, whenever you *want,* but if you are poor, whenever you *can*" (Diog. Laert. 6.40).

11. Seidensticker, *Gesprächsverdichtung* 185, 193.

12. Ibid., 196 (my translation). For the same effect of wordplay in Ovid see Galinsky, *Ovid's Metamorphoses,* 195. The wit of the epigram is thus for Seneca, as it is for Tacitus, a means for exposing the difference between "what is honorable and what is not" (*Ann.* 3.65.1, 4.33.2).

13. Tacitus' epigram leaves in doubt whether victory would make or prove the victor worse. The political irrationality in *systematic* triumph of the worse is the theme of the democratic contest between the Sausage Seller and Cleon in Aristophanes' *Knights.*

14. G. Kennedy, *The Art of Rhetoric in the Roman World* (Princeton, N.J., 1972), 312; Norden, *Antike Kunstprosa,* 1:273; Pratt, *Seneca's Drama,* 132.

15. See Wiseman, *Clio's Cosmetics,* 3; for Hellenistic historians' use of the matched speeches *pro* and *con* typical of *controversiae,* 28. The witty and dramatic display this permits undergoes further transformation in the epigrammatic dialogue of Senecan drama and receives its final "point" in Tacitean epigrams.

16. Pratt, *Seneca's Drama,* 141. G. Williams, *Change and Decline* (Berkeley, Los Angeles, and London, 1978) has a general discussion of the effect on morale of loss of freedom (153) and institutionalized cruelty (184); for characteristic thought and expression of the times, 192 (*sententiae,* 211). Norden, *Antike Kunstprosa,* 279,

remarks on the contemporary taste for the "monstrous." See Herington, "Senecan Tragedy," 429–31, for the surreal violence and contradictions of Seneca's age ("some found release in madness and crulty") and of his own life; also Ä. Bäumer, *Die Bestie Mensch,* Studien zur klassischen Philologie, 4 (Frankfurt and Bern, 1982); and E. Burck, *Vom römischen Manierismus* (Darmstadt, 1971), 94. Lefèvre, "Bedeutung des Paradoxen," 59–82, treats interest in paradox as in part symptomatic of social developments in the later Republic and early Empire. For pessimism about historical decline at Rome see Heldmann, *Antike Theorien über Entwicklung und Verfall der Redekunst,* 84.

17. F. Ahl, "The Art of Safe Criticism in Greece and Rome," *American Journal of Philology* 105 (1984): 174–208. Demetrius *On Style* (99–101) comments on the potentially sinister effect of "allegory," i.e., of metaphorical and therefore wittily indirect threats (e.g., "your grasshoppers will sing on the ground" meaning "I'll level your city"). This is the technique of omens, and Demetrius observes that mysteries use allegory of the same sort to create vague fear. G. Grube (*A Greek Critic: Demetrius on Style* [Toronto, 1961], 134) cites Cicero's remark that because of dangerous political conditions he will "be obscure by using allegories" *(allēgoriais obscurabo),* i.e., code words. For innuendo *(hyponoia)* see Demetrius, 287–95. Suetonius' *Life of Passienus Crispus* has an excellent example of prudence-cum-wit. Asked by Gaius if he had had intercourse with his own sister (as the emperor had had with his own sister), "Crispus replied, 'Not yet'—as decently and cautiously as you could wish so that he would neither criticize the emperor by denial ["no—and *you* shouldn't either"] nor disgrace himself by a false claim ["yes—for you have made it permissible"]." The "elegant balance between a husband's love and a senator's duty" in *Ann.* 11.4.3 is another case.

18. "In declamation everything is useless since declamation itself is useless"; declamations are like "struggling in one's dreams" (Sen. *Controv.* 3, pref. 12; cf. 9, pref. 1–2 for the freedom of declaimers from the consequences of real debate; 7, pref. 7–8 for an amusing intrusion of reality). "In the unreal atmosphere of the schools, with their mutual admiration and false values, it was hard to preserve one's balance, and a man who seemed sane within their walls would appear hardly normal outside" (M. Clark, *Rhetoric at Rome* [London, 1953], 88); "one's ordinary thought processes must come to a halt at times" (Norden, *Antike Kunstprosa,* 272).

19. L. Sussman, *The Elder Seneca, Mnemosyne* Supplement 51, [Leiden, 1978], 13.

20. Ibid., 33, 87.

21. Norden, *Antike Kunstprosa,* 28.

22. M. Nill, *Morality and Self-Interest in Protagoras, Antiphon and Democritus* (Leiden, 1985), 68. On paradoxical reasoning natural to law because of its implicit expectations, J. B. White, *Heracles' Bow* (Madison, Wis., 1985), 60.

23. The intricacy, paradox, and casuistry of Seneca's discussions throughout *Ben.* are often close to those of the declamations (in 3.6.1 he remarks that the question whether ingratitude should be actionable was debated in the rhetorical schools). The contention that slaves can do genuine favors for their masters is illustrated with striking *exempla* wittily narrated. Two slaves desert their mistress in a besieged city in order to return with the victors and pretend to take vengeance on her but actually to save her. She was thus "deserted by all but the deserters," who were determined that "their mistress seem to have been killed so that she not be killed" (3.23.4). Like

declaimers, Seneca concentrates on close personal relationships: is it a favor to one brother to save the life of another brother whom he dislikes (5.20.1); if a vicious person ransoms me, must I return the favor (2.21.1: treat it not as a favor but a loan to be repaid). For other examples of witty declamatory rhetoric, D. A. Russell, *Greek Declamation* (Cambridge, 1983), 43: A creditor demands return of loan and interest, the borrower claims that the money was a deposit and carries no interest; a revolution then cancels debts, and creditor and borrower reverse positions. When Alexander dreams that he should not trust dreams, he faces a puzzle like that posed by "All Cretans are liars." For later developments in declamation see G. Anderson, *Philostratus* (London, Sydney, and Dover, 1986), 29; for the atmosphere of witty conflict, 43.

24. For an outright joke about the complications of fidelity: a coward accuses his wife of adultery when their son turns out to be a brave man (Russell, *Greek Declamation,* 45). More commonly the wit of declamatory situations is nasty. The painter Parrhasius bought an aged prisoner of war and tortured him to provide himself with a model for Prometheus. This prompts a marvelous joke (oddly called "insane" by Seneca): "if you want to give Parrhasius what he deserves, have him do a self-portrait" (*Controv.* 10.5.24). *Ann.* 13.44 and 4.28 describe situations much like those that come up in declamations.

25. Pratt, *Seneca's Drama,* 146. Norden, *Antike Kunstprosa,* 320: since independent action was often impossible, the art of of analyzing inner events was taught in rhetorical schools. That could only reinforce the tendency to moral judgment.

26. Russell, *Greek Declamation,* 39; for further examples of oddity, 25, 28, 39, 69.

Chapter VI. Wit and Political Irrationality

1. "Active and Passive Negation: An Essay in Ibanskian Sociology," in *The Invented Reality,* ed. P. Watzlawick, (New York and London, 1984), 175–204; see also Elster, *Sour Grapes* (Cambridge, 1983), 19. *The Yawning Heights,* tran. G. Clough (New York, 1978); *The Radiant Future,* tran. G. Clough (New York, 1980). (These works cited hereafter as *IR, SG, YH,* and *RF,* respectively.)

2. Elster, *IR,* 176; cf. *SG,* 47, on the "tragi-burlesque aspects of Soviet society."

3. Elster, *IR,* 184; *SG,* 44, 60. See also P. Watzlawick, *How Real Is Real?* (New York, 1976), 15; and Watzlawick, "Components of Ideological 'Realities,'" in *IR,* 230.

4. E.g., instead of expressing amazement that the dog talks, someone corrects its diction. Absurd loss of contact with what normally would matter is the point of anecdotes about Nero inspecting the detached head of one of his victims and wondering how he could ever have feared a man with such a nose (*Ann.* 14.59.3; Dio 62.14.1) and assessing the attractions of his mother's body after he has had her murdered (*Ner.* 34.4; *Ann.* 14.9.1). See W. Trillitzsch, *Senecas Beweisführung* (Berlin, 1962), 54, on the use of *reductio* by Seneca. For the technique of accepting something only to permit it to destroy itself through its own absurdity in Juvenal (*Satire* 9) and comedy, G. Highet, *Juvenal the Satirist* (New York, 1961), 118; Rudd, *Themes in Roman Satire,* 37: "what Juvenal has done is to *assume* the moral dimension and then to pretend it isn't there, as Swift did in *A Modest Proposal.*" Highet's example of a drug dealer complaining peevishly about the extra work he has to do because of police measures (119) is close to Suetonius' story of Caligula handing down one sentence for forty defendants charged with different crimes, then going home and telling his wife that while she napped he had gotten a lot of work done (*Calig.* 38.3). For *reductio* in Jewish wit see below, n. 16.

5. Cf. Balsdon, *Emperor Gaius,* 165. For a study of flattery as a tactic of *reductio* to arouse hatred see Jerome, *Aspects of the Study of Roman History,* 280. Dio remarks that excessive honors were offered to Caesar as bitter jokes or to make him envied (44.7.2–3) and that they did in fact create his arrogance (54.8.4).

6. Cited by Elster *IR,* 196. In *Nichomachean Ethics* 1095b23 Aristotle observes that all honor is superficial because it is more dependent on those who give it than on those who receive it.

7. The imperative form of this ("I order you to be free") is what made Caesar's celebrated *clementia* so illusory to many. Cf. the Polish satirist cited in Watzlawick, "Components," 223: "If I may express my opinion, Engels said that . . ." Self-deception is only slightly better concealed in Galba's phrase at *Hist.* 1.16.1: "the fact that we [emperors] have begun to be chosen will serve as [take the place of] liberty [*loco libertatis*]." Such language is amusing because (if it is not ironic) it after all brings out the political doublethink it is trying to conceal or is unaware of. Baldwin, *Suetonius,* 300, remarks on the "wondrous formula" Pliny comes up with as he flounders with the fact that mimes expelled by Domitian and recalled by Nerva were expelled again by Trajan: "both rightly, since those whom an evil princeps had expelled should have been recalled and then—expelled" (the first because *he* was evil, the second because *they* were, *Pan.* 46.1–4).

8. R. Solomon, *In the Spirit of Hegel* (New York, 1983), 443. The recognition for which both struggle is at once internal self-assurance and external status *(Selbstbewußtsein).* The quandary of Groucho Marx with his club and of the emperor with the senate is essentially that "if another is [politically] conscious of me as a self but not of himself as the same, is my [political] selfhood authentic?" The slave's recognition of the master is questionable because it makes the master "dependent on dependence" (Q. Lauer, *A Reading of Hegel's Phenomenology of Spirit* [New York, 1976], 106–9). Hegel, of course, thinks of this as a dialectical and not historical relationship, though it is interesting that it is followed by Stoicism, i.e., purely internal freedom of thought permitting escape from the loop by withdrawal. Internal exile *(secessio)* was in fact one response to the political vicious circle at Rome. The reciprocal dialectic of fear is a favored subject of epigrams. "When Otho was afraid, he was feared" (*Hist.* 1.81.1); "what should we envy about informers, that they fear or that they are feared?" (*Dial.* 13.4). Cf. Sen. *De ira* 2.11.3; *Clem.* 1.19.5; *Oedipus* 705; *Ep.* 105.4. See also W-R. Heinz, *Die Furcht als politisches Phänomen bei Tacitus* (Amsterdam, 1975), 13.

9. Reciprocal dependence is thus also a form of reciprocal manipulation; R. Goodin, *Manipulatory Politics,* 35: "We may find ourselves in a situation of everyone manipulating everyone else." For the complex relationship between emperor and senate, B. Warmington, *Nero: Reality and Legend* (London, 1969), 21; M. Griffin, *Nero: The End of a Dynasty* (London, 1984), 94; F. Millar, *The Emperor in the Roman World* (Ithaca, N.Y., and London, 1977), 351; Veyne, *Le pain et le cirque,* 717: "there was conflict between Senate and Princeps, not because the Senate wanted his power but because it didn't"; Wirszubski, *Libertas as a Political Idea,* 124; P. Brunt, "The Senate in the Augustan Regime," *Classical Quarterly* 78 (1984): 442–44. Systematic contradiction in the structure of Roman politics has been traced back as far as the tension in the Republic between individual ambition and group restraint: B. Levick, "Morals, Politics, and the Fall of the Roman Republic," *Greece and Rome* 29 (1982): 53–62. "Any well-off Roman family might aspire to own a pedestal table, without making it impossible for others to do so; but there were only two hundred consulships

available every century" (54); this is a classic instance of the zero-sum game. The emperors exercised power through a combination of manipulation and open coercion, the former exploiting republican forms of government in particular.

10. R. Talbert, *The Senate of Imperial Rome* (Princeton, N.J., 1984), 87.

11. M. Arnheim, *The Senatorial Aristocracy in the Later Roman Empire* (Oxford, 1972), 21.

12. Too absolute a contrast between monarchy and dyarchy risks settling an issue through definition; cf. Fischer, *Historians' Fallacies,* 21. Tiberius has fairly been called the last republican, and the monarchic system, too, was in an equally odd way dyarchic.

13. Pitkin, *Wittgenstein and Justice,* 187.

14. Veyne, *Le pain et le cirque,* 718, on ritual refusal of power.

15. G. Orwell, *Nineteen Eighty-Four* (New York, 1949), 36, 215; Zinoviev, *YH,* 441.

16. Freud, *Jokes and the Unconscious,* 115; cf. 70; see below, sec. 5. For paralyzing circular regress in evaluation of concealed motive, J. Elster, *Ulysses and the Sirens,* 2d ed. (Cambridge, 1984), 111, 171. The principle of "tacit coordination" in game theory may entail revolving door regresses: "*I* must concede because *he* won't. He *won't* because he thinks that I *will.* He thinks that I *will* because he *thinks* I *think* that he *thinks* . . .": T. Schelling, *The Strategy of Conflict* (Cambridge, 1960), 22. The paradox of preemptive self-defense ("he was about to kill me in self-defense, so I had to kill him in self-defense," Schelling, 232) assumes even odder form at Rome in connection with more or less enforced political suicide, i.e., killing one*self* in self-defense. Drexler, *Grundzüge einer politischen Pathologie,* 79, has some remarks on vicious circles set up by layers of political motivation.

A few additional words about the bearing of traditional Jewish wit on the rhetoric of ancient historiography are perhaps in order. It is genuinely pertinent in this respect: its distinctive incoherence is historically a response to social and political oppression. More specifically, it is a form of self-defense combining resistance with resignation. Resistance lies in perception of situations as irrational, the point being that witty treatment of unreasonableness as though it were a fact of ordinary reality can also be serious, subversive protest that it *is* ordinary reality. At the same time, the sense of futility that naturally goes with this calls for resignation on the part of its victims, and the typically self-depreciatory, self-referential form of wit serves as a way of coming to terms with absurdity by talking and thinking about it in a peculiarly therapeutic way. (For a similar dimension to Seneca's witty diction see above p. 92.) Jewish humor thus embodies with unusual clarity an important property of political wit generally, including that at Rome, where the imperial system must have seemed senseless to many Romans.

17. Syme, *Tacitus,* 1:272, 1:299. For a vivid picture of opposition at Rome through pamphlets, literature, jokes, and anecdotes, G. Boissier, *L'opposition sous les Césars* (Paris, 1900), 69, 292. For an interesting comparison between the social contexts of ancient literature and the modern satiric samizdat on the score of informal transmission of ideas, M. I. Finley, *Democracy Ancient and Modern,* rev. ed. (New Brunswick, N.J., 1985), 146 (chap. entitled "Censorship in Classical Antiquity").

18. Syme, *Tacitus,* 272.

19. 4.71. For the political situation, B. Levick, *Tiberius the Politician* (London,

1976), 186, 199. For the sinister aspect of the ploy cf. "while many Germans thought that the Jews were no longer alive, they did not necessarily believe that they were dead," W. Laqueur, *The Terrible Secret,* cited in Elster, *SG,* 152. The peculiar force of such logic comes out in a special brand of pure wit, illustrated by a joke about subtle rabbinic modes of reasoning. "Two litigants . . . come before the rabbi. After hearing the first testimony, the rabbi says, 'It seems to me that you are right.' But after the second man speaks, the rabbi says, 'It seems to me that *you* are right, too.' 'How can this be?' says the rabbi's wife, who has been listening to the argument. 'How can both of these men be right?' 'H'm,' says the rabbi, '*You're* right, too.'"

20. Zinoviev has a man who on one and the same day receives the Order of Lenin, is expelled from the party, and is arrested (*RF,* 58). In Orwell's *Nineteen Eighty-Four* it is possible to be released after arrest only to be suddenly executed later. Something of the sort happens to a victim of Vitellius (*Vit.* 14.2), and when Piso was escorted home, "it was not certain whether for protection or execution" (*Ann.* 3.14.5). For the theme of unexpected death at the tyrant's hand see Walker, *Annals of Tacitus,* 220.

21. *Catch-22* (New York, 1966), Modern Library, 45. "He would be crazy to fly more missions and sane if he didn't, but if he was sane he had to fly them. If he flew them he was crazy and didn't have to; but if he didn't want to he was sane and had to" (46).

22. Elster, in *IR,* 177.

23. Ibid., 192; *SG,* 63.

24. Zinoviev, *YH,* 497.

25. Zinoviev, *RF,* 77.

26. Ibid., 262.

27. Heller, *Catch-22,* 79: "He was guilty of course, or he would not have been accused, and since the only way to prove it was to find him guilty, it was their patriotic duty to do so." Cf. *Ann.* 3.67.2: when Silanus was aggressively examined by the emperor "he often had to confess, so that Tiberius would not be asking in vain." Since Silanus is guilty, this may not be ironic. Yet the trial is rigged, and the remark calls up the odd notion of "official" as well as real guilt: even criminals can be railroaded. For eccentric jurisprudence see above, chap. 2, sec. 7, and chap. 3, sec. 4. Under Nero legal contests (mock trials?) led to real exile or death (Dio 61.10.1).

28. Zinoviev, *YH,* 819.

29. Ibid., 567. Tacitus mentions the case of a man who is assaulted by Nero in a senseless brawl at night and defends himself, then apologizes when he recognizes the emperor, but is forced to commit suicide because the apology is regarded as a reproach (*Ann.* 13.25.2). The point of the situation is not entirely clear. Perhaps the apology was taken to imply that Nero was above the law, whereas he wanted to pretend to be part of the give-and-take of street life. Suetonius' version is quite different; Nero is badly beaten because he has abused a senator's wife, and nothing is said about apology or suicide (*Ner.* 26.2). Tacitus' version, at any rate, suggests the madcap combination of a sense of propriety and official muggings ("at night the city was like a battlefield"). The victim of assault pretends to be the guilty party; that is taken as an accusation (seemingly without justification), and so he is executed for apologizing for something he did not do. The "guilty victim" appears in other anecdotes. After he had a man executed for his wealth and then learned that the man in fact had none, Caligula exclaimed, "Why, he tricked me! And for no reason; he could very well be alive!" (Dio 59.18.5).

When he suspected that his brother, whom he wanted to murder, had taken antidotes against poison, he was indignant: "What's that? An antidote against Caesar?" (*Calig.* 29.1). Quintilian mentions a formal joke on the theme: "I will hit you in the head and take you to court for having so hard a skull" (*Inst.* 6.3.83). The point of Caligula's joke about torturing Caesonia to find out why he loved her so much (*Calig.* 33) is that *he* is the victim, and so it parodies legal procedure in a different way.

30. Cf. *Hist.* 1.6.1 for confusion of guilt and innocence.

31. 67.4.2: "the worst thing about Domitian was that he wanted to be flattered and yet disliked equally those who did and those who did not do so—the one for seeming to flatter, the other for seeming to be contemptuous." Cf. 67.2.7 for the same pattern.

32. For a discussion of the facts in some of the cases mentioned and often distorted by Tacitus see Walker, *Annals of Tacitus,* 82–137; B. Baldwin, "Executions, Trials and Punishment in the Reign of Nero," *Parola del passato* 117 (1967): 425–39; and Baldwin, "Themes, Personalities and Distortions in Tacitus," *Athenaeum* 52 (1974): 70–81.

33. For the "comedy" of this interview, K. von Fritz, "Tacitus, Agricola, Domitian," *Classical Philology* 52 (1957): 74.

34. A. Wallace-Hadrill, "Civilis Princeps: Between Citizen and King," *Journal of Roman Studies* 72 (1982): 32–48. For a discussion of power relationships embodied in language generally, R. Fowler, *Language and Control* (London, Boston, and Henley, 1979): "power differential provides the underlying semantic for the systems of ideas encoded in language structure" (2). The concealment of intention and inversion of expression in *clementia* are signs of a particularly effective form of power. "When the language of control is backed up by the reality of power, the more massive the deletion, especially of the fact of power and coercion, the more powerful, mystified and irrational is the control. Anyone who can give orders without even acknowledging this in the surface of his utterance has access to an invidiously powerful form of command. For instance, someone who can say, 'the door is open' and be interpreted as saying 'close the door' has issued an imperative which has been totally deleted yet is fully effective. The person who obeys accepts the reality of a power that has not been claimed" (18). This was also felt to be true of the person who receives or asks for clemency.

35. For clemency as public relations, *Hist.* 1.71. M. Foucault traces the roots of the paradox to the very nature of political authority: "The right of life and death is a dissymmetrical one. The sovereign exercised his right of life only by exercising his right to kill, or by refraining from killing. . . . The right which was formulated as the 'power of life and death' was in reality the right to *take* life or *let* life" (*The History of Sexuality,* tran. R. Hurley [New York, 1978], 136; cf. *ius necis vitaeque civium, Hist.* 3.68.2). See also M. Fuhrmann, "Die Alleinherrschaft und das Problem der Gerechtigkeit," in *Prinzipat und Freiheit,* ed. Klein, 275.

36. Zinoviev, *YH,* 27. Zinoviev's writings are studded with self-contradictory antithetic epigrams with a distinctly Tacitean flavor of futility. "There was nowhere to go, but nowhere to stay either" (*YH,* 676); "the legalisation of a legal operation is illegal" (326); the right to stand in a queue "both for what was and what was not available" (16). In Tacitus, of course, such patterns are not simply about futility. Each part by itself makes a substantial point, as in the portraits composed of antithetic qualities contributing to carefully considered assessment of character. Cf. Aubrion, *Rhétorique et histoire chez Tacite,* 385–490. The added hint of futility comes when everything is taken together in larger perspective. Thus Sejanus' contradictory traits

include extravagance coupled with restraint "which is scarcely less harmful when faked in order to gain power" (*Ann.* 4.1.3). He really had self-discipline—Tacitus says so—yet not really and to no avail: restraint cancelled by extravagance, after all, comes to nothing.

37. Veyne, *Le pain et le cirque*, 787 n. 502.

38. "What was surprising was not vice but virtue: one praised people for the vices they did not have": Veyne, "Le folklore à Rome," 6. "Finally there is the universal propensity to assume the worst, a generalized maximin behaviour that might be called paranoid were it not so justified," Elster, *SG*, 89. This principle of negative virtue assumes even more oddly contorted form when Otho is blamed for virtues he does have: "Meanwhile, to everyone's surprise Otho did not bask at ease in idleness; he postponed his pleasures and dissembled his luxury . . . for that reason his false virtues and the vices which were bound to return were the more frightening" (*Hist.* 1.71.1). Even Tacitus' genuine admiration for Agricola's wife has sting to it. For if "praise for a good wife is all the greater in proportion to the greater blame for a bad one" (*Agr.* 6.1), the latter sets the norm. Cf. B. Baldwin, "Women in Tacitus," *Prudentia* 4 (1972): 83, also in *Studies on Greek and Roman History and Literature* (Amsterdam, 1985), 256.

39. A. Malissard, "Un exemple de composition Tacitéenne: Les deux batailles de Bedriac," *Hommages à Jean Cousin,* Annales littéraires de L'Université de Besançon, 273 (Paris, 1983), 163, 172 (my translation).

40. B. Marfurt, *Textsorte Witz* (Tübingen, 1977), 44 (n. 5) and 89, for *Metawitz,* also discussed as "shaggy dog" jokes by S. Stewart, *Nonsense* (Baltimore and London, 1978), 78.

41. Catullus' analogous *Odi et amo* is an instructive contrast, for there unaccountability is a climax with real substance, because passion is supposed to be irrational.

42. *What Is the Name of This Book?* (Englewood Cliffs, N.J., 1978), 3. Cf. "We suspect their famous atrocities of being, in a somewhat more profound way than is usually meant, entertainment, diversion in search of something to do . . . a game in which enemies are created and played with" (G. Braden, "The Rhetoric and Psychology of Power in the Dramas of Seneca," *Arion* 9 [1970]: 11).

43. Burck, *Vom römischen Manierismus.* There is a curious discussion in R. Koselleck (*Vergangene Zukunft,* Frankfurt, 1979, 288–93) of the effect of political terror on dreams—an affect perhaps implicitly recognized by Tacitus when he connects omens (including nightmarish dream omens?) with times of anxiety. The German woman who dreamt of herself prudently speaking Russian (which she did not know) to avoid saying or being heard to say anything reportable was dreaming the real-life absurdity of senators who spoke so as not to be understood (*Hist.* 1.85.3; cf. chap. 2 n. 30 and Koselleck, 289: "silence is part of the signature of a totalitarian state"). Overlapping of fact with fiction makes dreams a natural metaphor for what cannot be directly expressed, and in 1930s Germany they could actually foretell a reality equaling or outdoing the very worst fears. In the ancient historians the imagery of absurdity was still largely rhetorical and therefore still capable of exaggeration. As Tiberius stepped up his executions, he moved near Rome "to gaze, so to say, on the deluge of blood rushing through houses and on the hands of his executioners" (*Ann.* 6.40.2). For an imaginative reading of Lucan's "tasteless" rhetorical excess as a serious grasp of pervasive irrationality in Roman history see W. Johnson, *Momentary Monsters* (Ithaca and London, 1987).

44. Cf. H. Arendt, *The Origins of Totalitarianism* (New York, 1973), Harvest Books, esp. 460ff.

45. Ibid., 436.

46. For unrestricted *ira* as the dark side of *clementia* see Ä. Bäumer, *Die Bestie Mensch*, 122.

47. Arendt, *Origins of Totalitarianism*, 439.

48. Bäumer, *Bestie Mensch*, 96; 126; Arendt, 67.

49. *Eichmann in Jerusalem*, 2nd ed. (New York, 1965).

50. Ibid., 287.

51. Ibid., 252.

52. Ibid. 53, 135. For details (which often read like anecdotes in the historians) showing that "the horrible can be not only ludicrous but outright funny," 48.

53. J. Stanley, "Is Totalitarianism a New Phenomenon? Reflections on Hannah Arendt's *The Origins of Totalitarianism,*" *The Review of Politics* 49 (1987): 177–207. If totalitarian logic existed at all in ancient society, it was in the tendency of slavery as an institution to minimize the freedom of slaves as private moral agents too (197–203). Personal integrity is what the Stoics attempted to ensure with their doctrine of absolute inner freedom, which perhaps took some of its appeal from the disturbing possibility of slavery in the consciousness of those who were free. But talk of the relationship between emperor and senate as one between master and slaves was still a matter of moral rhetoric rather than formal political theory about power.

54. B. Mandeville, *The Fable of the Bees*, ed. F. Kaye (Oxford, 1924), 1:100–106; 1:25. Mandeville's aggressively witty way of formulating the paradoxes underlying social theory struck many at the time as alarmingly subversive, so much so that he was accused of achieving irrefutibility through absurdity. His position seemed to be a special "nonsense, neither true nor false" (D. Castiglione, "Considering Things Minutely: Reflections on Mandeville," *History of Political Thought* 7 [1986]: 466). Tiberius would surely have been deeply interested in this as a necessary and legitimate fact of politics. To some extent Dio, too, treats systematic contradiction in the Principate as an objective political fact (Manuwald, *Cassius Dio und Augustus*, 8ff, 167, 273). But such factors are again secondary to ethical ones: "Dio's attitude to monarchy, so far as it can be assessed, seems not to be of such decisive importance that the presentation and valuation of other factors are dependent on it. On the contrary, the picture that Dio gives of Octavian and his age led him, in spite of his basically positive view of monarchy, to include one-sidedly negative implications about that form of government" (20, my translation).

55. Goodyear, *Annals of Tacitus*, vol. 1, ad loc.

56. A. Camus, *The Rebel*, tran. A. Bower, New York, 1961, Introduction.

57. For the "paradigm change" in modern times see P. Gay, *The Enlightenment: An Interpretation* (New York, 1969), 2:456 (undermining of natural law); A. Hirschman, *The Passions and the Interests* (Princeton, N.J., 1977), 9ff; J. Pocock, *The Machiavellian Moment* (Princeton, N.J., and London, 1975), esp. 211, 463, 501; and J. Plamenatz, "In Search of Machiavellian *Virtù*," in *The Political Calculus*, ed. A. Parel (Toronto and Buffalo, N.Y., 1972), 157–58.

Selected Bibliography

Only modern works of which I have made the greatest use are included; other primary
and secondary literature is referred to in the notes.

Ahl, F. "The Art of Safe Criticism in Greece and Rome," *American Journal of Philology*
105 (1984): 174–208.

Ahl, F. *Metaformations*. Ithaca, N.Y., and London, 1985.

Arendt, H. *Eichmann in Jerusalem*. 2d. ed. New York, 1965.

Arendt, H. *The Origins of Totalitarianism*. New York, 1973.

Aubrion, E. *Rhétorique et histoire chez Tacite*. Metz, 1985.

Austin, J. L. *Philosophical Papers*. Oxford, 1961.

Austin, J. L. *How to Do Things with Words*. Oxford, 1962.

Baldwin, B. "Executions, Trials and Punishment in the Reign of Nero," *Parola del
passato* 117 (1967): 425–39. Also in *Studies on Greek and Roman History and
Literature*, 205–19.

Baldwin, B. "Themes, Personalities and Distortions in Tacitus," *Athenaeum* 52 (1974):
70–81. Also in *Studies on Greek and Roman History and Literature*, 220–31.

Baldwin, B. "Tacitean Humour," *Wiener Studien* 90 (1977): 128–44. Also in *Studies on
Greek and Roman History and Literature*, 232–48.

Baldwin, B. "Nero and His Mother's Corpse," *Mnemosyne* 32 (1979): 380–81. Also in
Studies on Greek and Roman History, 280–81.

Baldwin, B. *Suetonius*. Amsterdam, 1983.

Baldwin, B. *Studies on Greek and Roman History and Literature*. Amsterdam, 1985.

Balsdon, J. *The Emperor Gaius*. Oxford, 1934.

Bardon, H. "A propos des *Histoires:* Tacite et la tentation de la rhétorique," *Collection
Latomus* 44 (1960): 146–51.

Bäumer, Ä. *Die Bestie Mensch*. Studien zur klassischen Philologie, 4. Frankfurt and
Bern, 1982.

Benario, H. *An Introduction to Tacitus*. Athens, Ga., 1975.

Berlin, I., et al. *Essays on J. L. Austin*. Oxford, 1973.

Bicknell, P. "The Emperor Gaius' Military Activity in A.D. 40," *Historia* 17 (1968):
496–505.

Boissier, G. *L'opposition sous les Césars*. Paris, 1900.

Booth, W. *A Rhetoric of Irony*. Chicago and London, 1974.

Brunt, P. "The Senate in the Augustan Regime," *Classical Quarterly* 78 (1984): 423–44.

Burck, E. *Vom römischen Manierismus*. Darmstadt, 1971.

Chilver, G. E. F. *A Historical Commentary on Tacitus' Histories I and II*. Oxford,
1979.

Chilver, G. E. F., and G. B. Townend. *A Historical Commentary on Tacitus' Histories IV and V*. Oxford, 1985.

Cizek, E. *Structures et idéologies dans "Les vies des douz Césars" de Suétone*. Paris, 1977.

Clark, M. *Rhetoric at Rome*. London, 1953.

Cousin, J. "Rhétorique et psychologie chez Tacite," *Revue des études latines* 29 (1961): 228–47. Also in German in *Tacitus*, edited by V. Pöschl, 104–29. Wege der Forschung. Darmstadt, 1969.

Cox, P. *Biography in Late Antiquity*. Berkeley, Los Angeles, and London, 1983.

Danto, A. *Narration and Knowledge*. New York, 1985.

Dawson, H. "Whatever Happened to Lady Agrippina?" *Classical Journal* 64 (1968): 253–67.

Deroux, C. "Domitian, the Kingfish and the Prodigies," *Collection Latomus*, vol. 180, 283–98. Studies in Latin Literature and Roman History, 3. Brussels, 1983.

Devlin, R. "Tacitus and Techniques of Insidious Suggestion," *Antichthon* 17 (1983): 64–95.

Dillon, G. *Language Processing and the Reading of Literature*. Bloomington, Ind., and London, 1978.

Drexler, H. *Tacitus: Grundzüge einer politischen Pathologie*. Frankfurt, 1939.

Elster, J. *Sour Grapes*. Cambridge, 1983.

Elster, J. *Ulysses and the Sirens*. 2d ed. Cambridge, 1984.

Evans, E. "Roman Descriptions of Personal Appearance in History and Biography," *Harvard Studies in Classical Philology* 46 (1935): 43–84.

Fischer, D. *Historians' Fallacies*. New York, 1970.

Flach, D. "Dios Platz in der kaiserzeitlichen Geschichtsschreibung," *Antike und Abendland* 18 (1973): 130–43.

Flach, D. *Tacitus in der Tradition der antiken Geschichtsschreibung*. Hypomnemata 39. Göttingen, 1973.

Fowler, R. *Literature as Social Discourse*. London, 1981.

Fritz, K. von. "Tacitus, Agricola, Domitian," *Classical Philology* 52 (1957): 73–97.

Fuhrmann, M. "Die Alleinherrschaft und das Problem der Gerechtigkeit," *Gymnasium* 70 (1963): 481–514. Also in *Prinzipat und Freiheit*, edited by R. Klein, 271–320. Wege der Forschung. Darmstadt, 1969.

Gascou, J. *Suétone historien*. Bibliotheque des écoles françaises d'Athènes et de Rome, 255. Rome, 1984.

Goodyear, F. R. D. *The Annals of Tacitus, Books 1–6*. 2 vols. Cambridge, 1972–81.

Grant, M. *The Ancient Rhetorical Theories of the Laughable*. University of Wisconsin Studies in Language and Literature, 21. Madison, 1924.

Griffin, M. *Seneca, a Philosopher in Politics*. Oxford, 1976.

Grube, G. *A Greek Critic: Demetrius on Style*. Toronto, 1961.

Gugel, H. *Studien zur biographischen Technik Suetons*. Wiener Studien Beiheft 7. Vienna, Cologne, and Graz, 1977.

Hässler, R. *Tacitus und das historische Bewußtsein*. Heidelberg, 1965.

Heinz, W.-R. *Die Furcht als politisches Phänomen bei Tacitus*. Amsterdam, 1975.

Heller, J. *Catch-22*. Modern Library. New York, 1966.

Herington, C. J. "Senecan Tragedy," *Arion* 5 (1966): 422–71.

Heubner, H. "Sprache, Stil und Sache bei Tacitus," *Gymnasium,* Beiheft 4 (1964): 133–48.

Hock, R., and E. O'Neil. *The Chreia in Ancient Rhetoric.* Vol. 1. Texts and Translations, 27. Graeco-Roman Religion Series, 9. Atlanta, Ga., 1986.

Jens, W. "Libertas bei Tacitus," *Hermes* 84 (1956): 331–52. Also in *Prinzipat und Freiheit,* edited by R. Klein, 391–420. Wege der Forschung. Darmstadt, 1969.

Keitel, E. "Principate and Civil War in the *Annals* of Tacitus," *American Journal of Philology* 105 (1984): 306–25.

Kennedy, G. *The Art of Rhetoric in the Roman World.* Princeton, N.J., 1972.

Klinger, F. "Tacitus über Augustus und Tiberius," *Sitzungsberichte der Bayerischen Akademie der Wissenschaften* 7 (1953): 1–45. Also in *Tacitus,* edited by V. Pöschl, 496–539. Wege der Forschung. Darmstadt, 1969.

Klinger, F. "Beobachtungen über Sprache und Stil des Tacitus am Anfang des 13. Annalenbuches," *Hermes* 83 (1955): 187–200. Also in *Tacitus,* edited by V. Pöschl, 540–57. Wege der Forschung. Darmstadt, 1969.

Koestermann, E. *Cornelius Tacitus: Annalen.* 4 vols. Heidelberg, 1963–68.

Köhnken, A. "Das Problem der Ironie bei Tacitus," *Museum Helveticum* 30 (1973): 32–50.

Lefèvre, E. "Die Bedeutung des Paradoxen in der römischen Literatur der frühen Kaiserzeit," *Poetica* 3 (1970): 59–82.

Lounsbury, R. *The Arts of Suetonius.* American University Studies, Series XVII, Classical Languages and Literature, vol. 3. New York, 1987.

Manuwald, B. *Cassius Dio und Augustus.* Palingenesia, 14. Wiesbaden, 1979.

Marfurt, B. *Textsorte Witz.* Tübingen, 1977.

Martin, R. *Tacitus.* Berkeley and Los Angeles, 1981.

Millar, F. *A Study of Cassius Dio.* Oxford, 1964.

Millar, F. *The Emperor in the Roman World.* Ithaca, N.Y., and London, 1977.

Moss, R. "The Case for Sophistry." In *Rhetoric Revalued,* edited by B. Vickers, 207–24. Medieval and Renaissance Texts and Studies, 19. Binghamton, N.Y., 1982.

Norden, E. *Die antike Kunstprosa.* 2 vols. 5th ed. Stuttgart, 1958.

Orwell, G. *Nineteen Eighty-Four.* New York, 1949.

Pöschl, V. "Der Historiker Tacitus," *Die Welt als Geschichte* 22 (1962): 1–10. Also in *Tacitus,* edited by V. Pöschl, 161–76. Wege der Forschung. Darmstadt, 1969.

Pöschl, V. ed. *Tacitus.* Wege der Forschung. Darmstadt, 1969.

Pratt, N. *Seneca's Drama.* Chapel Hill, N.C., and London, 1983.

Raskin, V. *Semantic Mechanisms of Humor.* Dordrecht, Boston, and Lancaster, 1985.

Rogers, R. S. "Ignorance of the Law in Tacitus and Dio," *Transactions of the American Philological Association* 64 (1933): 18–27.

Rogers, R. S. "A Tacitean Pattern in Narrating Treason Trials," *Transactions of the American Philological Association* 83 (1952): 279–311.

Rose, M. *Parody//Meta-Fiction.* London, 1979.

Rudd, N. *Themes in Roman Satire.* Norman, Okla., and London, 1986.

Russell, D. A. *Greek Declamation.* Cambridge, 1983.

Saller, R. "Anecdotes as Historical Evidence for the Principate," *Greece and Rome* 27 (1980): 69–83.

Schelling, T. *The Strategy of Conflict*. Cambridge, 1960.

Seel, O. *Römertum und Latinität*. Stuttgart, 1964.

Segal, E. "Tacitus and Poetic History: The End of Annals XIII," *Ramus* 2 (1973): 107–26.

Seidensticker, B. *Die Gesprächsverdichtung in den Tragödien Senecas*. Heidelberg, 1969.

Shotter, D. "Ea Simulacra Libertatis," *Latomus* 25 (1966): 265–71.

Steidle, W. *Sueton und die antike Biographie*. Zetemata, 1. Munich, 1951.

Stewart, S. *Nonsense*. Baltimore and London, 1978.

Sullivan, J. P. *Literature and Politics in the Age of Nero*. Ithaca, N.Y., and London, 1985.

Sussman, L. *The Elder Seneca*. Mnemosyne Supplement 51. Leiden, 1978.

Syme, R. *Tacitus*. 2 vols. Oxford, 1958.

Syme, R. *Ten Studies in Tacitus*. Oxford, 1970.

Townend, G. "Suetonius and His Influence." In *Latin Biography*, edited by T. A. Dorey, 79–111. London, 1967.

Veyne, P. *Le pain et le cirque*. Paris, 1976.

Vogt, J. "Tacitus und die Unparteilichkeit des Historikers." Würzburger Studien zur Altertumswissenschaft, 9. *Studien zu Tacitus. Festschrift für Carl Hosius*, 1–20. Stuttgart, 1936. Also in *Prinzipat und Freiheit*, ed. R. Klein, 369–90. Wege der Forschung. Darmstadt, 1969.

Voss, B. *Der pointierte Stil des Tacitus*. Orbis antiquus, 19. Münster, 1963.

Walker, B. *The Annals of Tacitus*. 2d ed. Manchester, 1960.

Wallace-Hadrill, A. *Suetonius*. London, 1983.

Wallace-Hadrill, A. "Civilis Princeps: Between Citizen and King," *Journal of Roman Studies* 72 (1982): 32–48.

Wardman, A. E. "Description of Personal Appearance in Plutarch and Suetonius," *Classical Quarterly*, n.s. 17 (1967): 414–20.

Waters, K. "The Character of Domitian," *Phoenix* 18 (1964): 49–77.

Watzlawick, P., ed. *The Invented Reality*. New York and London, 1984.

Williams, G. *Change and Decline*. Berkeley, Los Angeles, and London, 1978.

Willrich, H. "Caligula," *Klio* 3 (1903): 85–118, 288–317, 397–470.

Wirszubski, Ch. *Libertas as a Political Idea at Rome*. Cambridge, 1950.

Wiseman, T. *Clio's Cosmetics*. Old Woking, 1979.

Zinoviev, A. *The Yawning Heights*. Translated by G. Clough. New York, 1978.

Zinoviev, A. *The Radiant Future*. Translated by G. Clough. New York, 1980.

Index

Index of Passages Cited